# Typographic Web Design

# Typographic Web Design

## How to Think Like a Typographer in HTML and CSS

**Laura Franz**

**WILEY**

A John Wiley & Sons, Ltd, Publication

This edition first published 2012

© 2012 Laura Franz

*Registered office*

John Wiley & Sons Ltd, The Atrium, Southern Gate, Chichester, West Sussex, PO19 8SQ, United Kingdom

For details of our global editorial offices, for customer services and for information about how to apply for permission to reuse the copyright material in this book please see our website at www.wiley.com.

The right of the author to be identified as the author of this work has been asserted in accordance with the Copyright, Designs and Patents Act 1988.

All rights reserved. No part of this publication may be reproduced, stored in a retrieval system, or transmitted, in any form or by any means, electronic, mechanical, photocopying, recording or otherwise, except as permitted by the UK Copyright, Designs and Patents Act 1988, without the prior permission of the publisher.

Wiley also publishes its books in a variety of electronic formats. Some content that appears in print may not be available in electronic books.

Designations used by companies to distinguish their products are often claimed as trademarks. All brand names and product names used in this book are trade names, service marks, trademarks or registered trademarks of their respective owners. The publisher is not associated with any product or vendor mentioned in this book. This publication is designed to provide accurate and authoritative information in regard to the subject matter covered. It is sold on the understanding that the publisher is not engaged in rendering professional services. If professional advice or other expert assistance is required, the services of a competent professional should be sought.

**Trademarks:** Wiley and the John Wiley & Sons, Ltd. logo are trademarks or registered trademarks of John Wiley & Sons, Ltd. and/or its affiliates in the United States and/or other countries, and may not be used without written permission. All trademarks are the property of their respective owners. John Wiley & Sons, Ltd. is not associated with any product or vendor mentioned in the book.

978-1-119-97687-5

A catalogue record for this book is available from the British Library.

Set in 9/14 Aller by Wiley Composition Services

Printed in the U.S. by Krehbiel

# About the Author

Laura Franz is an Associate Professor of Design at the University of Massachusetts Dartmouth, where she has taught web typography for 12 years.

She teaches a wide range of typography classes, including Typography I: History and Structure of Letterforms with an Introduction to Type on the Page; Typography II: Type as Information; Typography III: Type in Context: Print and Web; and Typography IV: Undergraduate Research Projects in Typeface Design. She is also Co-coordinator of The Graduate Certificate in Web and Interaction Design at UMass Dartmouth, in which she teaches a Web Typography class.

Professionally, she designs for both print and the web. Ongoing creative research projects include historictype.com, goodwebfonts.com, and The New Bedford Typeface project. She lectures and gives workshops on Typographic Web Design, and has written a course on the topic for Lynda.com.

She is particularly interested in how we teach future typographers the art and responsibilities of our craft.

# Publisher's Acknowledgments

Some of the people who helped bring this book to market include the following:

**Editorial and Production**
VP Consumer and Technology Publishing Director: Michelle Leete
Associate Director–Book Content Management: Martin Tribe
Associate Publisher: Chris Webb
Assistant Editor: Ellie Scott
Development Editor: Sara Shlaer
Copy Editors: Kathryn Simpson, Marylouise Wiack
Technical Editor: Simon Pascal Klein
Editorial Manager: Jodi Jensen
Senior Project Editor: Sara Shlaer
Editorial Assistant: Leslie Saxman

**Marketing**
Associate Marketing Director: Louise Breinholt
Marketing Executive: Kate Parrett

**Composition Services**
Compositor: Jennifer Mayberry
Graphics Tech: Sennett Vaughan Johnson
Proofreader: Melissa D. Buddendeck
Indexer: Potomac Indexing, LLC

*For Sam, Claire, and Phoebe—who love words even more than I do.*

# Acknowledgments

This book would never have been written if it weren't for some of the amazing people who have graced my life: Dan Boyarski (who showed me how to teach), David Kaufer (who convinced me I could write), my type students (especially those who questioned everything), Randy Apuzzo (who jotted down the first CSS description I ever saw, and reawakened my love for web design), Tom Boucher (who convinced me I should write a book, and edited my original version of the text), and all of my Second Sunday friends (who convinced me to stop and enjoy their company when I needed it most).

Related to the nuts and bolts of getting this book to its final printed form, thank you to Sara Shlaer (who kept me on top of the task at hand),

Jennifer Mayberry (who pulled the final book design together while I panicked over old-style figures and CMYK conversions) and Simon Pascal Klein (who consistently advocated for more semantic markup as opposed to the presentational markup I use in the lessons—he reminded me of my love for systems, both technical and typographic).

And finally, to my family—Samantha, Claire, and Phoebe—who gave me the physical, emotional, and psychological support to write this book. Without you, I never would have finished. Without you, none of it would matter.

# Contents

**CHAPTER 2**

**Aesthetics and Emotions: Does the Font Convey the Right Message?**

**CHAPTER 3**

**Contrast, Styles, and Characters: Can the Font Do the Job?**

# Part 2: Making Type Work: Scanning with Purpose

## Interlude 2: Tabular Information

## Part 3: Making Type Work: Casual and Sustained Reading

## Interlude 3: Building a Font Library

## Part 4: Designing with Type: Historical Styles

# Introduction

For decades, critics have predicted the end of the written word: "No one reads anymore! No one writes anymore!" Yet from birth certificates to gravestones, from T-shirts to text messaging, the written word—and thus reading—is woven into the fabric of our everyday lives.

Throughout history, we have used the written word to record and preserve who we are and what we care about: possessions, laws, commitments, ideas, and memories. Words and characters, once impressed in clay, written on papyrus, and printed with ink, are now manifest in pixels of light (Figure 1).

## People Still Read

The use of text messaging for casual conversation has exploded, surpassing phone conversation as the communication method of choice—suggesting our personal connection to reading and writing continues to thrive.

As Jessica Helfand wrote in 2000, "... words are ideas just waiting to be read. And reading will never die. Reading is your ticket to the world." [1] People read. They seek a connection to their community, answers to their questions, lessons to augment their skills, and new ideas to influence their lives.

People may not participate in sustained reading the way they used to (or the way we think they used to), but people read. They text, tweet, and post on Facebook. They search for things they need or want to know. They get lost in stories. People read what is important to them.

## Redefining Reading

If we define reading only as a sustained and literary activity, if we acknowledge only one kind of reading, then we measure ourselves against a fabricated truth. We ignore the actual activity and exclude people's needs and desires.

The truth is there are different ways to read, and they are all valid and important. As typographers, we can support them all.

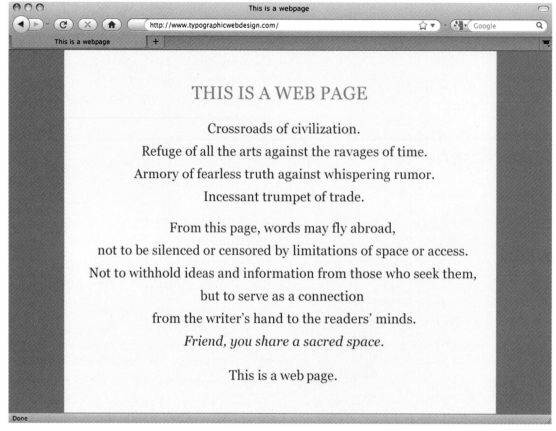

FIGURE 1 Information and ideas fly abroad, carried by words and characters now manifest in pixels of light. With respect to Beatrice Warde (en.wikipedia.org/wiki/Beatrice_Warde) who wrote and designed the original "This is a Printing Office" broadside in 1932.

People read in three ways:

- *Scanning with purpose* is scanning down or across a text, jumping from section to section, looking for a specific piece of information. The reader may glance only at the first letter or word of each section, dismissing incorrect matches and moving on.

- *Casual reading* is skimming over a text, reading sentences here and there (the first sentence of each paragraph, the caption, the pull quote) to get a general idea and flavor of the text.

- *Sustained reading* is engaged reading. It includes pleasure reading (pursued for its own sake) and reading for understanding. Readers slow down, read the entire text, and may go into a trancelike state.

**As typographers, our first responsibility is to our readers.** Our most important job is to help our readers find, understand, and connect with the words, ideas, and information they seek.

**Our second responsibility, then, is to honor the content.** We must help to clarify and share the meaning of the texts people read.

## Design from the Text, Not the Top-Left Corner

Designing a web page need not start with a blank screen and a prayer for inspiration. Knowing what the text says and how (and why) people will read it can and should influence the design.

### Designing from the Text

When scanning with purpose, readers need a left line down which to scan. They need words set in a font they can read easily and quickly.

They need information to be "chunked" for them, visually separated or grouped, so they can skip ahead if what they seek isn't in the current section. They need these chunks laid out in a consistent manner, so if they skip to the next section, they know what to expect.

When engaged in casual or sustained reading, readers need to feel comfortable. They shouldn't have to decipher words set in hard-to-read fonts (or font sizes). They need a comfortable line length so they don't get fatigued, and a generous line height to promote horizontal motion.

Casual and sustained reading benefit from chunking, too. Knowing when and where sections start and end gives readers a sense of the overall structure of a text. Chunking makes the text more manageable, providing readers with entry and exit points.

These are but a few of the things readers need. Understanding how people read leads to readable text blocks. Readable text blocks become the cornerstone for building a grid. Levels of hierarchy create emphasis. Captions and pull quotes become counterpoints to the text and create visual rhythm. Horizontal and vertical spacing create visual tension. Before you know it, a design develops, built upon your knowledge of how people read.

### Designing for Pleasure

We are pleasure-seeking creatures and appreciate fine things: beautiful colors, textures, and shapes; contrasts in rhythm; layers of complexity. But fine things cannot compensate for an unpleasant reading experience.

Instead of asking, "What can I do with this space?" ask, "What does a reader need from the text?"

Instead of asking, "What new font am I dying to use?" ask, "What does the text need from me?"

Instead of starting with visual inspiration, read the text you'll be working with. Design a pleasurable reading experience, and the other fine things will follow.

## What to Expect from This Book

This book will teach you how to think like a typographer in HTML and CSS.

**This is a book about typography.** It is a book about how to visually organize and design web pages based on how people read. It is a book about respecting, clarifying, and sharing the words, ideas, and information presented on a website.

This book shows how to choose fonts, create rhythm and tension, and create systems of vertical spacing and hierarchy. It shows how to sketch ideas, develop a grid, design a data chart, and integrate navigation. It also shows how historic approaches to typography can be used in web design.

**This is a book about typography for the web.** The content comes from hands-on exploration, from decades of using type on the printed page, from classic and contemporary typography books written by experienced book typographers, from over a decade of using type on the web, and from current blogs dedicated to web typography. This book combines typography tips established precomputer with instructions on using the relatively new `@font-face` property to incorporate web fonts.

**This book lets you practice what you're learning.** It gives you typography "rules" to follow, explains why they work, when to break them, and offers you the opportunity to test the rules with hands-on exercises in HTML and CSS.

Do the lessons. Designers are visual thinkers and makers. Many of us are kinesthetic learners. Doing the lessons will help you apply the concepts immediately. If you do not know HTML and CSS (or are feeling a bit rusty), use the step-by-step walk-throughs given with each lesson. I recommend using TextWrangler (a free text editor for the Mac available at `barebones.com/products/textwrangler/`) or Notepad++ (a free text editor for PCs available at `notepad-plus-plus.org`).

Read the walk-throughs, even if you're HTML/CSS savvy. I often draw attention to details, offering typographic tips that are best shown in the context of creating a layout.

**This is not a book about writing clean HTML and CSS syntax.** It is not a book about web compliance, testing across browsers, interactivity, or how to

structure a website. Excellent books and websites are available to learn about those issues. Every single one of the issues is integral to designing the best (accessible, usable) website possible, but they are not about how people read.

This is a book about typography.

## How This Book Is Organized

The book is organized into four parts.

**Part 1—Getting Started: How to Choose a Font.** The first section discusses the factors you should consider when selecting fonts for your web pages. It introduces choosing fonts based on legibility, aesthetic concerns, styles and weights, and even how to choose two fonts to work together. This section is followed by an Interlude chapter that raises a new topic: how to incorporate rhythm and tension in your layout.

Each chapter includes a lesson so you can practice the new typographic skills presented. In this section, you'll create a page exploring how to create multiple meanings for the same word, two bibliographies, and a page exploring rhythm and tension.

**Part 2—Making Type Work: Scanning with Purpose.** The second section discusses what to think about when designing a web page that people will scan quickly. It describes how to set text in a readable manner, and how to "chunk" text with space and hierarchy. It also covers some of the finer details of typography: working with punctuation, abbreviations, and rule lines. This section is followed by an Interlude chapter that raises another topic related to scanning with purpose: what to consider when setting tabular information. In this section, you'll create a web page for a campus film series and a ferry schedule for Martha's Vineyard.

**Part 3—Making Type Work: Casual and Sustained Reading.** The third section discusses what to think about when designing a web page that people will read in a more sustained manner. It offers more tips on setting text in a readable manner, and introduces typographic concepts for multipage websites: developing a grid, creating a navigation system, and applying systems across multiple pages. This section is followed by the final Interlude chapter that raises a new topic: what to consider when building a web font library. In this section, you'll create a multipage website highlighting the favorite recipes of a popular chef.

**Part 4—Designing with Type: Historical Styles.** The final section briefly introduces three general approaches to designing with type: the Traditionalist typographic page, the Modernist typographic page, and the Post-Modernist typographic page. It introduces formal characteristics of each approach, as well as the relationship between the typographer, the text, and the printed artifact. The chapters discuss examples of contemporary websites incorporating Traditionalist, Modernist, and Post-Modernist elements. In this section, you'll create three layouts (Traditionalist, Modernist, and Post-Modernist) for the same text and create a mini portfolio by linking together all of the lessons outlined in this book.

## About the Syntax in the Book

Unlike syntax typed into a text editor, syntax printed in a book is subject to space limitations. The following notes will help you navigate the code syntax as it appears in the book.

**How to Read the HTML Syntax**

The two-column layout of the book limits the length of code lines, so sometimes the HTML syntax runs onto multiple lines of code, like so:

```
<!DOCTYPE html PUBLIC
    "-//W3C//DTD XHTML 1.0 Strict//EN"
    "http://www.w3.org/TR/xhtml1/DTD
    /xhtml1-strict.dtd">
<html xmlns="http://www.w3.org/1999
    /xhtml">
<head>
<title>Lesson 16: Traditional
    Page</title>
<meta http-equiv="content-type"
    content="text/html;charset=utf-8" />
<link href="traditional_page.css"
    rel="stylesheet" type="text/css" />
</head>
<body>
</body>
</html>
```

Whenever a single line of HTML syntax is split into multiple lines, the syntax is indented. For example, these four lines of syntax should be on a single line:

```
<!DOCTYPE html PUBLIC
    "-//W3C//DTD XHTML 1.0 Strict//EN"
    "http://www.w3.org/TR/xhtml1/DTD
    /xhtml1-strict.dtd">
```

All line breaks occur at one of two places in the syntax. Most line breaks occur immediately before a space (one stroke of the spacebar). For example, these two lines of the syntax need to have a **space** between them when you type them in:

```
<!DOCTYPE html PUBLIC
    "-//W3C//DTD XHTML 1.0 Strict//EN"
```

Some line breaks occur immediately in front of a forward slash (/). When a line starts with a forward slash, **do not** add a space in front of the forward slash. For example, these two lines of syntax should **not** have a space between them when you type them in:

```
"http://www.w3.org/TR/xhtml1/DTD
    /xhtml1-strict.dtd">
```

So the rule is: Indented lines of HTML syntax belong on one long line. Add a space at the line break, **unless** there is a forward slash at the start of the line. Do not add spaces before the forward slashes.

### How to Read the CSS Syntax

Unlike HTML, the CSS code is purposely set on multiple lines to help you read the syntax. Most lines of CSS will end with a curly bracket ( { ) indicating the start of the description, or a semicolon ( ; ) indicating the end of a property value.

Very rarely you will see an example of CSS syntax that needs more than one line, like so:

```
body{
    background-image:url(images
        /background.jpg);
    }
```

Notice how the second line of syntax does not end in a semicolon, and the line below it is indented. This indicates that the two lines of syntax are actually a single line. When these line breaks occur, follow the same rules: if there is a forward slash, do not add a space!

Finally, very occasionally (only in the `@font-face` syntax shown in the book), line breaks occur before a dot ( . ). When a line starts with a dot, **do not** add a space in front of the dot. For example, these three lines of syntax should be typed in as a single line.

```
url('fonts/GrutchShaded-webfont
    .svg#webfontsyal6SUC')
    format('svg');
```

**Do not** add a space before the `.svg`. **Do** add a space before the word `format` (because there is not a dot or a slash in front of it).

When in doubt, copy and paste my syntax from one of the websites noted in the following section.

### Some of the Syntax Is in Bold

Bold syntax indicates where to add or change syntax in already-existing HTML or CSS.

In many lessons you'll write syntax over multiple steps. For example, when building your first web page in Chapter 2, you start by typing in some content:

```
<body>
yes
yes
yes
yes
</body>
```

Then you add heading tags around the content. The additional syntax is shown in bold:

```
<body>
<h1>yes</h1>
<h2>yes</h2>
<h3>yes</h3>
<h4>yes</h4>
</body>
```

## About the Lesson Files

You can download all the files needed to do the lessons in this book from the companion website at www.wiley.com/go/typographicwebde-sign. You can also download the examples I created and used for this book. Note that due to licensing issues, the examples available for download do not include any font files.

The project files are also available on my website, typographicwebdesign.com, along with the examples I created and used in this book. The

examples are not downloadable, so all font files are included. Instructions are provided on how to view, copy, and paste the HTML and CSS syntax. There are also examples of how others have completed the projects. See original student designs like the one shown in Figure 2, read my suggestions for improvement, and see the final revisions.

FIGURE 2 A film series by Josh Terciera, Spring 2010.

---

[1] *Sticks and Stones Can Break My Bones but Print Can Never Hurt Me: A Letter to Fiona on First Reading "The End of Print."* Jessica Helfand, 2000. PDF available at typeculture.com.

# PART 1

# How to Choose a Font

*First I had to learn the hard things, like . . . making letters—thousands and thousands of letters until I should know to perfection every curve, every serif, every thick element of a letter and every thin one, where it belonged and how it related to the form of the letter to which it belonged.*

BEN SHAHN, LOVE AND JOY
ABOUT LETTERS (1963)

# CHAPTER 1

# Anatomy and Legibility: Is the Font Easy to Read?

Text is meant to be read. If it feels difficult to read, people won't want to read it. How easily text can be read on the web depends on how type is used on the screen. One factor that affects readability, and a great place to start, is choosing a legible font.

## What Makes a Font Legible?

When we read, we don't see individual letters; we see (and read) the shapes of the words. These shapes are created primarily by two elements: the strokes of the letters and the spaces in and around the letters. If we lose either of these elements, legibility is compromised.

Did you ever try to read a poor photocopy of a photocopy of a photocopy? Experience tells you that type becomes harder to read with each generation of copying. Why does this happen? Sometimes, multiple-generation photocopies make the text lighter. Thinner strokes start to disappear, leaving only parts of letters and compromising the word shapes. At other times, multiple-generation photocopies make the strokes in the text thicker. The spaces in and around the letters start to disappear. Either way, when strokes

or spaces get lost, the legibility of the font changes, and reading becomes more difficult.

Web typographers need to pay particular attention to the strokes and spaces in a font because of screen resolution. Macintosh screens are 72 pixels per inch, or *ppi*, and Windows screens are 96 ppi. A font set at 12*px* (pixels) will appear approximately ⅙ inch tall on a Mac screen and less than ⅛ inch tall on a Windows screen. In either case, the screen will have (at most) 12px by 12px to render a letter. Thin strokes and small spaces in letterforms start to disappear, and as in the photocopy example, the text will be harder to read.

You'll often hear that "simple" fonts are better for the screen because of the resolution issues. That's a good rule of thumb, but it's not quite enough.

## Comparing Georgia and Helvetica

Helvetica is simpler and cleaner than Georgia, but Georgia is easier to read (Figure 1.1). Text set in Helvetica 12/18 (12px text with an 18px line height) is readable onscreen. Text set in Georgia 12/18, however, is more readable, even though it looks slightly smaller than Helvetica and is a more complex font. So why is it more readable?

Georgia, designed by type designer Matthew Carter, was designed for the screen. In typographical terms, it has a healthy x-height without sacrificing the ascenders and descenders. It also has open apertures, discernible terminals, and slightly looser letter spacing than Helvetica. I define all these terms in the following paragraphs.

Figure 1.2 shows that *descenders* [1] are the strokes of the letters that extend below the baseline. The *baseline* [2] is an invisible line that the letters appear to sit on. The descenders in Georgia and Helvetica are almost the same length [3], but Georgia's serifs give the descenders more presence.

*Serifs* [4] are little horizontal strokes, usually coming off the top and/or bottom of a *stem* [5], which is a vertical stroke in a letter. Georgia (Figure 1.2, top) is a *serif* font (it has serifs), whereas Helvetica (Figure 1.2, bottom) is a *sans serif* font (without serifs).

Web typographers need to pay attention to the strokes and spaces in a font due to screen resolution. Thin strokes and small spaces in letterforms will start to disappear.

Web typographers need to pay attention to the strokes and spaces in a font due to screen resolution. Thin strokes and small spaces in letterforms will start to disappear.

FIGURE 1.1 Text on the screen is not as clear as text printed on paper. Text may appear blurry or "jagged" depending on the reader's monitor. *Top:* Helvetica 12/18 on a 1440x900 Macintosh screen. *Bottom:* Georgia 12/18 on a 1440x900 Macintosh screen is more readable.

Figure 1.3 shows that *ascenders* [6] are the strokes of the letters that extend above the *meanline* [7]— an invisible line that would run along the top of a lowercase *x*. The meanline marks the font's *x-height* [8], which is the height of the lowercase letters between the baseline and the meanline.

Georgia has larger ascenders than Helvetica [9]. The generous ascenders make Georgia more legible. (Notice that the *f* and *t* in Helvetica look almost alike.) To compensate for the larger ascenders, Georgia's x-height is smaller. Unfortunately, this smaller x-height makes the text look smaller (even when it's set at the same size as Helvetica), but the larger ascenders are worth the sacrifice.

Figure 1.4 shows the *aperture* [10], which is the opening in letters such as *a* and *e*. *Terminals* [11] are the ends of strokes not terminated with a serif. Georgia's larger aperture and discernible terminals help with legibility. Helvetica's *e* and *a* look similar. They have a smaller aperture and lack distinctive terminals.

Overall, the letters in Georgia have more visual space around them. This space increases readability because it keeps letters in the text from blending together.

FIGURE 1.2 *Top:* Georgia. *Bottom:* Helvetica. 1 descender; 2 baseline; 3 length of baseline; 4 serifs; 5 stem.

It may seem odd that I've chosen to compare the web-safe font Georgia with Helvetica, which isn't web safe. Helvetica is famous for its simplicity and clarity, which makes it the perfect font to show that clean and simple aren't enough to guarantee legibility onscreen.

FIGURE 1.3 *Left:* Georgia. *Right:* Helvetica. 6 ascender; 7 meanline; 8 x-height; 9 height of the ascenders.

FIGURE 1.4 *Top:* Georgia. *Bottom:* Helvetica. 10 aperture; 11 terminal.

### Elements of Legibility

To summarize, reading text type (12 to 16px) is easier if the font has the following characteristics:

- A generous x-height
- Open apertures
- Prominent ascenders and descenders
- Slightly loose letter spacing
- Discernible terminals

## Comparing More Fonts

What makes Georgia, Times New Roman, Verdana, and Arial good choices for comparison? All four are web-safe fonts that are extremely likely to be on most computers, regardless of platform.

Georgia and Verdana are superior fonts for legibility of text on the web. They were designed for the screen and are easy to read. I use Georgia and Verdana in examples and lessons throughout this book—but they aren't the only acceptable fonts.

The number of fonts available to web typographers is increasing. Thus, an objective of this chapter is to show you how to look at and think about the parts of letters so that you can identify other legible fonts for text on the web.

Times New Roman is a visually smaller font than Georgia. In Figure 1.5, I've set Georgia at 63px and Times New Roman at 68px. The fonts' x-heights appear to be equal at these sizes, allowing you to see the differences clearly.

Times New Roman has narrower *bowls* (round shapes in the lowercase letters) [12] than Georgia does. A narrower bowl often results in smaller *counterforms* (spaces within a letterform) [13]. Smaller counterforms in text onscreen tend to get lost.

FIGURE 1.5 *Top:* Georgia. *Bottom:* Times New Roman. 12 bowl; 13 counterform.

Times New Roman also has thicker thick strokes and thinner thin strokes than Georgia does. The thin strokes have a tendency to get lost onscreen when the font is used for text. This tendency, combined with the narrower bowl, makes the text look more like a series of vertical strokes (Figure 1.6). The reader needs to work harder to read the word shapes in Times New Roman.

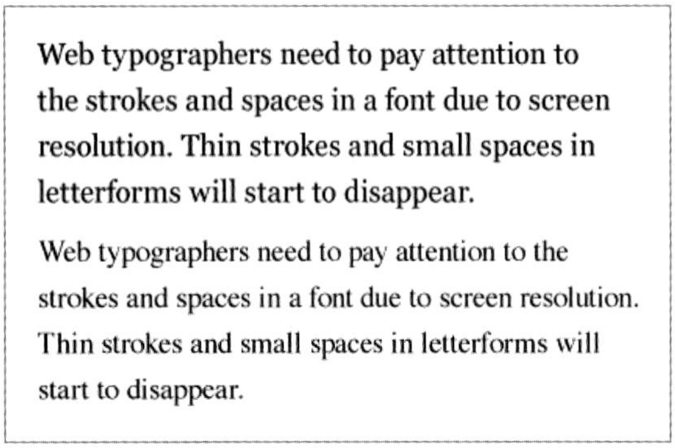

Web typographers need to pay attention to the strokes and spaces in a font due to screen resolution. Thin strokes and small spaces in letterforms will start to disappear.

Web typographers need to pay attention to the strokes and spaces in a font due to screen resolution. Thin strokes and small spaces in letterforms will start to disappear.

FIGURE 1.6 *Top:* Georgia 12/18 on a 1440x900 Macintosh screen is highly readable. *Bottom:* Times New Roman 12/18 on a 1440x900 Macintosh screen looks more like a series of vertical strokes and is hard to read.

Arial is a visually smaller font than Verdana. In Figure 1.7, I've set Verdana at 59px and Arial at 62px. The two fonts' x-heights appear to be equal at these sizes, allowing you to see the differences clearly.

FIGURE 1.7 Verdana (*top*) has more visual space than Arial (*bottom*) does.

Arial and Verdana both have generous bowls— neither is particularly narrow—but Verdana's bowl has a bit more visual space. Verdana's *shoulder* (the part of the bowl that connects to the stem) [14] connects to the stem differently. Notice that the counterforms in Arial's *h* and *p* are rounded, whereas Verdana's counterforms [15] have a corner, so Verdana's counterforms are more spacious. Verdana also has more space between letters.

Verdana's *a, c,* and *e* all have a larger aperture, giving the letters even more visual space (Figure 1.8). All these design decisions keep Verdana more legible at typical text sizes (Figure 1.9).

# a c e
# a c e

FIGURE 1.8 The larger apertures in Verdana (*top*) create more visual space than those in Arial (*bottom*), thus improving legibility.

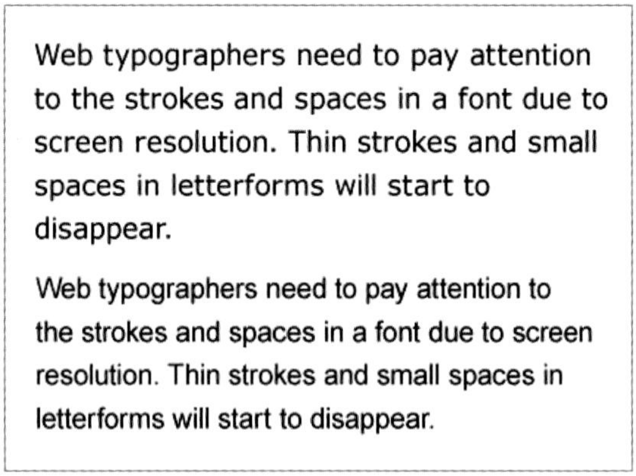

Web typographers need to pay attention to the strokes and spaces in a font due to screen resolution. Thin strokes and small spaces in letterforms will start to disappear.

Web typographers need to pay attention to the strokes and spaces in a font due to screen resolution. Thin strokes and small spaces in letterforms will start to disappear.

FIGURE 1.9 *Top:* Verdana 12/18 on a 1440x900 Macintosh screen is very readable. *Bottom:* Arial 12/18 on a 1440x900 Macintosh screen has less visual space than Verdana and is a bit harder to read.

**Recommended Reading**

To learn more about legibility, try the following resources:

- "It's About Legibility" by Allan Haley:
  www.fonts.com/aboutfonts/articles/
  typography/legibility.htm

- "Georgia & Verdana: Typefaces designed for the screen (finally)" by Daniel Will-Harris:
  www.will-harris.com/verdana-georgia.
  htm

- "Matthew Carter"
  en.wikipedia.org/wiki/Matthew_Carter

# Lesson 1: Compare and Contrast Fonts Online

This lesson helps you achieve the following objectives:

• Practice seeing and articulating the differences among fonts—what makes one font more legible than another.

• Build your vocabulary for describing fonts and defending font choices.

• Build your confidence in recognizing what makes a font more legible. As you discover new font options, you can analyze their legibility.

## Comparing Fonts on Typetester

The number of fonts available to web typographers has increased. Thus, an objective of this lesson is to practice analyzing parts of letters, articulating how the parts promote legibility on the web.

1  Open your browser, and go to the Typetester website at `www.typetester.org` (Figure 1.10).

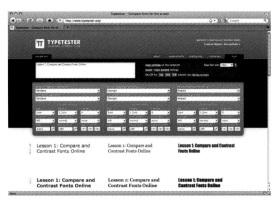

FIGURE 1.10 Typetester, created by Marko Dugonjić.

2  A paragraph of sample text loads automatically. Type your own text, if you prefer.

3  At the top of the left column, choose Georgia from the Choose Typeface from the List drop-down menu; at the top of the middle and right columns, choose Courier New and Times New Roman from the Choose Typeface from the List drop-down menus.

4  Compare these fonts with and contrast them to Georgia, writing about what you see (as I describe in the following section).

5  Repeat Steps 3 and 4, this time comparing and contrasting Impact, Arial, and Verdana, and writing about what you see.

6  Finally, compare and contrast two other fonts with Georgia or Verdana, writing about what you see.

You can choose Windows Default, Mac Default, or Windows Vista fonts, or any other fonts you have installed on your computer. Choose fonts that interest you—fonts you'd like to spend time analyzing.

A few popular fonts to try (not web safe, but good for this exercise) are Bodoni, Adobe Garamond, and Futura. Typetester may not list these fonts if you don't have them on your computer, however.

## Writing about What You See

When it comes to the anatomy and legibility of fonts, a great way to build your analytical skills is to notice carefully what you see and write down your observations. Writing forces you to slow down, notice details, and practice your vocabulary.

For each font pair you compare, ask yourself, "Which font is less legible? Why?" Use the following terms to explain your answers:

- Ascenders and descenders
- x-heights
- Bowls
- Apertures
- Terminals
- Counterforms
- Spaces between letters
- Thick and thin strokes

Other terms you may need to use are

- Baselines
- Meanlines
- Serifs
- Stems
- Shoulders

**Setting Font Sizes on Typetester**

Typetester uses a base font size method of setting font size and line height. This method is different from the one I recommend in this book.

On Typetester you will use *ems* to set the size and "leading" (or line height). In web design, ems are multipliers of the document's base font size. Typetester automatically uses a default base font size of 10px, so setting text on Typetester to 1.2 em means your font size = 12px. Line height is a multiple of font size. So in this example, 1.5 em line height = 18px (150 percent of the font size).

If this makes your head swim, don't worry. My method (pixels) is fine. In fact, I recommend using pixels when you start with web typography.

You can read a simple breakdown of the pros and cons of each font size method at `http://webdesign.about.com/cs/typemeasurements/a/aa042803a.htm`. For a more in-depth look at em spaces, read "How to Size Text in CSS," by Richard Rutter, at `www.alistapart.com/articles/howtosizetextincss`.

## Understanding How HTML, CSS, Web Servers, Browsers, and Personal Computers Work Together

HTML, CSS, web servers, browsers, and personal computers work together as a system. When building a website, you'll spend most of your time focusing on the HTML-and-CSS relationship, but fonts are controlled by servers and personal computers—and readers can't see your layouts without a browser—so you need to see how the system works as a whole.

### HTML

HTML stands for *Hypertext Markup Language.* You can use this markup language to structure content for a web page because it tells the browser what content is on the page and how each element has been defined. You could use HTML to tell a browser, "This is my main headline." In HTML, you'd write that information like this:

```
<h1>This is my main headline.</h1>
```

### CSS

CSS stands for *Cascading Style Sheets.* This style-sheet language describes how elements defined in HTML should look. You could use CSS, for example, to tell a browser, "All text between <h1>

and `</h1>` tags should be 24/32 Georgia," and you'd write it like this:

```
h1{
    font-family:Georgia;
    font-weight:normal;
    font-size:24px;
    line-height:32px;
    }
```

You start writing HTML and CSS in the next lesson.

## Browsers

*Browsers* are translators. They translate written HTML and CSS into something you can see (and understand) on your screen. Browsers follow a set of standards, but even standards contain gray areas, so Mozilla Firefox, Internet Explorer, Safari, and other browsers (even different versions of the same browser) don't necessarily display content the same way. It's best to test your pages in different browsers and operating systems to see how each one translates your HTML and CSS instructions.

## Personal Computers and Fonts

The individual web visitor has a lot of control of how he or she views web pages. A reader can have her screen resolution set higher or lower than yours, her browser window can be bigger or smaller than yours, and she can increase or decrease the font size you set in CSS.

Web typographers have to understand that fonts live in the operating system, not in the CSS or the web browser. Therefore, a font that you specify in CSS can be viewed only if the visitor has it on his computer (see Figure 1.11). If you have an unusual font installed on your system, it's easy to design a web page that includes the font; you can see it because the font is installed on your computer. But if your visitors don't have it installed too, their browsers will display a default font instead (see Figure 1.12).

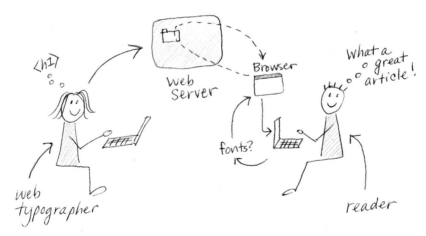

FIGURE 1.11 The web typographer writes code files in HTML and CSS. These files are put on a web server. Browsers download and translate the HTML and CSS so that readers see the designed content (instead of the markup and style-sheet languages). Fonts must be on the reader's computer—or linked from another source—to display correctly in the browser.

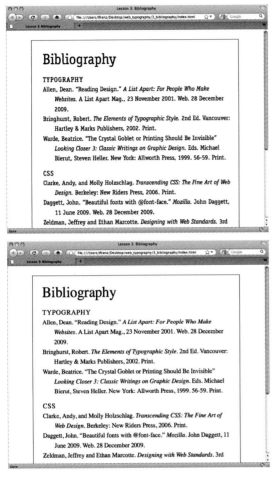

Most browsers now recognize the `@font-face` property in CSS. This property links to fonts, retrieves them from a web server, and displays them on a website. I cover this property in Chapter 4.

## Moving Forward

This chapter showed you how to choose a font based on legibility. It also introduced the system behind a web page.

In the next chapter, you read about choosing a font based on aesthetics and emotions. You also see how to write simple HTML and CSS files.

FIGURE 1.12 *Top:* If you use an unusual font that's installed on your computer, the font will appear to work fine. *Bottom:* Readers who don't have the font installed on their computers will see a default font—usually, Times New Roman.

# CHAPTER 2

# Aesthetics and Emotions: Does the Font Convey the Right Message?

Words have dictionary definitions *(denotations)* and emotional associations *(connotations)*. Fonts can help communicate both types of meaning.

Fonts are like clothing. We take them in and process their underlying meaning constantly—often not noticing them unless they are either really amazing or really "wrong." Sometimes the "wrongness" is related to legibility (letters are hard to recognize). Other times it's related to noticing a font is aesthetically or emotionally mismatched to the meaning of the word or text.

## Choosing a Font with Appropriate Aesthetic or Emotional Associations

The aesthetic and emotional associations that readers have with fonts are social constructs. Readers expect wedding invitations to use script fonts, just as they know how to dress for such occasions. On an intuitive level, they also know they shouldn't see the Declaration of Independence or the U.S. Constitution in Comic Sans (unless it's a political statement), and they probably won't ever see the Supreme Court justices wearing vintage Hawaiian shirts on the bench.

The trick is to remember that *no font can completely and clearly communicate the emotional associations of a text.* No perfect font exists to communicate the complexity of marriage or civil rights, for example, so don't go looking for a font with hearts or gavels in it. You'll only undermine the text by drawing readers' attention to odd elements in the letters. Instead, choose a font that feels like it *could* work—a font that doesn't jar readers because it's inappropriate or unexpected.

The words themselves communicate the message; the font plays a supportive role. It doesn't have to (and shouldn't try to) say, "Look at me! I'm ripe with meaning!"

In Figure 2.1, Comic Sans *looks* like what it is: an informal font designed to imitate comic-book lettering. It's not appropriate for the Declaration of Independence; that would just feel wrong. Caslon 540, on the other hand, is an interpretation of the font (by William Caslon) used to print official copies of the Declaration of Independence on the evening of July 4, 1776. Caslon 540 *feels* more appropriate, even though most people can't identify it and don't know its history. *Historic and other*

...nections aren't necessary for readers to ...ssociations between the font and the text.

...the end, however, Caslon 540 isn't an appropriate font either, regardless of its historical connection to the text. Legibility aside (smallish x-height, too-small closed counter in *e*), Caslon 540 isn't a web-safe font.

We hold these truths to be self-evident, that all men are created equal...

We hold these truths to be self-evident, that all men are created equal...

FIGURE 2.1 *Top:* Comic Sans is an informal font designed to imitate comic-book lettering. *Bottom:* Caslon 540 feels more appropriate for the Declaration of Independence.

## Choosing Serif Fonts for a Traditional Feeling and Sans Serif Fonts for a Modern Feeling

We've built emotional associations with serif and sans serif fonts, influenced by how letters and fonts have been used for hundreds of years.

Serif lettering has been part of the cultural landscape since at least the first century CE via inscriptions, handwritten documents, and fonts. The serif letters on Trajan's Column in Rome (see Figure 2.2) were originally brushed onto the stone before being chiseled out and repainted. Informal handwritten documents at the time were done in cursive, but formal documents and manuscripts were written in Latin Book Hand (which was based on the Roman Square Capitals used in inscriptions like Trajan's Column). The first successful serif typeface was cut in 1470 by Nicholas Jenson.

Thus, for centuries books and printed formal documents were set in serif fonts. Serif letters such as those used for inscriptions, formal documents, and books live in our collective subconscious. We think of them as "old" and "important."

FIGURE 2.2 An inscription on Trajan's Column, built in 113 BCE.

Sans serif lettering was also used in early inscriptions (as early as the fifth century BCE) but didn't have a presence in handwritten documents. Experimental sans serif fonts were used in the 1700s, but the first commercial Latin printing type to include lowercase sans serif letters wasn't in use until 1832.

Thus, sans serif letters took a cultural backseat to serif letters until the end of World War I. In the 1920s, after years of living in a country devastated by war, one group of German designers—the Modernists—wanted to look forward, not backward, to help society move toward a prosperous future. Influenced by industrialization, the Modernists lauded clarity over decoration and function over beauty. They saw all decoration as superfluous, including the serifs on letterforms, and they accused Traditionalists of living in the past, aping what went before.

For both artistic and economic reasons, Traditionalists and Modernists defended their typographic theories while verbally attacking the other camp. In the end, both groups continued to find work in the field. Traditionalism predominated in book design, whereas Modernism predominated in advertising and corporate design. Today, we see Traditionalism and Modernism as peacefully coexisting. We've been exposed to both Traditionalist and Modernist typography and have built our own associations with serif and sans serif fonts along party lines (see Figure 2.3).

We hold these truths to be self-evident, that all men are created equal, that they are endowed by their Creator with certain unalienable Rights, that among these are Life, Liberty and the pursuit of Happiness. That to secure these rights, Governments are instituted among Men, deriving their just powers from the consent of the governed.

We hold these truths to be self-evident, that all men are created equal, that they are endowed by their Creator with certain unalienable Rights, that among these are Life, Liberty and the pursuit of Happiness. That to secure these rights, Governments are instituted among Men, deriving their just powers from the consent of the governed.

FIGURE 2.3 *Top:* Georgia 13/20. *Bottom:* Verdana 12/20. Serif fonts feel "old" and "important." Sans serif fonts feel "functional" and "clear."

## Working with Formatting

Connotation isn't just about fonts. When you're using small bits of text (a word, a quote, or a heading, for example), it helps to consider how people read meaning into capital and lowercase letters, roman and italic type:

- **All caps:** Words set in all caps feel important, powerful, reliable, and enduring (see Figure 2.4). The letters are big and demanding. The letters tend to be square, with little variation in shapes and few round (soft) forms. Early Roman and Greek alphabets didn't have lowercase letters, so inscriptions were done in all caps. Because only the most important words and ideas were worthy of being carved into stone, people began to associate words set in all capital letters with power and importance.

- **All lowercase:** Words set in all lowercase letters are informal and tend to feel friendly. Variations in form, rounded shapes, and no initial capital letter give lowercase words a common, conversational feeling.

- **Italic:** Words set in italic feel humanist because they reference letters written by hand (see Figure 2.5). The letters often have curved endings and thick and thin strokes reminiscent of old pen-and-ink cursive handwriting. Terminals reference where ink may have pooled on the paper. Sans serif italics (often called *oblique* because they're slanted rather than italic in form) lack the organic, humanist quality of serif italics.

# JUSTICE   JUSTICE
## justice      justice

FIGURE 2.4 *Top:* Words set in all caps feel important, powerful, reliable, and demanding. *Bottom:* Words set in all lowercase letters feel less formal.

*justice justice*

FIGURE 2.5 Italic letters reference letters written by the human hand. Serif italics (*left*) look more like cursive than sans serif italics (*right*) do.

- **Quirky fonts:** Quirky fonts give additional meaning to a word and remind us that we cannot classify type by serif and sans serif alone. Impact, a sans serif font, feels very different from Verdana, as shown in Figure 2.6. Impact's bold strokes and condensed forms make it feel both powerful and constricting.

  Unlike Georgia, Courier (a serif font) does not feel traditional at all, as shown in Figure 2.6. It announces, "Hello. I was written on a typewriter." The presence of the imaginary typewriter becomes dominant, and the reader wonders whether this is some sort of potboiler justice doled out by Raymond Chandler's Philip Marlowe.

Justice **Justice**

FIGURE 2.6 You cannot classify all serif fonts as traditional and all sans serif fonts as modern. *Left:* Courier is dominated by the presence of an imaginary typewriter. *Right:* Impact is powerful and constricting.

## Conveying a Message

To summarize, when choosing a font to convey a message:

- Aesthetic and emotional associations are social constructs.

- No font can completely and clearly communicate the emotional associations of a text. Choose a font that seems to work.

- Serif fonts tend to feel traditional; sans serif fonts tend to feel modern.

- Caps are powerful, reliable, and enduring. Lowercase letters are informal and friendly.

- Serif italics feel humanist and more like cursive handwriting than sans serif italics do.

- Fonts play a supporting role to the author's words. Fonts should never shout, "Look at me! I am ripe with meaning!"

## Recommended Reading

To learn more about Modernism, try the Modernism page at

typophile.com/node/12610

# Lesson 2: Word Connotations

This lesson helps you achieve the following objectives:

- Practice using font, size, case, and style to communicate the emotional associations of words (see Figure 2.7).

FIGURE 2.7 Josh Terciera worked with the word *painful*. Visit www.typographicwebdesign.com to see similar explorations.

- Build your vocabulary for describing fonts and defending font choices.
- Build your confidence to communicate emotional associations in a subtle way (no hearts, daggers, or blood!) by using available resources (web-safe fonts).
- Take the time to find out how readers "read" the solutions you create for this lesson.
- Write your first HTML and CSS documents with a focus on type.

## Communicating Different Meanings of a Word

In this lesson, you will create four typographic versions of a single word.

1 Choose a word that you have an emotional association with.

2 Using typetester.org, test your word in various fonts and sizes.

Try to communicate different, or even opposite, connotations for the word. Experiment with case (capital and lowercase), style (roman and italic), and size. Take screen shots of your word as you experiment, jotting down fonts and sizes to document your process.

3 Choose four versions of the word to set in HTML and CSS.

All four versions must use web-safe fonts. If you want to work with other fonts, do more than four versions of the word.

4 Create an HTML document defining four versions of the word and a CSS document describing each of the four versions of the word.

If you are an HTML/CSS beginner (or feeling a bit rusty), follow my step-by-step instructions to build my version of this lesson.

5 Ask at least two people to look at your finished assignment and describe the emotional associations that they have with each version of the word.

The words themselves communicate the message; the font plays a supportive role. The fonts you choose don't have to (and shouldn't try to) shout, "Look at me! I am ripe with meaning!"

## Writing about What You See

When it comes to how fonts communicate, a great way to build your analytical skills is to carefully notice what you see and write down your observations. Writing forces you to slow down, notice details, and practice your vocabulary.

For each of the four versions of the word, ask yourself these questions:

- How do size, case, style, and font affect the meaning of this word?
- Did you choose a font that overshadows the word itself?
- Did other people have the same emotional associations with the word that you did?

## Writing Your First HTML and CSS Files

This lesson addresses the naming conventions and a recommended organizational structure for HTML files and folders. It also introduces five common IDs and elements: `<div>`, `<h1>`, `<h2>`, `<h3>`, and `<h4>`.

Before starting the lesson, you need a text editor to write your files, such as the following:

- For the lessons in this book, I used TextWrangler, from Bare Bones Software (available at `bare bones.com/products/textwrangler/ download.html`). The software is free, and works on Macs. It provides more text-editing control than BBEdit (another Bare Bones product) does and isn't weighed down by a lot of bells and whistles.
- If you're working on a PC, I recommend Notepad++, another free text editor (available at `notepad-plus-plus.org/download`).

- If you're working in a program such as Adobe Dreamweaver, you can still do all the lessons and follow along with my notes; simply work in code view.

**Naming Conventions**

The following list explains some basics about naming your files:

- Filenames need to be consistent, and HTML is case sensitive. I always use lowercase letters (no caps), so I know exactly what case I used for each filename.
- HTML balks at spaces. If you create a file, folder, or image name with a space in it, any links to that file, folder, or image may break. I always use an underscore character (_) instead of a space. Thus, I would name a folder *word_connotations* instead of *Word Connotations*.
- To keep filenames simple and links working, I recommend using only letters, numbers, and underscore characters.
- Periods (dots) should only be used with file extensions (*.html, .css,* and so on)
- Your home page should always be called *index.html.* A browser will look for and open the *index.html* file in any folder you send it to.
- Finally, name your files and folders something meaningful. You won't remember what the heck *new_page2.html* is tomorrow morning.

**Organizing Files**

HTML files reference other files. They link to images, other HTML documents, PDFs, CSS files, and so on. These links work only if the HTML file knows where to find the other files.

For now, you'll be working in a kind of closed system. Your HTML files will reference only other files on your desktop.

It's still important to keep everything organized so that links don't get broken.

Follow these steps:

1  Start by creating a main folder for all the lessons you'll do for this book, calling it *web_typography*.

2  In that folder, create a folder for this lesson, and call it *2_word_connotations*.

   You should include the lesson number that so folders stay in numerical order (for referencing). This structure may come in handy later if you want to review HTML or CSS you wrote in earlier lessons.

If you were creating a web page with images, you'd also need to make an *images* folder, but because this exercise doesn't call for you to incorporate any images, you can skip that step.

### Writing the HTML File

In your text editor, create a new document, and save it as *index.html* in your *2_word_connotations* folder.

Before you put content into the file, you need to type a few things.

#### Type the initial code

Type the following code, making sure not to skip any characters or spaces. The "About the Syntax in the Book" section in the Introduction gives tips on how to type in syntax so you don't skip necessary spaces or add unnecessary spaces.

```
<!DOCTYPE html PUBLIC "-//W3C//DTD
    XHTML 1.0 Strict//EN"
    "http://www.w3.org/TR/xhtml1/DTD
    /xhtml1-strict.dtd">
<html xmlns="http://www.w3.org/1999
    /xhtml">
```

```
<head>
<title>Title of the document</title>
<meta http-equiv="content-type"
    content="text/html;charset=utf-8" />
</head>
<body>
</body>
</html>
```

OK, so what the heck does all that mean?

### The DOCTYPE and DTD

Take a closer look at the first lines:

```
<!DOCTYPE html PUBLIC "-//W3C//DTD
    XHTML 1.0 Strict//EN"
"http://www.w3.org/TR/xhtml1/DTD
    /xhtml1-strict.dtd">
```

The DOCTYPE allows your HTML to be validated against a Document Type Definition (DTD), which tells the browser how to render your CSS. If you use an incorrect DOCTYPE, browsers will assume you've written invalid mark-up. The DTD you've typed is *DTD XHTML 1.0 Strict*. Your HTML will be valid only if you've used accepted elements and attributes. Because I'm not going to show you any deprecated (no longer acceptable) elements or attributes, this DTD is the correct one to use.

Notice that you're actually using XHTML for your syntax. XHTML uses a stricter syntax and promotes clean code. I refer to the syntax as HTML throughout this book, however, because of this line:

```
<meta http-equiv="content-type"
    content="text/html;charset=utf-8" />
```

You'll be serving (presenting for use) the XHTML as text/html. Browsers recognize the syntax as HTML, and you won't use any tags that aren't HTML compliant.

27

## Tags

HTML uses tags to define elements. Tags come in pairs: they open and close.

Look at the preceding HTML example closely. Find the `<html>` tag and the `</html>` tag. The first tag opens the definition; the second tag (with the `/`) closes the definition.

It may be hard to find the opening HTML tag because it actually looks like this:

```
<html xmlns="http://www.w3.org/1999
    /xhtml">
```

XHTML adds an `xmlns` declaration for the XHTML namespace in the `<html>` tag. The declaration is used to qualify attribute names. You don't need to know how the `xmlns` works; just know that you need to include `xmlns` in the `<html>` tag when using XHTML.

Whether or not an opening tag includes extra syntax, it still starts the definition. Thus, the `<html></html>` pair means that everything between these two tags is HTML.

### Head, Title, and Body Elements

You'll also see three other tag pairs, called *elements*:

```
<head></head>
<title></title>
<body></body>
```

The closing tag in each pair includes a slash (/).

An HTML document begins with a *head element*, which defines information about the document (what the title is, the link to the CSS file, metadata, scripts, and so on). Next is the `<title>` element, which lives in the head element. The tag pair `<title></title>` should be nested inside the `<head></head>` tags. In other words, the

`<title></title>` tags always go after the starting `<head>` tag but before the closing `</head>` tag, as follows:

```
<head>
<title>Title of the document</title>
</head>
```

There is also some metadata in the head element (right after the title element):

```
<meta http-equiv="content-type"
    content="text/html;charset=utf-8" />
```

This metadata defines the *character encoding*, which tells the web browser what set of characters (letters, numbers, and so on) to use when converting the bits to characters. You don't need to understand exactly how it works; just know that this line is required and should live in the head element. Notice that the metadata closes with `/>`. Because the `<meta>` tag isn't used for holding content, it doesn't come as a pair of tags. Because there's no closing tag, you close the single tag with `/>`.

The last pair of tags is the `<body>` element, which contains the content of the HTML document. You'll add content here as you progress through the lesson.

### View your web page

Take a moment to save your document.

Open the document in your browser. Do you see a blank screen, with the document's title at the top of the browser window? Perfect!

Now you can start putting in some content.

### Give the page a title

Between the `<title>` tags, change *Title of the document* to *Lesson 2: Word Connotations*.

### Add the content

Between the `<body>` tags, add your word four times. It will look something like this:

```
<body>
yes
yes
yes
yes
</body>
```

### View your web page

Save your HTML document, and view your document in your browser (if your browser is still open you can just click the Refresh button). You'll see the changes.

Now your web page has a meaningful title at the top of the browser window, and it has your word written four times. Unfortunately, the word runs across a single line, like this: yes yes yes yes (see Figure 2.8).

Why does it look like this? Browsers translate the HTML. Your browser will show only what you've given it. You haven't told the browser where to put line breaks, so it didn't add any.

### Define your headings

Usually, you'd use the paragraph element `<p></p>` to define paragraphs and break the lines. But since you aren't using whole paragraphs of text here, and I want you to set each of the four words differently, instead you'll use a variety of heading elements to define each word.

Put the following tag pairs in your HTML, using one pair around each word (note the bold code for the tags):

```
<body>
<h1>yes</h1>
<h2>yes</h2>
<h3>yes</h3>
<h4>yes</h4>
</body>
```

### View your web page

Save your HTML document, and view the changes. You should see your words in a column along the left edge. The words are bold and get smaller as they go down (see Figure 2.9).

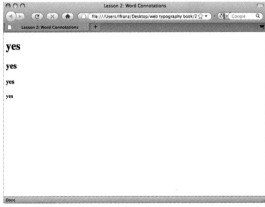

FIGURE 2.9 Headline elements (<h1> to <h6>) have default stylistic values. All <h> tags, for example, default to bold. You need to describe elements differently in CSS if you don't want items to be displayed with default settings.

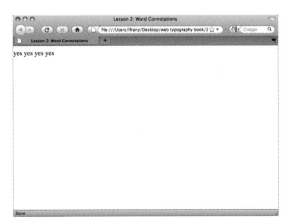

FIGURE 2.8 The word runs across a single line because you haven't told the browser where to put line breaks.

29

Why does each word look a little different from the others? The heading elements (`<h1>` to `<h6>`) have default stylistic values that browsers use to display the headings—unless *you* describe the elements differently. That's exactly what you are going to do next.

### Writing the CSS File

The CSS document is where you can, among other things, *describe how elements defined in* HTML *should look.* For this assignment, you tell the browsers what the `<h1>`, `<h2>`, `<h3>`, and `<h4>` elements should look like.

In TextWrangler (or another text editor), create a new document, and save it as *word_connotations. css* in your *2_word_connotations* folder.

### Describing an Element

CSS descriptions have three parts:

- **Selector:** The element/ID/class you want to describe
- **Property:** The attribute you want to affect
- **Value:** The value you want to assign to the property

Written together, they look like this:

```
selector{property:value;}
```

If you want to set your `<h1>` in Georgia, for example, you would write it like this:

```
h1{font-family:georgia;}
```

To set your `<h1>` in 24px Georgia, you would write it like this:

```
h1{font-family:georgia;font-
size:24px;}
```

Notice that the two properties—`font-family` and `font-size`—are separated by a semicolon.

Also notice that there are no spaces anywhere in the syntax. If you ever need to type a value with two or more words (such as `Comic Sans MS`), put that value in quotation marks (as in `font-family:"Comic Sans MS"`).

If you want to set your `<h1>` in 24/32 Georgia and remove the bold (default) setting associated with the `<h1>` element, your syntax is going to get longer. To make the CSS easier to read, it's customary to put one `property:value` pair on each line, separated with a semicolon, like this:

```
h1{
    font-family:georgia;
    font-weight:normal;
    font-size:24px;
    line-height:32px;
    }
```

It is also customary to indent the `property:value` pairs. This helps make the syntax easier to read.

### Describe the first element: `<h1>`

In this lesson, you will create four typographic versions of a single word you choose. But to learn the HTML/CSS, an example is provided using four versions of the word *yes* (see Figure 2.10).

Make the top version of *yes* to be 48/48 Georgia italic, regular weight, and centered. Type the following CSS syntax and then save the CSS file:

```
h1{
    font-family:georgia;
    font-style:italic;
    font-weight:normal;
    font-size:48px;
    line-height:48px;
    text-align:center;
    }
```

# YES
# *yes* YES
# yes

FIGURE 2.10 Four versions of the word *yes*. *Top:* Impact. *Middle left:* Georgia italic. *Middle right:* Georgia. *Bottom:* Verdana.

Now look at the web page in the browser again. Wait! Nothing changed! What went wrong?

**Tell the HTML file to reference the CSS file**

The browser doesn't know to use the CSS file. You need to tell it to do so. Add the following line in the head element (that is, between the <head> </head> tags) of the HTML file:

```
<link href="word_connotations.css"
    rel="stylesheet" type="text/css" />
```

You'll put this syntax in the head element of any HTML file that references a CSS file. Notice that you're telling the HTML file to reference *word_connotations.css,* which is the CSS file you just created. This filename is a variable. Use the correct name of the CSS file for each project.

Save the HTML file, and reload the file in the browser window. It works!

**Describe the second element: <h2>**

You want the second version of *yes* to be 60/60 Georgia, regular weight, all caps, with 5 pixels of letterspacing, and centered. Type the following CSS syntax:

```
h2 {
    font-family:georgia;
    font-weight:normal;
    font-size:60px;
    line-height:60px;
    text-transform:uppercase;
    letter-spacing:5px;
    text-align:center;
    }
```

Save the CSS file, and view the web page in the browser again.

**Describe the third element: <h3>**

Make the third version of *yes* 120/120 Impact, regular weight, all caps, and centered. Type this CSS syntax:

```
h3 {
    font-family:impact;
    font-weight:normal;
    font-size:120px;
    line-height:120px;
    text-transform:uppercase;
    text-align:center;
    }
```

Save the CSS file, and view the web page in the browser again.

### Describe the fourth element: <h4>

Make the fourth version of *yes* 24/24 Verdana, regular weight, and centered onscreen. Type this CSS syntax:

```
h4{
    font-family:verdana;
    font-weight:normal;
    font-size:24px;
    line-height:24px;
    text-align:center;
    }
```

Save the CSS file, and view the web page in the browser again.

You've described all four elements. Everything looks good, but the words have unexpected white spaces between them (see Figure 2.11). These spaces are caused by default margins in the <h1> to <h6> elements. Leave these margins alone for now (I cover them in the next lesson) and move on to creating a "div."

FIGURE 2.11 Headings (<h1> to <h4>) described in CSS. Notice the white spaces between words, which are caused by default margins in the elements.

### Creating a div

*Div* is short for *division*. Think of a `<div></div>` pair as a container (or layout box) you can use to create structure in your web page (see Figure 2.12).

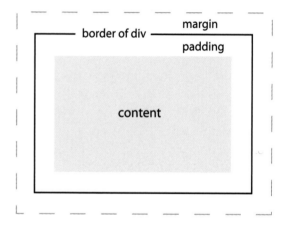

Your div will take up the entire space, even if the content or bordered area looks smaller.

FIGURE 2.12 A div has margins and padding, even if readers see only the border and content.

You often see a div referred to as a *wrapper*. You can use either term when referring to a div.

A div is a box to hold content. It has a border. It also has padding inside the border and a margin between the border and other elements in the layout. You'll become more acquainted with margins, padding and borders later, but for right now, add and describe a simple div.

#### Add a div in your HTML

You want the four words to live inside the div, so add the `<div>` tags around your content. Type the following syntax inside your body element and before your `<h1>` element:

```
<div id="main_container">
```

32

Notice that you didn't type just `<div>`. Why? Most web pages contain more than one div to structure the content (just as most magazines have more than one column of text). Unlike headlines, in which you have six (`<h1>` to `<h6>`) tags to work with, you have only one `<div>` tag to use, so you need to identify (ID) which div you want to use when you add a div to your HTML.

I've named the div `main_container` because it's the main div that *contains* all the other elements in the layout. In HTML and CSS, you can name divs whatever you want to. I find that `main_container` is most meaningful for me, but use `wrapper` if you prefer. Just make sure that the div name in your HTML matches the div name in your CSS.

As your web page compositions become more complex, you'll need to identify multiple divs to build your pages (div IDs are unique and can only be used once on a page). You should always name your divs in a meaningful way: `header`, `footer`, `page`, `main_navigation`, and so on.

You still have to close the div. After your `<h4>` element, still inside your body element, type `</div>`.

### Describe the div ID

If you were to save and view your *index.html* file in the browser, you wouldn't see any changes, because you haven't described the `div id` in CSS.

To make your `main_container` div a white rectangle (400px wide) with a black border (1px), centered in the browser, write the syntax like this:

```
#main_container{
    width:400px;
    border-width:1px;
    border-style:solid;
```

```
    margin-top:20px;
    margin-right:auto;
    margin-bottom:0px;
    margin-left:auto;
    background-color:#ffffff;
}
```

The `div id` selector looks different from the `<h1>` selectors because you're dealing with an ID. You're describing a specific ID applied to a div, so you create and describe the ID #main_container, not div. To create and describe an ID in CSS, you must precede the name with a hash mark (#).

There are also some new properties in this syntax:

- You set the size of the container to 400px wide and put a solid, 1px border around it.

- You set the margins of the `main_container`. The margins are the spaces between the container and elements next to it. The only element next to your `main_container` is the browser window. You put 20px between the top edge of the `main_container` and the browser window. You put 0px between the bottom edge of the `main_container` and the browser window. Most important, you told the browser to automatically calculate the amount of margin to put between the sides of the `main_container` and the browser window. This keeps the `main_container` centered left to right, regardless of the width of the browser window (see Figure 2.13).

- Finally, you made the `main_container` background color white. CSS uses hexadecimal color codes to represent RBG (red, green, blue) colors, and #ffffff means white. (Plenty of color charts are available online. My favorite is Hues Hub, at `www.december.com/html/spec/colorhues.html`.)

33

FIGURE 2.13 Setting the left and right margins to auto keeps the main_container centered in the browser.

You're almost done. Next, you add the background color.

### Add a background color to the page

After you learn the syntax for a property, you can use it across selectors. In the preceding section, for example, you gave `main_container` a white background by adding a line to the syntax describing the `#main_container`:

```
background-color:#ffffff;
```

To add a background color to the page, use the same property syntax but apply it to the body element. In the CSS file, type the following:

```
body{
background-color:#999999;
}
```

Save the CSS file, and view the web page in the browser again. It should look like Figure 2.14.

FIGURE 2.14 The background-color syntax changed the background color of the body (the whole page) to gray.

You have created and described four heading elements, described the body element, and created and described an ID for a div. Congratulations!

For more practice, go back and redo the lesson, using your own word connotations.

If you need to use syntax for a property I haven't covered, HTML Dog (`htmldog.com/reference/cssproperties`) has typographer-friendly resources for finding and setting properties and values.

## Recommended Resources

For this lesson, I recommend the following online resources:

- To download TextWrangler, go to barebones.com/products/textwrangler/download.html

- To download Notepad++, visit notepad-plus-plus.org/download

- To copy and paste the doctype declaration, go to www.w3.org/QA/2002/04/valid-dtd-list.html

- To see examples of this lesson, visit typographicwebdesign.com

- For a full range of colors, visit Hues Hub: december.com/html/spec/colorhues.html

- For articles about using color, visit Design Festival at designfestival.com/category/color/

- To build your own color schemes, go to Color Scheme Designer at colorschemedesigner.com/

- For more CSS syntax, go to htmldog.com/reference/cssproperties/

## Moving Forward

This chapter showed you to how to choose a font based on aesthetics and emotion. It also showed you how to write some basic HTML and CSS.

In the next chapter, you read about choosing a font based on whether it can do the job. You also work with more text and see how to create and apply a class in HTML and CSS.

# CHAPTER 3

# Contrast, Styles, and Characters: Can the Font Do the Job?

Deciding whether the font can do the job starts with reading the text. Is the text complex? Does it have multiple sections and subsections in need of headings and subheadings? Does the author want to emphasize certain ideas? Do you need or want to italicize titles, quotes, or other items?

If you answer "yes" to any of these questions, you need to choose a font that can do the job; you need to find a font family with all the styles and weights you need. A *font family* is made up of all the styles in the font. Most families include regular, bold, italic, and bold italic (see Figure 3.1). More complex families include more styles.

| Regular | Regular |
|:---:|:---:|
| **Bold** | **Bold** |
| *Italic* | *Italic* |
| ***Bold Italic*** | ***Bold Italic*** |

FIGURE 3.1 Two font families. *Left:* Georgia. *Right:* Verdana. Most basic font families include regular, bold, italic, and bold italic.

## What Should I Look for in a Bold Style?

You should consider two factors when looking for a bold style:

- **Contrast:** Is there enough difference between the bold and regular styles to create visual contrast (see Figure 3.2)? Will bold words catch the reader's eye as he scans the text? Will bold words create emphasis without overwhelming the regular text or screaming at the reader?

> Is there enough contrast to create **emphasis** where you need it?
>
> Is there enough contrast to create **emphasis** where you need it?

FIGURE 3.2 *Top:* Sans serif fonts tend to have visually heavier bolds than serif fonts, with greater contrast between bold and regular. *Bottom:* Serif fonts traditionally have less contrast between bold and regular.

Not every bold is alike. Sans serif fonts tend to have visually heavier bolds. Why? Sans serif fonts tend to be *monoline* (all the strokes have similar thickness). When a bold version is designed, every stroke gets significantly thicker, resulting in a visually heavier bold than one designed for a serif font.

A visually heavier bold could be exactly what you're looking for if words or ideas must really jump out at the reader. On the other hand, your text may call for a more subtle contrast.

• **Legibility:** Sometimes, the strokes in bold styles get so thick that the counterforms get lost (see Figure 3.3). This situation can happen if a font was designed for print (the designer didn't build in enough counterspace) or a font family wasn't designed as a system (the designer paid more attention to the regular weight, simply thickening strokes when a bold style was needed).

---

**Do counterforms (spaces) fill in?**

**Do counterforms (spaces) fill in?**

**Do counterforms (spaces) fill in?**

**Do counterforms (spaces) fill in?**

---

FIGURE 3.3 *Top to bottom:* Verdana Bold, Arial Bold, Georgia Bold, and Times New Roman Bold. Choose a bold style with open counterforms. If spaces in and around the letters are too small, the text is harder to read onscreen.

## What Should I Look for in an Italic Style?

Three factors should influence your choice of an italic style: letter shapes, legibility, and contrast.

• **Shapes of letters:** Not all "italic" styles are italic (see Figure 3.4). Some are actually oblique (slanted). True serif italic letters feel like handwriting; they have curved endings, and thick and thin strokes. Sans serif italics feel like regular letters that have been slanted.

---

*Serif italics feel like handwriting.*

*Sans serif italics (oblique) feel like regular letters that have been slanted.*

---

FIGURE 3.4 Not all italic styles are really italic. Most sans serif italics are oblique. Notice the different forms of the *i* and *f* in the serif italic and the sans serif oblique.

• **Legibility:** Sometimes italics lose legibility (see Figure 3.5). The spaces inside and around the letters can get smaller as the letters get narrower. Oblique letters become more illegible as the forms of the letters are squished over on an angle.

---

*Some obliques are harder to read.*
*Some obliques are harder to read.*

*Some italics are harder to read.*
*Some italics are harder to read.*

---

FIGURE 3.5 *Top to bottom:* Compare Verdana Italic, Arial Italic, Georgia Italic, and Times New Roman Italic. Choose an italic (oblique) style with open counterforms. If spaces in and around the letters are too small, text is hard to read.

• **Contrast:** The contrast between regular and italic text is subtle. Italic is often used for titles and quotes that are meant to be read as part of the overall text, rather than for catching a reader's eye as he scans.

## What Else Should I Consider in a Font?

Here are a few other factors to consider when choosing a font:

• **Legibility at small sizes:** Sometimes, text includes captions, footnotes, or other elements that you want to deemphasize. Choose a font that continues to be legible even at small sizes (see Figure 3.6).

> Fonts with larger x-heights, such as Verdana, hold up better even at smaller sizes. This text is set at 10/15 pixels. It's still easy to read.
>
> Fonts with smaller x-heights, such as Georgia, are hard to read at smaller sizes. This text is set at 10/15 pixels. It's more difficult to read.

FIGURE 3.6 Fonts with large x-heights remain legible at small sizes.

• **Capital letters:** If the text includes a lot of capital letters, or if you want to use all caps for a heading, consider what the capital letters in the font look like (see Figure 3.7). Are the forms pleasing and easy to read, or do they take up too much space?

> M.F.K. Fisher        M.F.K. Fisher
> HD DVD movies    HD DVD movies
> New York, NY       New York, NY

FIGURE 3.7 Capital letters in a font should be easy to read and shouldn't stand out too much.

• **Numbers:** There are two kinds of numbers: *lining* and *old style* (see Figure 3.8). *Lining* figures are based on the proportions of capital letters. Old-style figures (also called text figures or non-lining figures) have ascenders and descenders. They blend into text better than lining figures do because they resemble lowercase letters.

> LINING FIGURES        Old style figures
> 1234567890 LOOK      1234567890 look
> LIKE CAPITALS.            like lowercase.

FIGURE 3.8 Lining figures blend in with capital letters, whereas old-style figures blend in with lowercase text.

Poet Robert Bringhurst wrote in *The Elements of Typographic Style*, "[Old-style figures] are basic parts of typographic speech, and they are a sign that dollars are not really twice as important as ideas, and numbers are not afraid to consort on an equal footing with words."

• **Width of the font:** Fonts take up different amounts of horizontal space. They have narrower or wider bowls, and more or less space around the letterforms. A wide font will fit comfortably in a wide column, whereas a narrow font will fit comfortably in a narrow column. I cover column width (line length) in detail in Chapter 6.

## Can the Font Do the Job?

To summarize, to decide whether a font can do the job, read the text, and figure out what you need the font to do. Here are a few tips:

- Look for a bold that provides enough contrast but is still legible.

- Look for an italic that has the shapes/quality you want and retains legibility.

- See whether the font remains legible at small sizes.

- Look at the capital letters. Ask yourself whether they're pleasing and easy to read or too big.

- Look at the numbers. Ask yourself whether they blend in with the text or are lining figures and look more like caps.

- Look at the width of the font. The wider the font is, the longer the line length (column width) will be.

## What If I Can't Get Everything I Want from a Font?

You have many things to consider when choosing a font: bold, italic, caps, numbers, font width, legibility at small sizes, and so on. What if you can't get everything you want?

The truth is, you probably won't. As a typographer, you need to balance everything the text needs with everything you want and decide what characteristics are most important. The font I use in this book, for example, is Aller, but Aller wasn't my first choice.

## Deciding to Use Aller

I originally wanted to use a sans serif font for text and a serif font for headings because this is a book about a contemporary, technology-driven approach to creating typography that is based on traditional typographic theory. I felt that combining the two forms of fonts (modern and traditional) would represent the essence of typographic web design.

But I ran into some problems. The two-column layout in this book (which is the best layout for incorporating the images) results in narrow columns. The first sans serif fonts I tried had bowls that were too wide for the column width. I couldn't fit enough words on each line, and the text got choppy. When I tried condensed sans serif fonts, they didn't look right with any of the serif fonts. There was too much contrast between the fonts. The serif fonts looked wide, open, and traditional. The sans serif fonts looked narrow, tight, and modern.

After testing dozens of fonts, I settled on using a single font: Aller. It's a sans serif font, but it has a lovely, traditional-looking italic and old-style figures. As a contemporary font, it was designed with qualities from both modern and traditional fonts; the final page doesn't feel too modern or too traditional.

In addition, Aller's bowl is narrower than most noncondensed sans serif fonts; more words fit on each line. This improves the flow of the text for reading. Aller has a large x-height, so it can be set fairly small in the captions and retain readability. It has a strong bold for contrast and a pleasing italic; both are important because

italic and bold are needed throughout the text for emphasis. Finally, Aller has pleasing capital letters. This is important because the text is peppered with the acronyms HTML and CSS.

While I gave up the original concept of using both a serif and a sans serif font, in the end I found a font that met the needs of the text while retaining a bit of a traditional feeling and a bit of a modern feeling. Every project is different, as you see in Figure 3.9.

**BREAD & BLESSINGS SANDWICH PROGRAM**
The Bread & Blessings Sandwich Program is a mi
poor and homeless in Providence. Three times a v
volunteers of all ages serve coffee, hot chocolate, |
more than two hundred (200) men, women and c
Congregational Church at 300 Weybosset Street i
Those lunches are made three times a week by an

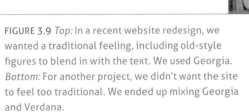

FIGURE 3.9 *Top:* In a recent website redesign, we wanted a traditional feeling, including old-style figures to blend in with the text. We used Georgia. *Bottom:* For another project, we didn't want the site to feel too traditional. We ended up mixing Georgia and Verdana.

41

# Lesson 3: A Short Bibliography, Part 1

This lesson helps you achieve the following objectives:

1   Practice choosing a font based on what it has to offer: roman, italic, bold, caps, and numbers.

2   Practice creating a simple hierarchy for headings, subheadings, titles, and text.

3   Build your vocabulary for describing the differences between two fonts and how they do a job.

4   Write slightly more complex HTML and CSS documents than in the preceding chapters, incorporating a `<span class>`. Even if you're already HTML/CSS savvy, follow the walk-through provided in this section because I share typographic tips as I show the HTML/CSS.

You'll find instructions for Part 2 of the bibliography in Chapter 4.

## Create a Bibliography Using One Font Family

In this lesson, you will create a bibliography with section headings and italicized titles.

1   Use the text file 3_bibliography.doc provided at www.wiley.com/go/ typographicwebdesign.

2   Typeset the bibliography, using either the Verdana or Georgia font family (see Figure 3.10). Use only one font family.

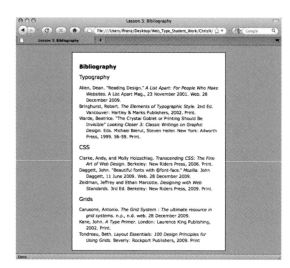

FIGURE **3.10** Working with the text provided, Chris Nelson designed the bibliography shown here. Visit the Typographic Web Design site to see other explorations.

3   The bibliography has the main heading Bibliography. This heading should stand out the most. Make the main heading big, bold, or all caps. Use only one characteristic—size, weight, or case—to emphasize the heading. Changing only one characteristic to create emphasis is more subtle and more difficult, and forces you to balance the elements in the bibliography more carefully.

4   The bibliography is separated into three sections: Typography, CSS, and Grids. These subheads should stand out more than the text but not as much as the main heading. Again, pick one way to emphasize the subheads: size, weight, or case.

5   Within each section are three resources. Each resource includes capital letters, italics, and numbers, so you'll get a chance to use all three elements in the text.

6   When you finish designing the bibliography, take a screen shot and then change the font family. Take a screen shot of the bibliography showing the new font family.

## Writing about What You See

Compare and contrast the two screen shots. How are they different? Analyze the caps, numbers, bold, and italic of each font. Use terms such as *emphasis, contrast,* and *counterforms* in your descriptions. You can also use more colloquial terms, like *gets lost* or *stands out.*

## Using HTML and CSS to Design the Bibliography

This lesson introduces the `<p>` tag for setting your text, the `<span>` tag and classes for italicizing titles, and padding, margins, and text-indent for controlling space around the text.

In the *web_typography* folder, create a folder for the lesson. Call it *3_bibliography.*

### Start the HTML File

In your text editor, create a new document, and save it as *index.html* in your *3_bibliography* folder.

#### Type the basic HTML syntax and title

Add the following code to your *index.html* file (a template for the Doctype Declaration is available for copying and pasting at `w3.org/QA/2002/04/valid-dtd-list.html`):

```
<!DOCTYPE html PUBLIC "-//W3C//DTD
    XHTML 1.0 Strict//EN"
    "http://www.w3.org/TR/xhtml1/DTD
    /xhtml1-strict.dtd">
```

```
<html xmlns="http://www.w3.org/1999
    /xhtml">
<head>
<title>Lesson 3: Bibliography</title>
<meta http-equiv="content-type"
    content="text/html;charset=utf-8" />
</head>
<body>
</body>
</html>
```

#### Add the content

Between the body tags, paste the text from *3_bibliography.doc.*

#### View your web page

Save your HTML document, and drag the icon into your browser. Without `<h1>`, `<p>`, and `<br />` tags, the text runs together (see Figure 3.11). Quotation marks from the Word document flow in as weird syntax (see Figure 3.12), which you will fix later.

**FIGURE 3.11** Without `<h1>`, `<h2>`, and `<p>` tags, the text runs together.

Allen, Dean. â€œReading Designâ€ A List
ake Websites. A List Apart Mag., 23 November
2009. Bringhurst, Robert. The Elements of
. Vancouver: Hartley & Marks Publishers, 2002.
thing else. Warde, Beatrice. â€œThe Crystal
Be Invisible.â€ Looking Closer 3: Classic
n. Eds. Michael Bierut, Steven Heller. New
9. 56-59. Print. CSS Clarke, Andy, and Molly
CSS: The Fine Art of Web Design. Berkeley:

**FIGURE 3.12** Quotation marks from the Word document flow in as weird syntax.

### Add line breaks

You'll use a variety of tags to organize the text.

First, define the main heading (Bibliography) with
<h1> tags, as follows:

```
<h1>Bibliography</h1>
```

Define each subheading (Typography, CSS, and
Grids) with <h2> tags:

```
<h2>Typography</h2>
<h2>CSS</h2>
<h2>Grids</h2>
```

Define each item (book, article, or blog) with <p>
tags:

```
<p>Allen, Dean. "Reading Design."
A List Apart: For People Who Make
Websites. A List Apart Mag., 23
November 2001. Web. 28 December
2009.</p>
```

### View your web page

Save your HTML document, and view the changes.
The bibliography is broken up into the main
heading, subheadings, and individual items.

You still need to fix some things, though:

1   Put the text in a div so you can control the line
    length of the text and center it in the browser.

2   Start writing the CSS file.

3   Improve the typography.

4   Italicize the titles by using a class.

5   Fix the quotation marks.

6   Describe your headings.

The following sections walk you through the
preceding tasks.

### Put the div in your HTML

You want the bibliography to live inside a div, so
add the <div> tags around your content. Type the
following syntax inside your body element and
before your <h1> element:

```
<div id="main_container">
```

After the final item, still inside your body element,
type the closing tag:

```
</div>
```

### Start Writing the CSS File

The CSS document is where you describe how
elements defined in HTML should look. Start by
describing what the div should look like.

In your text editor, create a new document, and
save it as *bibliography.css* in your *3_bibliography*
folder.

### Describe the div ID

To make your main_container div a white rectangle (400px wide) with a black border (1px),
centered in the browser, write the syntax like this:

```
#main_container{
    width:400px;
    border-width:1px;
    border-style:solid;
    margin-top:20px;
    margin-right:auto;
    margin-bottom:0px;
    margin-left:auto;
    background-color:#ffffff;
    }
```

**Tell the HTML file to reference the CSS file**

In the HTML file, add the following line in the head element (between the `<head></head>` tags):

```
<link href="bibliography.css"
    rel="stylesheet" type="text/css" />
```

Remember to put this syntax in the head element of any HTML file that references a CSS file. Notice that you're telling the HTML file to reference *bibliography.css*, which is the CSS file you just created. In Chapter 2, you linked to a different CSS file.

---

### About the HTML and CSS in This Book

The lessons in this book focus on web typography, not on writing clean, expert syntax. This is not a book about web compliance, testing across browsers, interactivity, or how to structure a website. All of these issues are integral to designing the best (most accessible, most usable) website possible, but they are not the focus of these lessons.

If you are new to writing HTML and CSS, these lessons were written for you. Every step in the process is explained, and new techniques are introduced in each chapter so you can build your HTML and CSS skills with confidence. I avoid HTML and CSS that assumes prior knowledge. I want to help you get up and running quickly so you can revel in your successes. You can learn more advanced techniques once you have mastered the basics.

If you are experienced writing HTML and CSS, some of the syntax and semantics used in the lessons might not match your expectations of how HTML and CSS should be written. For instance, I don't use shorthand or introduce reset stylesheets. I don't show how to use more than a couple of techniques in each chapter, so semantically, HTML markup might feel a "step behind" in some places. I use naming conventions meant to help new HTML and CSS writers recognize what they are doing in their syntax.

If you already know how to complete a lesson using more advanced techniques or using different semantics, please do so! This is the perfect time to weave together your new typographic skills and your existing HTML and CSS knowledge. But I still recommend you take the time to read through the walk-throughs; you have the opportunity to see what a typographer looks for on the screen.

**Save your HTML document and view the changes**
The text is in a reasonable column, but it's too close to the border of the div (see Figure 3.13). Next, you add some padding (space inside the div) to give the text a little breathing room.

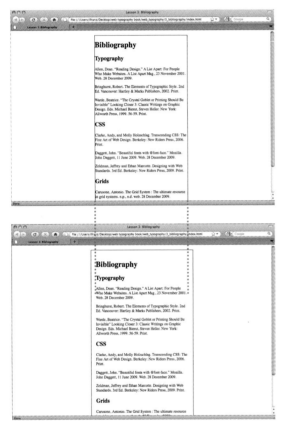

FIGURE 3.13 *Top:* Without padding, the text is right up against the border of the div. *Bottom:* With 20px padding all around, you have space between the text and the border of the div. Notice that the padding increased the amount of space occupied by the div. The 400px div now takes up 440px.

**Add padding**
To add the same amount of padding all the way around (20px, for example), add the following

syntax to the list of property:values; for the `#main_container` in CSS:

```
padding:20px;
```

Now your `#main_container` syntax looks like this:

```
#main_container{
    width:400px;
    border-width:1px;
    border-style:solid;
    margin-top:20px;
    margin-right:auto;
    margin-bottom:0px;
    margin-left:auto;
    background-color:#ffffff;
    padding:20px;
    }
```

To add different amounts of padding on each side, set individual properties, moving clockwise from the top:

```
padding-top:10px;
padding-right:20px;
padding-bottom:30px;
padding-left:40px;
```

*Note:* If you already know how to write CSS shorthand, feel free to use it instead. I don't use shorthand in this book.

**Improve the Typography**
Now that the div is set properly, it's time to attend to the typography. Continue working in your CSS file.

**Style the <p> tag**
For this example, I used Georgia. You may choose to use Verdana, so write your syntax accordingly.

Style the <p> just like you styled the heading elements in Chapter 2. If you want the text to be Georgia 13/20px, left aligned, with no spaces between the paragraphs, write the syntax like this:

```
p{
    font-family:georgia;
    font-size:13px;
    line-height:20px;
    text-align:left;
    margin:0px;
    padding:0px;
    }
```

By specifically setting margins and paddings to 0px, you override any default spaces that browsers add to <p> tags. Again, you can alter this syntax to include the values you prefer.

### Change the left margin to outdent

Bibliographies are set so that all lines except the first are indented; the first line of each item is outdented.

To outdent the first line, you add a left margin to the text and then remove the extra left margin on the first line only.

The syntax styling the <p> tag simply describes the margin as margin:0px;. You need to change the margin so that the left margin is 20px but all the others remain 0px. Use the following code to do so:

```
margin-top:0px;
margin-right:0px;
margin-bottom:0px;
margin-left:20px;
```

Next, to remove the extra left margin on the first line only, add the following line:

```
text-indent:-20px;
```

Your CSS syntax for the <p> tag now looks like this:

```
p{
    font-family:georgia;
    font-size:13px;
    line-height:20px;
    text-align:left;
    text-indent:-20px;
    margin-top:0px;
    margin-right:0px;
    margin-bottom:0px;
    margin-left:20px;
    padding:0px;
    }
```

**Save your HTML document and view the changes**
Now when you view your code in the browser, each item in the list outdents (see Figure 3.14).

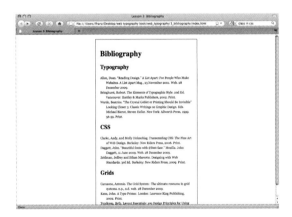

FIGURE 3.14 Each item in the list outdents on the first line. You added a left margin and removed it for the first lines only using the text-index property. A common rule in typography is to set your indent equal to your line height. The line height in this example is 20px, so the left margin is also 20px.

Next, you will italicize the title of each item by creating a class in CSS and applying it in the HTML document.

## Italicize the Titles by Creating a Class

Sometimes, you want to change the look of some words in a single line of text. Thus far, you've used heading tags and the `<p>` tag, all of which automatically add a line break to the text. How do you make some words italic without inserting a line break? You create a class.

### Create a class in the CSS

In the CSS file, add the following syntax:

```
.titles{
    font-style:italic;
    }
```

The class you created looks different from the heading and `<p>` selectors because in a sense, you're creating your own selector. There's no `<titles>` tag, but you want to control how the titles in the bibliography look. By creating this class, you're telling the CSS, "I want a new selector. I'm calling it *titles*."

To create and describe a class in CSS, you must precede the name with a dot (.).

Note that you can also create a class specifically attached to an existing selector. `p.intro` might be an introductory paragraph with a different look from the rest of the paragraphs on a page. You'll see classes used this way a lot. Don't worry about it yet; you'll do this in Chapter 13.

### Apply the class in the HTML

To apply the class in the HTML, use the `<span>` tag.

You want to apply the class to each book or website title, so add the `<span>` tags around each title. (*Note:* Don't italicize titles of articles, which already use quotation marks.) Type the following

syntax (don't include the dot) before each book or website title:

```
<span class="titles">
```

After each title, type the closing tag:

```
</span>
```

### Save your HTML document and view the changes

After you save the document and open it in your browser, you'll see that all the book and website titles are italicized (see Figure 3.15). If it didn't work, go back and check your syntax character by character.

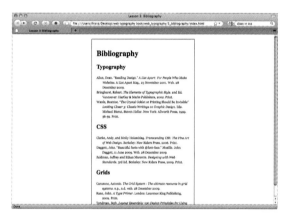

FIGURE 3.15 Book and website titles are italicized by means of the <span class="title"></span> syntax. Don't italicize the titles of articles, which are already in quotation marks.

From here, finish the page on your own, fixing quotation marks and describing your headings.

### Fix the quotation marks

When you specified Georgia or Verdana, the quotation marks may have appeared to fix themselves because both fonts recognize the smart (curly) quotes imported from the Microsoft Word document.

But the quotation marks will still show up as weird syntax in some browsers. If the quotation marks are still coming in all wonky, go into your HTML and replace all left quotation marks with the following code:

```
&ldquo;
```

Then replace all right quotation marks with this code:

```
&rdquo;
```

Save your file, and view your document in the browser to see the changes. I talk about quotation marks in detail in Chapter 9.

### Describe your headings

I leave you to do this last part—describing your headings—on your own. The steps are described in detail (if in a different context) in Chapter 2. You'll internalize the process better if I don't walk you through it step by step.

You've already defined your main heading and subheadings by using the <h1> and <h2> tags. Now you need to go into your CSS document and describe what <h1> and <h2> should look like. You can describe font, size, weight, case, line height, margin, and padding.

Remember that the <h1> (main heading) should stand out most. The <h2> should stand out more than the text but not as much as the <h1>.

In addition, continue using only one font. Try to emphasize the headings by using only size, weight, or case.

Good luck!

### Recommended Resources

For this lesson, I recommend the following online resources:

- To download the text for this lesson, go to www.wiley.com/go/typographicwebdesign

- To see examples of this lesson, visit typographicwebdesign.com

- To see more CSS syntax, visit htmldog.com/reference/cssproperties

- To copy and paste the Doctype, go to w3.org/QA/2002/04/valid-dtd-list.html

## Moving Forward

This chapter introduced you to choosing a font based on the needs of the text. It also showed you how to apply and style a <p> tag and a class.

In the next chapter, you read about choosing two fonts to work together, as well as adding a web font to your bibliography by using the @font-face syntax.

# CHAPTER 4

# Choosing Two Fonts to Work Together

A common misconception is that text should be set in a serif font and headlines should be set in a sans serif font. This isn't always necessary. You didn't need two fonts (one serif, one sans serif) to make the bibliography work in the preceding chapter's lesson. When you use size, case, and style wisely, you can create elegant, well-organized solutions for almost any project with only one font.

At times, though, you need (or want) to use two fonts. In this chapter, I show you how to choose two fonts to work together.

## Display Type: Using a Second Font

*Display type* (18px or bigger, usually used for headings and pull quotes) is a common way to bring in a second font.

### Identifying What You Need from a Second Font

The first step in choosing a second font for display type is asking yourself why you want to use one. If your only reason is to create contrast, I recommend that you reconsider. You can create contrast with a single font by using size, color, case, weight, and placement.

A second font adds more than just contrast; it also adds a voice to the text. A second font communicates an aesthetic or emotion that the original font doesn't.

To pick the style of second font you need, answer a couple of questions:

- What extra layer of meaning (connotation) do you want to communicate?
- What do you need the second typeface to do for you?

After you answer these questions, you're ready to look for a second font that will go with your text face.

### Considering Concord and Contrast

When two fonts are used together, they need to have the right balance of concord and contrast. Too much similarity or contrast between the fonts creates discord.

If two fonts are too similar, they're like two shades of a color that don't quite match, even though you feel that they should (see Figure 4.1). If they have nothing in common, they feel like they don't belong together (see Figure 4.2 and Figure 4.3).

# Display Type

Too much similarity or contrast between fonts creates discord. If too similar, they are like two shades of a color that don't quite match... but feel like they should. If they have nothing in common, they feel like they don't belong together.

# Display Type

Too much similarity or contrast between fonts creates discord. If too similar, they are like two shades of a color that don't quite match... but feel like they should. If they have nothing in common, they feel like they don't belong together.

# DISPLAY TYPE

Too much similarity or contrast between fonts creates discord. If too similar, they are like two shades of a color that don't quite match... but feel like they should. If they have nothing in common, they feel like they don't belong together.

# DISPLAY TYPE

Too much similarity or contrast between fonts creates discord. If too similar, they are like two shades of a color that don't quite match... but feel like they should. If they have nothing in common, they feel like they don't belong together.

FIGURE 4.1 *Top:* Nadia Serif (in the heading) combined with Georgia. The fonts are too similar to work well together. There's not enough contrast. *Bottom:* Nadia Serif with Verdana is a better match. The fonts contrast in strokes and serifs but have similar letter structures and x-heights.

FIGURE 4.2 *Top:* NeoRetroDraw combined with Georgia. The fonts are too different to work together. NeoRetroDraw is hand-drawn, sans serif, all caps, geometric. Georgia is none of these things. *Bottom:* NeoRetroDraw with Verdana is a better match if the typographer is looking for a hand-drawn second font; both fonts are sans serif.

A good rule of thumb for choosing a second font is "Don't settle." If a display font doesn't match the mood of the text or work with the text type, keep looking. Always be willing to go back and develop new solutions rather than settle for a font that's not right.

In Chapter 3, you achieved concordance by using the same font throughout. You achieved contrast with size, weight, or case.

When working with two fonts, consider their structures (x-height, bowl shape), strokes (monoline, thicks/thins), styles (script, retro, distressed, hand-drawn), and serifs. If too many characteristics are the same, the fonts are probably too similar. If too many characteristics are different, there's probably too much contrast.

*Display Type*

Too much similarity or contrast between fonts creates discord. If too similar, they are like two shades of a color that don't quite match... but feel like they should. If they have nothing in common, they feel like they don't belong together.

*Display Type*

Too much similarity or contrast between fonts creates discord. If too similar, they are like two shades of a color that don't quite match... but feel like they should. If they have nothing in common, they feel like they don't belong together.

FIGURE 4.3 *Top:* Beautiful ES combined with Verdana. The fonts are too different to work together. In addition to the contrast between script and roman forms, Beautiful ES has thick and thin strokes that are usually associated with more traditional fonts. Verdana's strokes are more uniform, so the font feels less traditional. *Bottom:* BlackJack with Verdana is a better match if the typographer is looking for a script second font. BlackJack has less contrast between thick and thin, less slant, and a less-traditional feel than Beautiful ES.

## Text Type: Using a Second Font

*Text type* (12–16px, usually used for text) is another way to bring in a second font. It's becoming more common to use a second font for text—as more legible, well-designed fonts that are legal to use in web pages, contain a full family, and work well together become available. And I expect that more fonts will become available in the future.

### Identifying What You Need from a Second Text Font

The first step in choosing a second font for text is asking yourself why you want to use one. If your only reason is to add flavor because Georgia and Verdana are so ubiquitous, I recommend that you reconsider. Ubiquitous type is like ubiquitous air. Choosing to add a second font to add flavor is like spraying air freshener because you want to draw attention to the smell of a room. Sometimes, you want people to notice what a room smells like (especially if you're a fantastic cook), but usually not. Smell can be intrusive, distracting people from the intended experience. Trying to read information and ideas through a typeface with flavor is like trying to enjoy a movie when the guy behind you is wearing too much cologne.

To pick the second font you need, ask yourself a couple of questions:

- How will the second typeface help you respect, clarify, and share the information and ideas in the text?

- What do you need the second typeface to do for you?

### Considering Balance and Continuity

Concord and contrast are even more important when you're choosing a second text type font. Display type is intended to stand out; it's meant to be read separately from the text. Text type, however, is usually meant to be read as a continuous unit.

A second font brings another voice to the text. It can emphasize or deemphasize; it can provide the voice of reason or create a dreamlike state. It shouldn't make readers stop in their tracks (unless, of course, the writer intended to have that effect).

As with display type, two text-type fonts shouldn't be too similar. One of the fonts will look like a mistake (see Figure 4.4) or have too much contrast (see Figure 4.5).

A second font brings another voice to the text. It can emphasize or deemphasize; it can provide a voice of reason or create a dreamlike state.

It shouldn't make readers stop in their tracks (unless, of course, the writer intended to have that effect).

As with display type, two text type fonts should not be too similar (one will look like a mistake) or have too much contrast.

A second font brings another voice to the text. It can emphasize or deemphasize; it can provide a voice of reason or create a dreamlike state.

It shouldn't make readers stop in their tracks (unless, of course, the writer intended to have that effect).

As with display type, two text type fonts should not be too similar (one will look like a mistake) or have too much contrast.

FIGURE 4.4 *Top:* DejaVu Serif combined with Georgia. The fonts are too similar to work well together. *Bottom:* DejaVu Serif combined with Verdana is a better match. The fonts contrast in strokes and serifs but have similar letter structures.

A second font brings another voice to the text. It can emphasize or deemphasize; it can provide a voice of reason or create a dreamlike state.

It shouldn't make readers stop in their tracks (unless, of course, the writer intended to have that effect).

As with display type, two text type fonts should not be too similar (one will look like a mistake) or have too much contrast.

A second font brings another voice to the text. It can emphasize or deemphasize; it can provide a voice of reason or create a dreamlike state.

It shouldn't make readers stop in their tracks (unless, of course, the writer intended to have that effect).

As with display type, two text type fonts should not be too similar (one will look like a mistake) or have too much contrast.

FIGURE 4.5 *Top:* Walkway Bold combined with Georgia. The fonts are too different to work together. In addition to the contrast between serif and sans serif, Walkway Bold has geometric forms (the bowl is a perfect circle) and a thinner stroke. Even the bold version feels light compared with Georgia. *Bottom:* PT Sans with Georgia is a better match. The fonts contrast in serifs, but their bowl shapes are less extreme in contrast, and their stroke weights complement one another.

When mixing text fonts, try to find two fonts with similar structures. Avoid significant variance in bowls (narrow/circular/wide), extensions of ascenders and descenders (long/short), x-heights (generous/small), and apertures (open/closed). If one of the fonts feels larger or smaller than the other, balance the fonts optically rather than mathematically (see Figure 4.6).

# fonts fonts fonts

FIGURE 4.6 Balance fonts optically. Size fonts so that their x-heights match. Unfortunately, this guideline isn't always achievable when you're using pixels because you can't work in increments smaller than a pixel, but get as close as you can. Verdana 36px (*left*) needs to be reduced to 32px (*center*) to match Georgia 36px (*right*).

## Selecting a Second Font

To summarize, when you choose a second display font, you should

- Identify what you expect the font to communicate.
- Balance concord and contrast (not too similar; not too different).
- Consider structures (x-heights, bowl shapes), strokes (monoline, thicks/thins), styles (script, retro, distressed, hand-drawn), and serifs.
- Avoid settling for a font that doesn't work.

When you choose a second font for text, you should

- Identify how a second font will help respect, clarify, and share the information and ideas in the text.
- Create continuity by balancing concord and contrast.
- Avoid significant variances in bowls, extensions of ascenders and descenders, x-heights, and apertures.
- Balance fonts optically rather than mathematically.

## About the Fonts Used in This Chapter

The seven new fonts used in this chapter are available free from fontsquirrel.com.

All seven fonts are legal to use with `@font-face` in CSS. I cover `@font-face` later in this chapter and show you what to look for in fonts (which aren't always good for online use) in Chapter 15, "Building a Font Library."

# Lesson 4: A Short Bibliography, Part 2

This lesson helps you achieve the following objectives:

1 Practice choosing a second font to use for display type.

2 Practice creating hierarchy with headings and subheadings, making changes as needed.

3 Build your vocabulary for describing why two fonts work together.

4 Use @font-face in your CSS. Even if you are HTML/CSS savvy, follow the walk-through provided in this section because I share typographic tips as I show the HTML/CSS.

## Use a Script Font for the Title

In the first part of the lesson, you will choose and apply a script font to the main heading in your bibliography from Chapter 3.

1 Go to www.fontsquirrel.com and choose a script font. Many kinds of script fonts are available; choose one that works with your text type (Georgia or Verdana).

2 Make a copy of the folder from the last lesson. Rename it *4_bibliography_script*. Rename your CSS file *bibliography_script.css*, and link to it.

3 Download the @font-face syntax, and insert it into your new CSS document for the <h1> tag. (I explain how to do this in the HTML and CSS walk-through.)

4 Adjust the size, weight, and case of <h1> as needed.

## Use a Font of Your Choice for the Title

To practice using @font-face, you will repeat the steps with a font of your choice.

1 Go to www.fontsquirrel.com and choose another font. Make sure that it works with your text type. If it doesn't, change your text type to the other standard (Georgia or Verdana).

2 Make a copy of the folder from the last lesson. Rename it *4_bibliography_choice*. Rename your *CSS bibliography_choice.css*, and link to it.

3 Download the @font-face syntax, and insert it into your new CSS document for the <h1> tag. (I go over how to do this in the HTML and CSS walk-through.)

4 Adjust the size, weight, and case of <h1> as needed (see Figure 4.7).

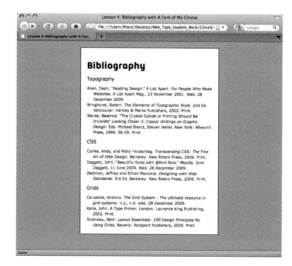

FIGURE 4.7 Chris Nelson added a font of his choice. He added Ubuntu Titling Bold (from Betatype) for the main heading. Visit the Typographic Web Design site to see other explorations.

## Write about What You See

- Choose one of the preceding exercises.
- Which font did you choose? Why?
- What text type does the font work best with? Why?
- Use words such as *concord, contrast, structure* (x-height, bowl shape), *stroke* (monoline, thick/thin), *style* (script, retro, distressed, hand-drawn), and *serif.*

## Use @font-face and Font Stacks

In this exercise, you modify the bibliography from the lesson in Chapter 3, so just make a copy of that lesson's folder, and name the new folder *4_bibliography_script*. Keep the new folder inside the *web_typography* folder.

Rename the CSS file *bibliography_script.css*. Link it to the *index.html* file by going into the HTML file and changing the syntax in the head element to the following:

```
<link href="bibliography_script.css"
    rel="stylesheet" type="text/css" />
```

Change the title to

```
<title>Lesson 4: Bibliography with
    Script Font</title>
```

Create a new folder in the *4_bibliography_script* folder called *fonts*. Font files for this lesson will go here.

### Understanding @font-face

Most browsers now recognize the @font-face property in CSS. This property enables web designers to use more than the limited number of web-safe fonts. The @font-face property links to fonts, retrieves them from a web server, and displays them on a website.

### Legal Issue: Linking Is Not Embedding

The capability to link fonts with the @font-face property has been around for a while, but not every browser has supported it. Now that most browsers support it, one of the main problems is that not every font's EULA (End User License Agreement) allows it.

When you're purchasing or downloading a font to use on your website, read the EULA or other license that accompanies the font. If the license doesn't *explicitly* allow web linking (or if a license isn't provided), don't do it. Contact the foundry or designer to negotiate or clarify permission.

Web linking is *not* the same as web embedding. *Web embedding* means that the font has been embedded in a file (text in an image, a font used in Adobe Flash). *Web linking* means that the font is downloaded to the browser and used to render the text on the web page. Fonts that allow web embedding don't allow web linking unless explicitly stated in the license.

For this lesson, you obtain your fonts from fontsquirrel.com. At this writing, the site provides only free fonts and states whether the fonts give permission to web-link (most of them do). Thus, you may legally use almost all the fonts on the site. Each font has a EULA; it's your responsibility to read the license and respect its provisions.

### Technical Issue: Different Browsers Use Different File Types

If you want the @font-face property to work across all browsers, you need to have access to multiple font files: Embedded OpenType (EOT) files for Internet Explorer 4+; TrueType (TTF/OTF) for Mozilla Firefox 3.5+, Opera 10+, Safari 3.1+, and Chrome 4.0.249.4+; Scalable Vector Graphics (SVG) for iPad and iPhone; and Web Open Font Format

(WOFF), the emerging standard of web fonts for Firefox 3.6+, Internet Explorer 9+, and Chrome 5+.

I don't cover how to save the different file types. That's not the objective of this lesson. Instead, I show you how to use `@font-face` kits provided by fontsquirrel.com. These kits provide all the preceding files plus *demo.html* and *stylesheet.css* files so you can get going fast.

**Choosing Your Font**

The first part of the lesson asks for a script font. Find one at `www.fontsquirrel.com` that you think will work. View and test-drive the font by typing the word *Bibliography* (see Figure 4.8). Some fonts look great until you string letters together to form words. If a font doesn't look right to you, don't settle. Keep looking.

FIGURE 4.8 Test-drive a font before you download it. Some fonts look great until you string letters together. After you've picked your font, click the @ font-face Kit link (circled) to start building and downloading the kit.

Download the @font-face kit

Every approved and available web font has a link to the font's `@font-face` kit, as noted in Figure 4.8. Click the link and then follow these steps:

1 When you're asked to choose font formats, choose all of them (TTF, EOT, WOFF, and SVG).

2 Click the Download `@font-face` Kit button.

3 Find the kit on your desktop or in your Downloads folder.

4 Open the *demo.html* file (or in some cases, the file with the word "demo" in the name) in your browser to make sure that all files downloaded correctly.

Put the EOT, TTF, SVG, WOFF, and license files in your fonts folder

Put the font files in the *fonts* folder you created in *4_bibliography_script*. Put the license file in the folder as well. It's good to keep the license agreement with the fonts. (Read it, too!) Leave the other files; you won't need them in the *fonts* folder. The *stylesheet.css* file is a valuable reference file, so keep track of where you store it.

Describe @font-face in your CSS document

Find the *stylesheet.css* file provided by Font Squirrel in the `@font-face` kit. Open the file in your text editor. Find and copy the following syntax:

```
@font-face{
font-family:'ChopinScriptRegular';
    src:url('ChopinScript-webfont
        .eot');
    src:url('ChopinScript-webfont
        .eot?iefix') format('eot'),
    url('ChopinScript-webfont.woff')
        format('woff'),
    url('ChopinScript-webfont.ttf')
        format('truetype'),
    url('ChopinScript-webfont
        .svg#webfontBrisyAdb')
        format('svg');
font-weight:normal;
font-style:normal;
}
```

58

Open your CSS file for this lesson (*bibliography_script.css*), and paste the syntax at the top of the file.

This syntax isn't going to work... yet. You need to tell the various browsers to find the files they need in the *fonts* folder. Thus, you need to add `fonts/` to all the URLs, like so:

```
@font-face{
font-family:'ChopinScriptRegular';
    src:url('fonts/ChopinScript-webfont
        .eot');
    src:url('fonts/ChopinScript-webfont
        .eot?iefix') format('eot'),
    url('fonts/ChopinScript-webfont
        .woff') format('woff'),
    url('fonts/ChopinScript-webfont
        .ttf') format('truetype'),
    url('fonts/ChopinScript-webfont
        .svg#webfontBrisyAdb')
        format('svg');
    font-weight:normal;
    font-style:normal;
    }
```

Whoa! What does that all mean?

Line 1: This syntax defines `@font-face`.

Line 2: I'm naming this font ChopinScriptRegular so that I can use it to describe an element (such as an `<h1>`).

Lines 3 and 4: IE9-compatible browsers can find the .eot file in the *fonts* folder.

Lines 5 and 6: IE6 to IE8 can find the .eot file in the *fonts* folder.

Lines 7 and 8: Firefox 3.6+ and Chrome 5+ can find the .woff file in the *fonts* folder.

Lines 9 and 10: Firefox 3.5+, Opera 10+, Safari 3.1+, and Chrome 4.0.249.4+ can find the .ttf file in the *fonts* folder.

Lines 11, 12, and 13: iPads, iPhones, Firefox 3.5+, Chrome 0.3+, and Opera 9+ can find the .svg file in the *fonts* folder.

Line 14: This font has a normal `font-weight`. (*Note:* Font Squirrel will set `font-weight` to "normal" even if the font itself is bold. FontSquirrel does this to increase support in browsers that ignore `font-weight`. This method works, because if you use a bold font, its "normal" weight is bold. The font weight won't lighten.)

Line 15: This font has a normal `font-style`. (*Note:* Font Squirrel will set `font-style` to "normal" even if the font itself is italic. Font Squirrel does this to increase support in browsers that ignore `font-style`. This method works, because if you use an italic font, its "normal" style is italic. The font style won't straighten out.)

Line 16: This line closes the `@font-face` definition.

To learn more about the `@font-face` syntax and why it it must be written in the order shown, I highly recommend the article "The New Bulletproof @font-face Syntax" by Ethan Dunham at `fontspring.com/blog/the-new-bulletproof-font-face-syntax`.

## Notes about the Syntax

In the syntax, I used the font Chopin Script. Use your own font information wherever I use Chopin-specific information.

You can type this syntax if you prefer, but because it's available in the *stylesheet.css* provided by www.fontsquirrel.com, I recommend copying and pasting it. The code contains a lot of details, and one missing piece of punctuation will prevent `@font-face` from working.

If you choose to type in the syntax, remember, indented lines belong together on a single line, and do not add spaces before periods (.) or forward slashes (/). Thus the following syntax would be typed in as a single line, with no space between "webfont" and ".ttf":

```
src:url('fonts/ChopinScript-webfont
    .ttf') format('truetype'),
```

**Use the font-family name in your h1 element**
You've named the `font-family` and told browsers where to find the font. You're ready to use it.

Change your `h1 font-family` syntax to include the new font. My `h1 font-family` was Georgia for the last bibliography (in Chapter 3), as follows:

```
h1{
    font-family:georgia;
    }
```

I add Chopin Script to my `font-family` options:

```
h1{
    font-family:'ChopinScriptRegular',
    georgia;
    }
```

## Building a Font Stack

In the preceding section, I added Chopin Script, but kept Georgia as an alternative, separating the fonts with a comma. This arrangement is called a *font stack*. A font stack tells the browser, "If for any reason you can't use the first font, use the second one."

It's a good idea to build font stacks. This practice keeps your websites from defaulting to Times or Arial. I also recommend deliberately removing your first choice from the stack during the design process just to see what the page would look like with the second font (see Figure 4.9). Try to avoid unpleasant surprises.

**Provide copyright information**
CSS allows you to write comments in the syntax. Comments show up in the CSS file but don't affect the HTML file.

Comments start with these characters:

```
/*
```

Comments end with these characters:

```
*/
```

Use a comment to identify any fonts linked in your file. Most EULAs require you to provide the copyright information. It's especially important to give recognition to designers who provide their fonts free for web linking.

Providing copyright information also helps web typographers identify and find good fonts! You'll appreciate it when others do this in their CSS.

**Bibliography**

TYPOGRAPHY

Allen, Dean. "Reading Design." *A List Apart: For People Who Make Websites.* A List Apart Mag., 23 November 2001. Web. 28 December 2009.

Bringhurst, Robert. The Elements of Typographic Style. 2nd Ed. Vancouver: Hartley & Marks Publishers, 2002. Print.

TYPOGRAPHY

Allen, Dean. "Reading Design." *A List Apart: For People Who Make Websites.* A List Apart Mag., 23 November 2001. Web. 28 December 2009.

Bringhurst, Robert. *The Elements of Typographic Style.* 2nd Ed. Vancouver: Hartley & Marks Publishers, 2002. Print.

# Bibliography

TYPOGRAPHY

Allen, Dean. "Reading Design." *A List Apart: For People Who Make Websites.* A List Apart Mag., 23 November 2001. Web. 28 December 2009.

Bringhurst, Robert. *The Elements of Typographic Style.* 2nd Ed. Vancouver: Hartley & Marks Publishers, 2002. Print.

FIGURE 4.9 *Top:* The original h1, Georgia 30/40px. The main heading stands out but isn't overwhelming. *Middle:* The h1 in Chopin Script 48/40px. *Bottom:* Georgia 48/40px. If a browser can't use Chopin Script, it will use Georgia. The font will change, but not the size. The main heading is huge—not great, but acceptable. Keep an eye on font stacks when you're setting text type!

The following syntax is modified only slightly from Font Squirrel's copyright comment. Again, read the EULA to see what you're expected to include for each font.

```
/*
 * Chopin Script is copyrighted by
   the vendor listed below.
 *
 * @vendor:     Dieter Steffmann
```

```
 * @vendorurl:  http://www.steffmann.de
 * @licenseurl:
   http://www.fontsquirrel.com
   /license/Chopin-Script
 */
```

*Note:* The asterisks that start every line aren't required for the comments to work. They act as visual elements to draw attention to the copyright information.

**Repeat the lesson with a font of your choice**

Make a copy of the folder you just finished. Name it *4_bibliography_choice.* Keep it in the *web_typography* folder.

Rename the CSS file *bibliography_choice.css.* Link it to the *index.html* file by going into the HTML file and changing the syntax in the head element to the following:

```
<link href="bibliography_choice.css"
    rel="stylesheet" type="text/css" />
```

Change the title to the following:

```
<title>Lesson 4: Bibliography with
    A Font of My Choice</title>
```

Repeat the lesson you just completed for the script font, this time using a font of your choice. Try to do the lesson without referring to the instructions, using them as needed.

As always, you can view other results and solutions at the Typographic Web Design site.

Good luck!

### Recommended Resources

For this lesson, I recommend the following online resources:

- To choose and download fonts, visit `fontsquirrel.com`

- To see examples of this lesson, visit `typographicwebdesign.com`

## Moving Forward

This chapter explained how to choose two fonts to use together. It also showed how to link to a web font using the `@font-face` syntax.

In the next chapter, you read about creating rhythm and tension on the typographic page. You also see how to use more than one div in your layout.

# Rhythm and Tension

*What determines the result is the way in which the diverse elements are organized in relation to each other, the contributions each makes to form, texture, and weight, and the effect of their relation with the space in which they exist.*

CARL DAIR,
DESIGN WITH
TYPE (1967)

# CHAPTER 5

# Rhythm and Tension in the Typographic Layout

Imagine a song with a rhythm that never changes (tap, tap, tap, tap, tap, tap, tap).

Pretty boring.

Imagine a song with a dynamic rhythm that shifts, contrasting changes in volume and pace. Some beats are soft; others are loud. Some come slowly; others, quickly. Sometimes, the beats stop altogether, and the rhythm falls silent, creating tension as we wait for the beats to start again (tap, tap, tappity-tap. BAH BAH BAH BAH......BAH!).

Like good music, successful dynamic typographic layouts—whether simple or complex—need a basic rhythm (created by repetition), counterpoints (created by contrast), and spatial tension (created by spatial relationships). This chapter explores the methods you can use to add those features to your layouts.

## Repetition and Counterpoints

Text has an inherent rhythm created by the repetition of horizontal lines. This rhythm is composed with a consistent use of font, size, line length, and line height.

To compose a dynamic rhythm, you need to break the basic horizontal repetition with counterpoints. Two fundamental counterpoints are the focal point and strong vertical lines (see Figure 5.1).

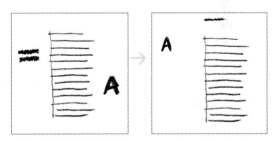

FIGURE 5.1 *Left:* Equal margins and competing focal points undermine rhythm and tension. *Right:* A single focal point and strong vertical line improve rhythm and tension.

## Web Designers Need to Sketch!

Now is the perfect time to start sketching. Get the ideas out of your head, and visualize possible solutions quickly and easily before building a layout. *Writing syntax is easier when you know what your layout looks like.*

If you listen to music, watch films, or enjoy art, you already have experience with rhythm and tension. Try to create rhythm and tension on paper rather than hope that the CSS/HTML will provide them when you place elements in the layout.

All images in this chapter are sketches for Lesson 5: *A is for Alignment.*

## The Focal Point

We understand our world in terms of contrasts: light and shadow, hot and cold, bitter and sweet. When an element contrasts with the rest of the composition, it becomes a *focal point* and acts as a counterpoint to the rhythm of the text.

You can create contrast in many ways. I introduce five possibilities in this chapter: size, color, space, weight, and shape. You'll find that these methods for creating contrast are hard to separate from one another; for example, you might create a focal point by making an element big (size) and placing it apart from the rest of the elements on the page (space). You'll often use two or more methods for creating contrast at the same time. The trick is to not use them all at once.

**Contrast of size:** An element (letter, word, title, sentence, or paragraph) is bigger or smaller than the others (see Figure 5.2).

**Contrast of color:** An element is brighter, darker, or a different hue from the others (see Figure 5.3).

**Contrast of space:** An element is on its own, away from the others. Two or more elements are bundled, creating a physical relationship apart from the others (see Figure 5.4).

**Contrast of weight:** An element is heavier/bolder (or thinner/lighter) than the others (see Figure 5.5).

**Contrast of shape or form:** An element has a different shape or form from the others (see Figure 5.6). Shape/form can refer to the form of a font or the shape of a text block.

Contrast works best when a limited number of elements are emphasized. If everything is emphasized, nothing stands out. For a counterpoint to work, you must have the repetition of the other elements. A song with nothing but contrasts in tone, volume, and rhythms becomes chaotic. The same is true of typographic layouts.

**Caution: Avoid making shapes with text blocks.** Text blocks that say, "Hey, look at me—I'm a triangle!" are similar to fonts that say, "Hey, look at me—my *i* is dotted with a heart!" Remember that the words themselves communicate the message. You only undermine the text by drawing the reader's attention to oddly shaped text blocks.

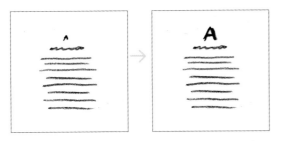

FIGURE 5.2 *Left:* A peaceful layout. *Right:* Contrast of size creates a counterpoint to the rhythm of the text.

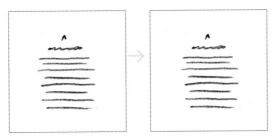

FIGURE 5.3 *Left:* A peaceful layout. *Right:* Contrast of color creates a counterpoint to the rhythm of the text.

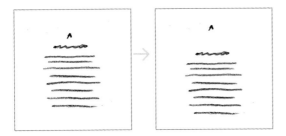

FIGURE 5.4 *Left:* A peaceful layout. *Right:* Contrast of space creates a counterpoint to the rhythm of the text.

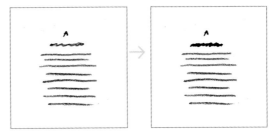

FIGURE 5.5 *Left:* A peaceful layout. *Right:* Contrast of weight creates a counterpoint to the rhythm of the text.

FIGURE 5.6 *Left:* A peaceful layout. *Right:* Contrast of shape creates a counterpoint to the rhythm of the text.

## Strong Vertical Lines

We see our world in terms of lines: horizontal (the horizon) and vertical (what grows up from the horizon, either natural or manmade). When a strong vertical line acts as a counterpoint to the horizontal rhythm of text, the typographic layout becomes more dynamic.

You can create a strong vertical line in many ways. I introduce four methods in this chapter: alignment, creating a gutter, continuation, and shape. Again, you'll find that the methods for creating strong vertical lines are hard to separate from one another; often, you'll use two or three at the same time.

**Alignment:** A visible vertical line is created between the even edge of the text and the white space surrounding it (see Figure 5.7).

**Gutter:** A visible vertical line is created when two text blocks with even edges are bundled. A *gutter* is the white space between the text blocks. The narrower the space, the stronger the vertical line (see Figure 5.8 and Figure 5.9). When working with two columns of text, always keep your gutter a bit wider than your line height; this keeps the two columns from blending into a single column.

**Continuation:** An invisible vertical line is created when two or more elements are lined up along the same line. *Continuation* is a principle of how we read objects: Any line tends to be seen as continuing in its original direction. Use continuation to extend the visible vertical lines created by alignment and gutters (refer to Figure 5.8, and see Figure 5.10 and Figure 5.11).

**Shapes of text blocks:** A vertical shape is created when text blocks are long and narrow. Vertical text blocks are the weakest method for creating a vertical line. You'll find that you need to pair this method with alignment and gutters to achieve a good counterpoint to the horizontal rhythm of the text (see Figure 5.12).

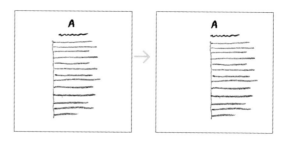

FIGURE 5.7 *Left:* A layout with a vertical line. *Right:* Aligning all the elements (and slightly shifting the text block) emphasizes the vertical line.

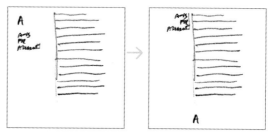

FIGURE 5.8 *Left:* A layout with a vertical line. *Right:* A narrow gutter and continuation work together to emphasize the vertical line.

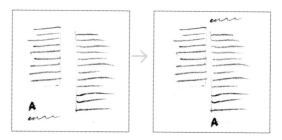

FIGURE 5.9 *Left:* A layout with a vertical line. *Right:* Tightening the gutter (and moving elements out of the corner) emphasizes the vertical line.

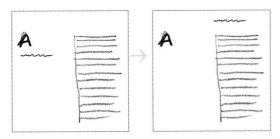

FIGURE 5.10 *Left:* A layout with a vertical line. *Right:* Moving one element creates continuation. It turns a side-by-side layout into one with a strong vertical line coupled with a strong focal point.

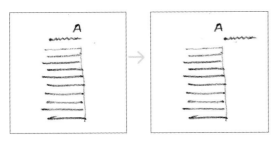

FIGURE 5.11 *Left:* A layout with a vertical line created using continuation. *Right:* Moving one element further emphasizes the invisible vertical line.

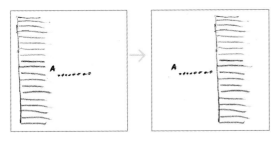

FIGURE 5.12 *Left:* A layout with a vertical line. *Right:* Moving the vertical text block away from the edge emphasizes the vertical line created by the even edge of the text.

## Spatial Tension

Compositions with a focal point and a strong vertical line can still feel static if you don't pay attention to the space around the elements.

You can create spatial tension in many ways. I introduce six in this chapter: avoid the center, create a sense of direction, avoid repetition of form, contrast the sizes of white shapes, consider the z-axis, and consider the edges. Once again, you'll find that the methods for creating spatial tension are hard to separate from one another; often, you'll use two or more at the same time.

**Avoid the center.** Place your focal point and/or your strong vertical line off-center. Centering a strong element creates balance and stability, which you may not always want (see Figure 5.13).

**Create a sense of direction.** Directional movement tends to start at the edge of a page. Vertical movement starts at the top edge; horizontal movement starts on one side or the other (see Figure 5.14).

**Avoid repetition of form: Create unequal white spaces.** Use your white space as a counterpoint to the rhythm of the text. When appropriate, keep space at the top, right, bottom, and left of the composition unequal. Avoid creating white spaces equal to the sizes and shapes of other elements, such as text blocks or titles (refer to Figure 5.13).

**Contrast the sizes of white shapes.** Contrasting large and small white spaces creates a more dynamic composition than repeating a midsize white space does (see Figure 5.15).

**Consider the z-axis.** When working in two dimensions, you can suggest a third dimension by changing size (smaller, more tightly spaced elements look farther away), opacity (lighter elements recede), and intensity (dull elements recede, while brightly colored elements come forward). (See Figure 5.16 and Figure 5.17.)

**Consider the edges.** The edges help define space (2D and 3D), define margins, and suggest direction/motion. Don't let the edges go to waste or disappear; they're valuable elements (refer to Figure 5.14 and Figure 5.16)!

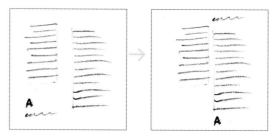

FIGURE 5.15 *Left:* The white spaces (top, right, bottom, and left margins; the gutter) are almost equal. *Right:* Shifting elements to create contrast between large and small white spaces improves spatial tension.

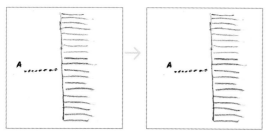

FIGURE 5.13 *Left:* A good start, but the vertical line is centered, and the text block is the same size as the right margin. *Right:* Shifting the entire composition to the right improves spatial tension.

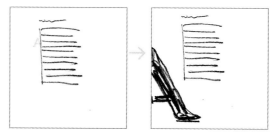

FIGURE 5.16 *Left:* The letter *A* recedes because it's small, light, and cropped by the text box. *Right:* The letter *A* comes forward because it's big, dark, and cropped by the outside edge. In both versions, the use of the z-axis helps create spatial tension.

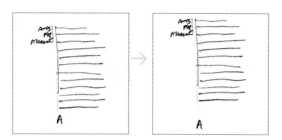

FIGURE 5.14 *Left:* A good start, but the composition feels clustered in the center of the page. *Right:* Using a tighter top and bottom margin helps create vertical movement on the page. The text feels like it's hanging from the top edge, creating spatial tension.

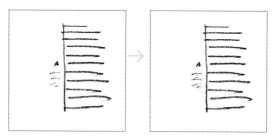

FIGURE 5.17 *Left:* The use of space and the gutter help create a strong vertical line. *Right:* Using a bright color brings the small text forward and helps create spatial tension.

*Note:* Keep your balance. Dynamic compositions still need balance. Balance is a product of visual weight (size, weight, color, and shape) and placement. If the layout feels like it wants to fall off the page, keep rearranging the elements, increasing or decreasing their visual weight as needed to create balance.

---

### Creating Counterpoints

To summarize, to break the horizontal repetition with counterpoints:

- Create a focal point with contrast (size, color, space, weight, and shape).
- Create strong vertical lines with alignment, gutters, continuation, and the shape of text blocks.

### Creating Spatial Tension

To summarize, to create spatial tension in the layout:

- Avoid the center.
- Create a sense of direction.
- Use unequal margins.
- Contrast the sizes of white spaces.
- Consider the edges.
- Consider the z-axis.

---

# Lesson 5: A is for Alignment

This lesson helps you achieve the following objectives:

1 Create rhythm and tension with various elements. Consider size, shape, the visual texture created by the strokes and spaces in and around the letterforms in the text, white spaces, invisible lines, and relationship to the edge of the box.

2 Create counterpoints by using a focal point (with contrast) and a strong vertical line.

3 Sketch out a variety of solutions. Make a list of things to try (refer to how to create a focal point, strong vertical lines, and spatial tension earlier in the chapter). Then sketch a solution for each.

4 Work with multiple divs to create a composition. Even if you're already HTML/CSS savvy, follow the walk-through provided in this lesson because I share typographic tips as I show you the HTML/CSS.

5 Add depth and visual tension to the composition by adding a background image in Part 2 of the lesson.

6 Add a layer of rhythm (adding minor counterpoints) by emphasizing words in the text in Part 2 of the lesson.

7 Practice making changes (even subtle ones) to improve the overall composition as extra elements are added.

## Overview of the Lesson

This lesson is divided into two parts. In Part 1, you design a dynamic typographic composition using the following elements: the letter *A*, a heading that reads *A is for Alignment*, a paragraph of text, and a white square (650px × 650px) on a gray background. Other elements will emerge as you lay out your composition: an invisible line created by how you align elements and the edges of the box holding your composition.

Think of type as creating shapes and visual textures. The capital *A* is a shape (a triangle) and also has shapes within it (the counterforms). The short line of text *(A is for Alignment)* has a shape (a kind of line), but it also has a texture. The text block has a shape (tall or wide, even on one side, ragged on the other), but it's filled with visual texture created by the strokes and spaces in and around the letterforms. Even the white spaces around the elements are shapes!

Use the shapes and textures to create a focal point (with contrast) and a strong vertical line. Strive for spatial tension.

Here are a few points to keep in mind as you begin formatting your text:

• **Use a left or right alignment for your text.** There are five ways to align type; each way has pros and cons (which I cover in Chapter 6), and all can be appropriate and beautiful. In this lesson, however, I want you to create a strong vertical line, and using left or right alignment helps you do that.

• **Start at 12/18px for your text.** Your size and line height may need to change to create the texture and text block you want. If you make your font size bigger, increase the line height too. The lines of text should feel like lines, not like tightly woven fabric.

- **Keep an eye on your line length (width of the** `text_container`**).** If your line length gets too short, you end up with a really ragged edge *(rag)* on one side of your text. Also, avoid creating shapes with your rag. No triangles or silhouettes!

In Part 2, you add an image to your composition to increase visual tension (see Figure 5.18). You also add minor counterpoints to the rhythm by emphasizing the kinds of alignment described in the text:

- Justified
- Flush left
- Flush right
- Centered
- Asymmetrical

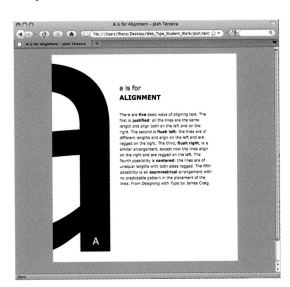

**FIGURE 5.18** Working with the text provided, Josh Terciera designed the typographic layout shown in this figure. Visit the Typographic Web Design site to see additional explorations.

Consider bolding, capitalizing, or changing the size of the words. What happens? Your type may reflow because some words in the text are now taking up more horizontal space. The shape of the text may change (getting longer or wider, or starting to form an odd shape). Does the shape of the text still work? Change the `text_container` width as needed.

The relationships among elements may change as well. Does the rhythm still work? Is the tension as strong? If not, move elements as needed to increase rhythm and tension again.

## Creating a Dynamic Composition, Part 1

In this part of the lesson, you will create a dynamic composition using multiple divs, applying the float property, and working with the universal selector.

To begin, in the *web_typography* folder, create a folder for this lesson. Call it *5_alignment*.

### Start the HTML File

In your text editor, create a new document, and save it as *index.html* in your *5_alignment* folder.

Copy and paste in the basic HTML syntax, add the title, and link to the CSS file:

```
<!DOCTYPE html PUBLIC "-//W3C//
    DTD XHTML 1.0 Strict//EN"
    "http://www.w3.org/TR/xhtml1/DTD
    /xhtml1-strict.dtd">
<html xmlns="http://www.w3.org/1999
    /xhtml">
<head>
<title>Lesson 5: A is for Alignment
    </title>
```

```
<meta http-equiv="content-type"
   content="text/html;
   charset=utf-8" />
<link href="alignment.css"
   rel="stylesheet"
   type="text/css" />
</head>
<body>
</body>
</html>
```

Add your `"main_container"` div between the `<body></body>` tags:

```
<div id="main_container"></div>
```

### Start the CSS File
In your text editor, create a new document, and save it as *alignment.css* in your *5_alignment* folder.

#### Describe the div ID for main_container
The `main_container` div is a white square (650px wide) centered in the browser. Write the syntax like this:

```
#main_container{
   width:650px;
   height:650px;
   margin-top:20px;
   margin-right:auto;
   margin-bottom:0px;
   margin-left:auto;
   background-color:#ffffff;
   }
```

#### Give the web page a gray background
To add a background color to the entire page, apply it to the `body` element, as shown:

```
body{
   background-color:#999999;
   }
```

### View your web page
Save your HTML document, and drag the icon into your browser. You should see a white square on a gray background (see Figure 5.19).

FIGURE 5.19 This 650px white square is where you'll build your dynamic typographic composition.

### Make and Describe the Divs (Containers)
You already know how to make a `main_container` div and how to describe what it looks like. In this lesson, you make and describe multiple divs so that they work together to build your composition.

To make and describe the divs, you need to know what they should look like. Use the sketches you made for this lesson to identify a general size and placement for each div (Figure 5.20).

*Note:* If this is your first time working with multiple divs, I recommend that you follow along with my example. After you've worked out the lesson using my example, go back and redo it, using your own composition.

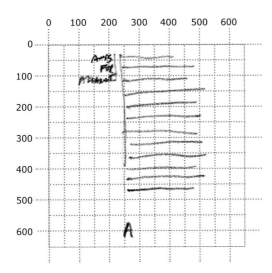

FIGURE 5.20 A grid overlay divides the composition into 13 equal 50px units (13 × 50px = 650px). Use a grid like this one (drawing it over your sketch with a pencil is fine) to estimate the size and placement of elements in a hand-drawn sketch.

**Make three more divs for the layout**

`#a_container` (which will contain the letter *A)* looks like it's about 50px × 50px. Start there. Add a border so that you can see the div when you put it in the HTML.

```
#a_container{
    width:50px;
    height:50px;
    border:1px solid #000000;
    }
```

`#text_container` (which will contain the text) looks like it's about 275px wide and 450 pixels tall. Again, add a border so that you can see the div when you put it in the HTML.

```
#text_container{
    width:275px;
    height:450px;
    border:1px solid #000000;
    }
```

`#alignment_container` (which will contain the words *A is for Alignment)* looks like it's about 125px × 100px. Again, add a border:

```
#alignment_container{
    width:125px;
    height:100px;
    border:1px solid #000000;
    }
```

**Put the three divs in the HTML**

Browsers place divs in the order in which they appear in the HTML. Browsers place the divs in rows, starting in the top-left corner (see Figure 5.21).

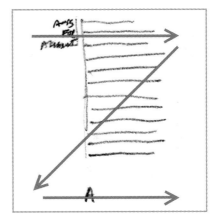

FIGURE 5.21 Browsers place the divs in rows, starting in the top-left corner.

Add the divs inside the `main_container`:

```
<div id="main_container">
    <div id="alignment_container">
        </div>
    <div id="text_container">
        </div>
    <div id="a_container">
        </div>
</div>
```

75

## View your web page

Save your HTML document, and view the changes. Yikes! This is not what you want at all. The divs fall in a single column along the left edge (see Figure 5.22).

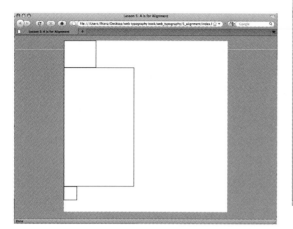

FIGURE 5.22 The divs fall in a single column along the left edge.

You need to tell browsers to place the divs in rows. You do this next, using the `float` property.

### Place divs with the float property

To fix the placement of the divs, use the `float` property. You can tell a div to float left or right. For now, you use only a `float:left`.

In the CSS document, add the line `float:left;` to each of your divs, as in this example:

```
#alignment_container{
    float:left;
    width:125px;
    height:100px;
    border:1px solid #000000;
    }
```

## View your web page

Save your HTML document, and view the changes. Now the divs run in a single row across the top (see Figure 5.23).

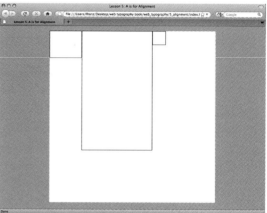

FIGURE 5.23 With float:left added to the CSS, each div attaches itself to the item on its left.

Why? By adding the `float:left`, you told each div to attach itself to the item on its left. `Alignment_container` is attached to the edge of the `main_container`, `text_container` is attached to the `alignment_container`, and `a_container` is attached to the `text_container`.

### Use the universal selector to clear margins and padding

You've broken the single column. Now you need to get the divs where you want them by adding margins and padding where you need them. But first, you should clear all margins and padding to 0 so that you can add space back only where you want it.

The CSS universal selector applies a value to all properties in all elements in the HTML document. It's represented by an asterisk (*).

76

To set all margins and padding to 0 using the universal selector, add it at the top of your CSS document, as follows:

```
* {
    margin:0;
    padding:0;
}
```

All margins and padding—for all classes, divs, and tags (h1, h2, p, and so on)—are now set to 0. This gives you complete control of the spaces between elements. You can add back exactly the amount of space you want back—only where you want it.

**Put space back in with margins and padding**
Starting at the top of the composition, you need approximately 40px between the top edge of the main_container and the top elements. You could add a top margin to each of the two top elements, but it would be easier to add top padding inside the main_container, as shown in the following code:

```
#main_container{
    width:650px;
    height:650px;
    margin-top:20px;
    margin-right:auto;
    margin-bottom:0px;
    margin-left:auto;
    padding-top:40px;
    background-color:#ffffff;
}
```

Next, you need approximately 100px of space between the left edge of the main_container and the alignment_container. Add that by using margin-left: as follows:

```
#alignment_container{
    width:125px;
    height:100px;
    margin-left:100px;
    border:1px solid #000000;
}
```

Next, you need approximately 15px of space between the right edge of the alignment_container and the left edge of the text_container. Notice that you're adding a space between two divs. Add the space using by margin-left: as follows:

```
#text_container{
    width:275px;
    height:450px;
    margin-left:15px;
    border:1px solid #000000;
}
```

**View your web page**
Save your HTML document and view the changes. You have a couple of problems to fix. First, the main_container is no longer a square (see Figure 5.24). Why? When you added padding-top, the amount of padding was added to the overall height of the div. To keep the original height of the main_container (or any div), you need to remove an equal amount of space from the height.

Change the height of the main_container as follows:

```
height:610px;
```

You still need to get the a_container down to the next row. You have a couple of ways to do this. In this exercise, you do it by force.

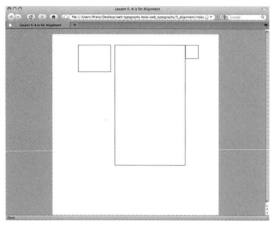

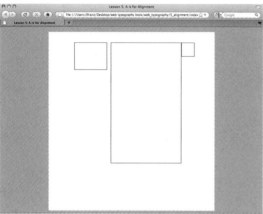

FIGURE 5.24 *Top:* The padding-top added to the main_ container made it taller. To fix this, remove an equal amount of space from the height of the container. *Bottom:* The corrected square main_container.

### Force a div to the next row

If a browser doesn't have enough room to fit a div, the div will be forced down to the next row. This situation can wreak havoc if you don't expect it, but you're going to use it to your advantage.

You want the a_container on the next row. Force it out of the top row by adding margin-right to the text_container. You don't have to fill the entire space; in fact, I highly recommend that you don't!

```
#text_container{
    width:275px;
    height:450px;
    margin-left:15px;
    margin-right:100px;
    border:1px solid #000000;
    }
```

### Place the last div with margins

With a_container in the next row, you need to place it where you want it.

You need approximately 250px of space between the left edge of main_container and the left edge of a_container. You also need approximately 100px between the bottom of text_ container and the top of a_container, as follows:

```
#a_container{
    width:50px;
    height:50px;
    margin-top:100px;
    margin-left:250px;
    border:1px solid #000000;
    }
```

### View your web page

Save your HTML document and view the changes. The divs aren't placed exactly where you want them, but they're pretty close (see Figure 5.25). You'll adjust margins as needed after the text is in.

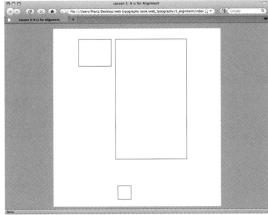

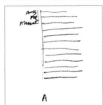

FIGURE 5.25 *Top:* The divs aren't exactly placed but are pretty close. *Bottom:* The original sketch.

## Add the Content and Define the Elements

Now that you have the divs set, it's time to add the content.

In the HTML document, type the *A* and *A is for Alignment* in their proper divs:

```
<div id="a_container">
    A</div>
<div id="alignment_container">
    A is for Alignment</div>
```

Paste the text from *5_alignment.doc* into the text_container:

```
<div id="text_container">
    paste text here</div>
```

Define the *A* as a h1 element:

```
<div id="a_container">
    <h1>A</h1></div>
```

Define *A is for Alignment* as a h2 element:

```
<div id="alignment_container">
    <h2>A is for Alignment</h2></div>
```

Define the text as a p element:

```
<div id="text_container">
    <p>text is here</p></div>
```

### Describe the elements in CSS

In the CSS document, type the syntax that defines how each element should look.

Make the text Georgia, 12/18px:

```
p{
    font-family:georgia;
    font-size:12px;
    line-height:18px;
}
```

Make the *A* Georgia 48/48px:

```
h1{
    font-family:georgia;
    font-weight:normal;
    font-size:48px;
    line-height:48px;
}
```

Make *A is for Alignment* Georgia, bold, 24/36px, and right-aligned:

```
h2{
    font-family:georgia;
    font-weight:bold;
    font-size:24px;
    line-height:36px;
    text-align:right;
}
```

After all the elements are defined, remove all the borders from the CSS syntax, and see how it looks.

79

## View your web page

Save your HTML document, and view the changes. It's not exactly how you envisioned it in your sketch (see Figure 5.26); you still have some work to do. You need change font size, line height, and margins. After everything you've already done, this extra work may be discouraging, but you can tackle each element one at a time.

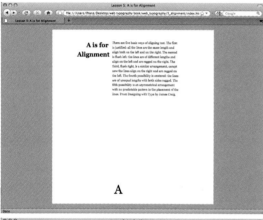

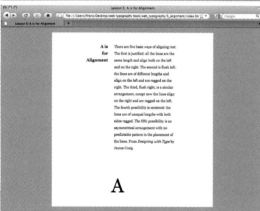

FIGURE 5.26 *Top:* Everything is placed, but the text is too small; the *A* is too small; and *A is for Alignment* is too big. *Bottom:* This is how the document should look. You want a little more room between *A is for Alignment* and the text block; you want *A is for Alignment* on three lines (to create a longer gutter); and you want *A is for Alignment* to line up horizontally with the lines of text in the text block (to keep the horizontal underlying rhythm of the text).

## Improve the Typography

The text is too small (it should take up more room), and the left margin should have a little more space. Georgia 14/26px will work best. Make the div a little narrower, increase `margin-left`, and add a slight `margin-top` (1px) to line up the text with *A is for Alignment*.

Use the following CSS syntax to make the changes described:

```
#text_container{
    float:left;
    width:255px;
    height:450px;
    margin-top:1px;
    margin-left:25px;
    margin-right:100px;
    }

p{
    font-family:georgia;
    font-size:14px;
    line-height:26px;
    }
```

The *A* is too small (it should be the focal point) and a little too close to the bottom edge. It also needs to visually line up better with the text block. Because the *A* has a triangular shape, it can't line up exactly on the edge of the letter. It should be pushed a little to the left.

Make those changes by using this CSS syntax:

```
#a_container{
    float:left;
    width:75px;
    height:75px;
    margin-top:60px;
    margin-left:240px;
    }
```

```
h1{
    font-family:georgia;
    font-weight:normal;
    font-size:75px;
    line-height:75px;
}
```

*A is for Alignment* is too big (it shouldn't over-power the *A*), and you want *A is for Alignment* on three lines (to create a longer gutter). Finally, make *A is for Alignment* line up horizontally with the lines of text in the text block.

Georgia, bold, 16/26px works best. Add a couple of <br /> tags to break it into three lines.

<br /> tags are *line-break tags;* they break lines of text. <br /> tags should be used sparingly because they create problems if a viewer increases or decreases the text size in his browser. It's okay in this instance because the headline is short.

Notice that the line-break tag doesn't come in a pair. The single tag closes itself and ends in />. There's a space between <br and />. Now the HTML syntax looks like this:

```
<div id="alignment_container">
    <h2>A is<br />
    for<br />
    Alignment</h2></div>
```

Even though you used the same line height for the h2 and p (to help them line up), the h2 is a little bigger than the p, so the h2 keeps looking lower. Add a slight margin-top (1px) to the text_container to push the text down a pixel to line up with *A is for Alignment* (see Figure 5.27).

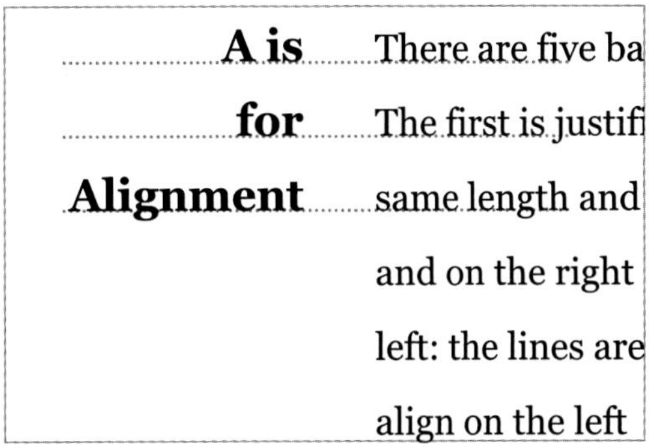

FIGURE 5.27 The baselines of *A is for Alignment* and the body text line up. This helps keep the horizontal underlying rhythm of the text. You used the same line height for h2 and p but still had to add a slight top margin to the text_container to get them to work.

Here's the new CSS syntax related to *A is for Alignment*:

```
#alignment_container{
    float:left;
    width:125px;
    height:100px;
    margin-left:100px;
}

h2{
    font-family:georgia;
    font-weight:bold;
    font-size:16px;
    line-height:26px;
    text-align:right;
}
```

**Italicize the title of the book with a class**
To make some words italic without inserting a line break, create a class. (You did this in Lesson 3: Bibliography.) In the CSS, add the following syntax:

```
.titles{
    font-style:italic;
}
```

To apply the class to the book title, add the <span> tags around the title. Before the book title, type this syntax:

```
<span class="titles">
```

After the title, type this syntax:

```
</span>
```

Now you're ready to go back and redo the lesson, using your sketch, multiple divs, and elements as shown. When you're done, move on to Part 2 of the lesson.

## Creating a Dynamic Composition, Part 2

In this part of the lesson, you will add a background image and emphasize words in the text.

You modify the composition that you created in Part 1 of this lesson, so make a copy of the *5_alignment* folder, and name the copy *5_alignment_counterpoints*. Keep it in the *web_typography* folder.

Create a new folder in the *5_alignment_counterpoints* folder called *images*. Image files for the lesson will go in this folder.

Rename the CSS file *alignment_counterpoints.css*. Link it to the *index.html* file by going into the new HTML file and changing the syntax in the head element to the following:

```
<link href="alignment_counterpoints
    .css" rel="stylesheet"
    type="text/css" />
```

Change the title as shown:

```
<title>Lesson 5: A is for Alignment,
    with Counterpoints</title>
```

**Layer an A in the Background with an Image**

You have many ways to suggest depth (the z-axis) in a composition, including size, color, placement, and opacity. You can do all these things by using the skills I've already shown you. But if you want to suggest layering by placing an *A* behind other elements, you need to make an image with the *A* and put it in the background of the main_container.

Make the image

In the photo-editing software of your choice (I use Adobe Photoshop), create a 72 ppi image of the *A* at the size you think you'll use it, and save it as a .gif file. As with the text, you may need to go back and edit it later.

If you're not familiar with photo-editing software, you have a couple of options:

- Free tutorials are available online, but you have to search for them. Most of these tutorials cover how to save an image for the web but don't get you started on the software itself. Lynda.com offers video tutorials for a reasonable price.

- Another option is to work with text only. A dynamic composition doesn't require an image.

In Photoshop, I made an *A* (Georgia, 450px) on a 450px square canvas with 72 ppi resolution. I saved it as *background_a.gif* and brought it into the main_container background by adding a line of syntax (type it in as a single line of syntax; it's broken below to fit in the book) in the CSS for the main_container:

```
background-image:
    url(images/background_a.gif);
```

This syntax tells the browser, "Put a background image in my main_container." Use *background_a.gif* in the images folder for this lesson.

## View your web page

Save your HTML document and view the changes (see Figure 5.28). Yikes! The image is *tiling* (repeating) across the background. Why? By default, background images repeat. Tiling is great when you want it, but you don't want it for this example.

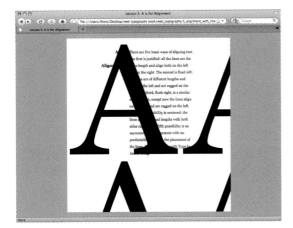

FIGURE 5.28 Background images repeat by default. To position a single version of the *A*, you need to add a couple more lines of syntax to the main_container.

## Position a single version of the A

First, get rid of the repeat. The syntax is

```
background-repeat:no-repeat;
```

Then position the image. You position the *A* both horizontally (the first number in the syntax) and vertically (the second number in the syntax):

```
background-position:-140px 300px;
```

Add all three lines of syntax to the `main_container` so that your final syntax looks like this:

```
#main_container{
    width:650px;
    height:610px;
```

```
    margin-top:20px;
    margin-right:auto;
    margin-bottom:0px;
    margin-left:auto;
    padding-top:40px;
    background-color:#ffffff;
    background-image:
        url(images/background_a.gif);
    background-repeat:no-repeat;
    background-position:-140px 300px;
}
```

## View your web page

Save your HTML document, and view the changes (see Figure 5.29). This is much better!

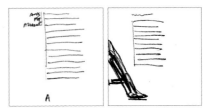

FIGURE 5.29 *Top:* The result isn't a perfect match for the ideas sketched. *Bottom:* The original sketch.

The final composition may not look exactly as you sketched it. You could make changes to make it match your sketch more faithfully, but you may find that you're happy with the composition as is. Sometimes, an unexpected result is delightful.

## Make and Apply a Class to Create Counterpoints in the Text

You used a class (`.title`) earlier in the lesson to italicize the book title. Now you want to emphasize the five ways to align text. You don't want to insert a line break, so you create another class to emphasize the words with bold. In the CSS, add the following syntax:

```
.emphasis{
    font-weight:bold;
    }
```

You want to apply the class to the names of different ways to align text, so add the `<span>` tags around those names. Before each name (justified, flush left, flush right, centered, and asymmetrical), type the following line:

```
<span class="emphasis">
```

After each name, type

```
</span>
```

Notice that the `<span>` tag ends before the punctuation immediately following each word. It's usually best to not emphasize the punctuation, allowing each word to come forward on its own without drawing attention to the punctuation. At times, you'll want to break this "rule," but I recommend following it for now.

It's also a best practice to name your classes based on their roles in the composition. Whenever possible, stay away from naming classes `italic` or `bold`. As a composition progresses, styles and weights may change, but titles and emphasis remain.

### View your web page

Save your HTML document, and view the changes. The minor counterpoints add an extra beat to the rhythm of the text (see Figure 5.30). The extra beats can change the rhythm or tension in the composition. Make changes as needed.

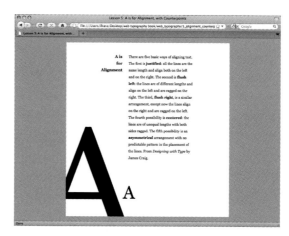

FIGURE 5.30 The minor counterpoints add an extra beat to the rhythm of the text while highlighting vocabulary words and breaking up a complex paragraph. In addition to bold, you can use size, case, or opacity to emphasize words. The emphasized words add a ripple effect down the text. To take advantage of this result, I slightly changed the size and placement of my smaller *A;* it feels more like an extension of the ripple.

Congratulations! You've finished Part 2!

For more practice, go back and redo the background image as needed . . . and redo the class using your own method of emphasis.

This lesson was a complex one, and you covered a lot of ground. You worked with multiple divs, made changes as needed to improve typography, incorporated all that you found out earlier about elements and classes, and even added a background image. Great job!

**Recommended Resources**

For this lesson, I recommend the following online resources:

- To download the text for this lesson, go to `www.wiley.com/go/typographicwebdesign`

- To see examples of this lesson, go to `www.typographicwebdesign.com`

- To learn how to use imaging software (such as Photoshop), go to `www.lynda.com`

- To download GIMP, a freely distributed image manipulation program, go to `www.gimp.org`

## Moving Forward

This chapter introduced you to creating rhythm and tension in a composition. You also saw how to use multiple divs and place a background image.

In the next chapter, you find out about establishing a good font size, line height, and line length. You also work with more complex text.

# Making Type Work: Scanning with Purpose

*The most devastating experience for me as a magazine writer is seeing my work in print. . . .*

*I can't figure out why anyone would want to read what I wrote. The text is only texture, a decorative element. The type is too small, the lines too long, the title too obscure, and the layout too complicated. I get nauseous just staring at it—loss of creative control feels a lot like a hangover.*

VERONIQUE VIENNE, "SOUP OF THE DAY," METROPOLIS (1995)

# CHAPTER 6

# How We Read, Part 1

This chapter covers how font size, line height, line length, alignment, and color (black and white) affect readability (how easily text can be read). As I said at the beginning of Chapter 1, text is meant to be read—and if it feels difficult to read, people won't want to read it. Readability on the web depends on how type is used on the screen.

In previous chapters, we explored legibility, and the importance of choosing fonts with strokes and spaces that hold up on the screen. But creating readable text is more than just working with legible fonts.

Reading is a complex activity. Readers use both their foveal (central) vision and their peripheral vision to process more than one word at a time; they fixate on certain words while filling in the rest. Readers scan across lines of text while also scanning down the text, either to the next line or the next paragraph. Readable text promotes both horizontal and vertical scanning; readability is a function of size, line height, line length, alignment, and color.

## Size

If type is too small, it loses legibility. The shapes of letters (both the strokes and spaces) are less pronounced at small sizes. Readers have to slow down to recognize individual letters or word shapes. It is difficult to process more than one word at a time if text is too small.

If type is too large, it undermines the horizontal flow of the text. Large words take up more space in our foveal vision, making it difficult for readers to process more than one word at a time. Figure 6.1 illustrates this point.

If text is too small or too large, it is more difficult to read. Small type loses the shapes of letters. Large type loses the horizontal flow of the text.

If text is too small or too large, it is more difficult to read. Small type loses the shapes of letters. Large type loses the horizontal flow of the text.

FIGURE 6.1 Small type (11px or smaller) and large type (17px or bigger) are too difficult to read and should not be used in text. They are more appropriate for captions, pull quotes, and headlines. *Top:* Georgia 10px. *Bottom:* Georgia 20px.

I recommend setting text type at 12 to 16px (using the `font-size` property). Fonts with a large x-height look bigger and will work fine at 12 to 15px. Fonts with a small x-height look smaller, and need to be set at 13 to 16px (see Figure 6.2). I rarely set large amounts of text at 12px; it's harder to read.

> Fonts with generous x-heights look larger. They're more comfortable to read at smaller sizes. Fonts with smaller x-heights need to be set a little bigger. This is Verdana 12 px.
>
> Fonts with generous x-heights look larger. They're more comfortable to read at smaller sizes. Fonts with smaller x-heights need to be set a little bigger. This is Georgia 13 px.

FIGURE **6.2** Fonts with smaller x-heights need to be set a little bigger to remain legible. *Top:* Verdana 12px. *Bottom:* Georgia 13px.

## Line Height

Line height (the `line-height` property) controls the amount of space between lines of text. The lines of text should feel like horizontal lines, not like a tightly woven fabric.

Readers scan both horizontally and vertically, and if the line height is too tight, it undermines the horizontal flow of the text; readers will find themselves scanning down the text, even when they don't want to.

If the line height is too loose, the lines of text start to "float away" from each other. They no longer feel like a cohesive unit of text, and vertical scanning becomes more difficult.

A good rule of thumb is to set your line height at no less than 150 percent of your text size. For example, 12px text needs at least an 18px line height, 13px text needs at least a 19px line height, and so on (see Figure 6.3).

> If the line height is too loose, the lines start to float away from each other. It makes vertical scanning difficult. If the line height is too tight, readers will start scanning down the text, even if they don't want to. This is too tight.
>
> If the line height is too loose, the lines start to
>
> float away from each other. It makes vertical
>
> scanning difficult. If the line height is too tight,
>
> readers will start scanning down the text, even
>
> if they don't want to. This is too loose.
>
> If the line height is too loose, the lines start to float away from each other. It makes vertical scanning difficult. If the line height is too tight, readers will start scanning down the text, even if they don't want to. This is just right.

FIGURE **6.3** Set line height at approximately 150 percent of font size to promote both sustained and casual reading. *Top:* Georgia 12/15. *Middle:* Georgia 12/24. *Bottom:* Georgia 12/18.

Text fonts designed for the screen tend to have slightly larger x-heights—this creates more internal space in the letters, which is necessary to promote legibility in low-resolution conditions. A large x-height means there is less "automatic" space between lines of text. The space is taken up by the letters themselves. Thus a font with a generous x-height also needs a generous line height; a font with a smaller x-height can work with a smaller line height (see Figure 6.4).

A font with a larger x-height needs more line height. Verdana 12/17 px looks tighter than Georgia 12/17.

A font with a larger x-height needs more line height. Verdana 12/17 px looks tighter than Georgia 12/17.

FIGURE 6.4 Verdana has a larger x-height (and looser letterspacing) than Georgia, and so Verdana needs an ample line height. *Top:* Verdana 12/17. *Bottom:* Georgia 12/17.

Small type (below 12 px) needs a looser line height than 150%. When the reader has to work harder to read the shapes of words, a little extra line height helps. This is 164%.

Small type (below 12 px) needs a looser line height than 150%. When the reader has to work harder to read the shapes of words, a little extra line height helps. This is 145%.

FIGURE 6.6 Small type needs a looser line height. *Top:* Georgia 11/18. *Bottom:* Georgia 11/16.

Depending on the amount of text, the line length, the font size, the size of a font's x-height, and so on, you may find that the line height needs to be tightened or loosened slightly to promote comfortable reading. That's okay. You don't have to follow the 150-percent rule to the letter. It's there as a guideline. Read the text, see how the lines of text relate to each other, and make adjustments as needed (see Figures 6.5 and 6.6).

Large type can use a line height tighter than 150%. This is set at 135%.

Large type can use a line height tighter than 150%. This is set at 150%.

FIGURE 6.5 Lines of large type, used for small amounts of text like headlines and pull quotes, can use a line height tighter than 150 percent. *Top:* Georgia 20/27. *Bottom:* Georgia 30/30.

## Line Length

Long lines of text are harder to read because they force readers to change their eye movement. Readers want to scan across and down the text at the same time, focusing on a couple of words and filling in the rest. When lines of text are long, readers need to work harder to scan across an entire line, and then go back to find the start of the next line (see Figure 6.7).

Short lines can make text feel chopped up, causing a reader's scanning to become more vertical than horizontal. Short lines break up the intended rhythm of a text meant for sustained reading. In addition, short lines can undermine the shape of a text block, creating extremely ragged edges on one side of the text, or creating large white spaces in justified text. Use short lines for captions and lists (see Figure 6.8).

Contrary to what you may have read or heard elsewhere, line length should not be based on the width of the page. Nor is it only a factor of font size. Due to bowl shape and letterspacing, each font needs a slightly different line length. The line length of this paragraph is too long.

Contrary to what you may have read or heard elsewhere, line length should not be based on the width of the page. Nor is it only a factor of font size. Due to bowl shape and letterspacing, each font needs a slightly different line length. This line length is better.

FIGURE 6.7 *Top:* A 100+ character line length. Long lines of text are harder to read. *Bottom:* A 75-character line length is easier to read.

Contrary to what you may have read or heard elsewhere, line length should not be based on the width of the page. Nor is it only a factor of font size. All fonts are different. Due to bowl shape and letterspacing, each font needs a slightly different line length. This line length is comfortable to read.

Contrary to what you may have read or heard elsewhere, line length should not be based on the width of the page. Nor is it only a factor of font size. Due to bowl shape and letterspacing, each font needs a slightly different line length. This length is too short.

FIGURE 6.8 *Top:* A 46-character line length is comfortable to read. *Bottom:* A 22-character line length can make the text feel chopped up.

### Avoid Doubling

Have you ever found yourself reading the same line over and over? This is called *doubling*. It is usually caused by lines of text that are too long. The long lines undermine our ability to scan down the text.

Contrary to what you may have read or heard elsewhere, line length should *not* be based on the width of the page (that is, how much space you have to fill). Nor is it only a factor of font size. All fonts are different. Due to bowl shape and letterspacing, each font needs a slightly different line length.

The best way to determine line length is to count the number of characters on a line. Reading text on the screen is most comfortable at 75 to 85 characters (including punctuation and spaces) per line.

## Count Characters

Line length is measured in characters, not pixels. A comfortable line length is 75 to 85 characters. When counting characters, include all punctuation marks and spaces. Count the characters in two or three typical lines of text. The average number of characters is your line length.

## Alignment

There are five ways to align text: left aligned, right aligned, centered, justified, and asymmetrical. The copy used in the lesson in Chapter 5 (An Interlude: Rhythm and Tension) describes each method of alignment. Each method has pros and cons related to ease of reading and formal beauty and integrity.

**Right aligned, centered, and asymmetrical** alignments are more difficult to read. The starting point for each line varies. Readers have to find the start of each line, which undermines vertical scanning (see Figures 6.9 to 6.11).

Yet these alignment methods add pleasing shapes (form and counterform) and visual interest when they are done well. They are great for small amounts of text that do not require sustained reading or purposeful scanning. Consider these alignments for captions, pull quotes, and headlines.

Asymmetrical alignment is not available as a CSS value. Lines of text have to be individually placed to create asymmetry.

Right aligned text has lines of different lengths. The text is even on the right and ragged on the left. Harder to scan because of the uneven left edge, right justified text can keep a layout from feeling too "blocky." Avoid a ragged edge that is too obvious or too even. Use for captions and pull quotes.

Right aligned text has lines of different lengths. The text is even on the right and ragged on the left. Harder to scan because of the uneven left edge, right justified text can keep a layout from feeling too "blocky." Avoid a ragged edge that is too obvious or too even. Use for captions and pull quotes.

FIGURE 6.9 Right aligned text. *Top:* A good ragged edge. *Bottom:* Lines are too even, creating a less successful ragged edge.

Centered text has lines of unequal lengths with both sides ragged. Harder to scan because of the uneven left edge, centered text can add a traditional feeling to a layout. Use for captions, pull quotes, and headings.

Centered text has lines of unequal lengths with both sides ragged. Harder to scan because of the uneven left edge, centered text can add a traditional feeling to a layout. Use for captions, pull quotes, and headings.

FIGURE 6.10 Centered text. *Top:* Good ragged edges. *Bottom:* Lines form a slightly triangular shape, creating less successful ragged edges.

> Asymmetrical text
> has no predictable
> pattern in the placement
>                                of the lines.
>
>
> Asymmetrical text
> has no predictable
> pattern in the placement
> of the lines.

FIGURE **6.11** Asymmetrical text. *Top:* Harder to read because of the uneven left edge, asymmetrical text can add a sense of motion or transition to a layout. Use this alignment for headings and pull quotes. *Bottom:* A less successful asymmetrical alignment with a predictable pattern.

**Left aligned and justified** alignments are easier to read because each line starts at the same place. Readers do not have to find the start of each line, which promotes vertical scanning (see Figures 6.12 and 6.13).

Unfortunately, both alignments can add unwanted visual elements if they are not set well, such as a misshapen ragged edge, or white "rivers" of space within a block of type. These problems are more prevalent if the line length is too short.

**The shape of the text block** does matter. Text is for reading. If text blocks add shape, it should be for a purpose, and the shapes created should be beautiful and meaningful. The best text blocks are those that contribute to the rhythm and tension of a page without screaming, "Hey, look at me, I make a triangle!"

> Left aligned text has lines of different lengths. The text is even on the left and ragged on the right. Easier to scan because of the even left edge, left justified text can keep a layout from feeling too "blocky." The ragged edge can become obvious if the line length is too short.
>
> Left aligned text has lines of different lengths. The text is even on the left and ragged on the right. Easier to scan because of the even left edge, left justified text can keep a layout from feeling too "blocky." The ragged edge can become obvious if the line length is too short.

FIGURE **6.12** The ragged edge on left aligned text shouldn't be too equal or too obvious. *Top:* A good ragged edge. *Bottom:* A less successful ragged edge, creating a concave shape.

> Justified text has lines of equal lengths with both sides even. Easier to read because of the even left edge, justified text forms a strong block shape in a layout. Rivers of white space can appear in the text if the line length is too short to fit enough words.
>
> Justified text has lines of equal lengths with both sides even. Easier to read because of the even left edge, justified text forms a strong block shape in a layout. Rivers of white space can appear in the text if the line length is too short to fit enough words.

FIGURE **6.13** Word spaces in justified text open and close to keep line lengths even. *Top:* Good word spacing. *Bottom:* A shorter line length creates awkward rivers of space.

## Color (Black/White)

White type on a black background is more difficult to read because the white letters glow and "sparkle" in the black background. The sparkle makes word shapes more difficult to recognize. Readers slow down and scanning is compromised (see Figure 6.14, top).

I highly recommend *never* setting white text on a black background. If you must use a dark background, try using a gray background (such as #333333). This lessens the contrast between the black and white, thus reducing the sparkle and eye strain (see Figure 6.14, bottom).

> White type on a black background is more difficult to read because the white letters glow and sparkle on the black background. Reduce the contrast between the black and white to reduce the sparkle and eye strain.
>
> White type on a black background is more difficult to read because the white letters glow and sparkle on the black background. Reduce the contrast between the black and white to reduce the sparkle and eye strain.

FIGURE 6.14 *Top:* White text on a black background sparkles. *Bottom:* White text on a dark gray (#333333) background is easier to read.

Some people report that reading black type on a white background is more difficult on a computer screen than on paper (see Figure 6.15, top).

This may be the result of the light emitted from the screen. It may be because of the fact that we read best what we read most, and not everyone is used to reading text on the screen. It may also be the result of inappropriate fonts set too small or too big, with too little line height and too long a line length!

Using a legible font, set with a size, line height, line length, and alignment intended to promote comfortable reading, will go a long way to solve the discomfort of reading on the screen. If necessary, however, consider using a gray like #333333 for the text. This lessens the contrast between the black and white, thus reducing the "brightness" of the white (see Figure 6.15, bottom).

> Black type on a white background is easier to read, but some people find it difficult to read type on a screen. If necessary, reduce the contrast between the black and white to reduce eye strain.
>
> Black type on a white background is easier to read, but some people find it difficult to read type on a screen. If necessary, reduce the contrast between the black and white to reduce eye strain.

FIGURE 6.15 *Top:* Black text on a white background is easier to read than white text on a black background. *Bottom:* Dark gray (#333333) text on a white background may be even easier to read.

### Creating Readable Text

To summarize, reading text is easier when:

- Font size is 12 to 16px
- Line height is at least 150 percent of font size
- Line length is about 75 to 85 characters
- Text is aligned left or justified
- Text is *not* white on black

# Lesson 6: A Film Series, Part 1

In the *A is for Alignment* lesson in Chapter 5, letters and text are visual elements used to create rhythm and tension.

In this exercise you will design a page—an announcement for a campus film series—by understanding how the reader might interact with text (scanning with purpose). You'll start by setting text to promote that kind of reading (see Figure 6.16), establishing a font, font size, line height, and line length.

This lesson helps you achieve the following objectives:

1   Practice choosing a font, font size, line height, and alignment to promote horizontal and vertical scanning.

2   Practice setting line length (and thus column widths) based on the text—not based on how much space you have at your disposal.

3   Practice sketching solutions that combine promoting readability with creating rhythm and tension.

4   Practice building a composition using more than one div, and use `overflow:hidden;` to force open a div with an auto height. Even if you are already HTML/CSS savvy, follow the walk-through provided. I show you what a typographer looks for in the process.

French Film Festival: 6 Short Films from France

Thursday, March 12, 2009

3:00 - 4:45 PM

CVPA Auditorium (Room 153)

This program of six French short films features a range of genres and reflects the diversity of contemporary French filmmakers and of the people of France. The films portray foundry workers in Brest, Algerian immigrants transplanted to Paris, the malaise of everyday life for an upper-class married couple, and flirtatious youths in the capital's subway system. Titles include

"Kitchen" by Alice Winocour

"Gratte-papier" (Pen-Pusher) by Guillaume Martinez

"Ma mere: Histoire d'une immigration" (My Mother: Story of an Immigration) by Felipe Canales

"Je suis une voix" (One Voice, One Vote) by Jeanne Paturle and Cécile Rousset

"La dernière journée" (The Last Day) by Olivier Bourbeillon

"L'Origine de la tendresse" by Alain-Paul Mallard.

Between them, the films have been honored with numerous awards and nominations at festivals from Cannes to Berlin to Montreal and beyond.

Sponsored by: Foreign Lit. and Languages

---

French Film Festival: 6 Short Films from France

Thursday, March 12, 2009

3:00 - 4:45 PM

CVPA Auditorium (Room 153)

This program of six French short films features a range of genres and reflects the diversity of contemporary French filmmakers and of the people of France. The films portray foundry workers in Brest, Algerian immigrants transplanted to Paris, the malaise of everyday life for an upper-class married couple, and flirtatious youths in the capital's subway system. Titles include

"Kitchen" by Alice Winocour

"Gratte-papier" (Pen-Pusher) by Guillaume Martinez

"Ma mere: Histoire d'une immigration" (My Mother: Story of an Immigration) by Felipe Canales

"Je suis une voix" (One Voice, One Vote) by Jeanne Paturle and Cécile Rousset

"La dernière journée" (The Last Day) by Olivier Bourbeillon

"L'Origine de la tendresse" by Alain-Paul Mallard.

Between them, the films have been honored with numerous awards and nominations at festivals from Cannes to Berlin to Montreal and beyond.

Sponsored by: Foreign Lit. and Languages

**FIGURE 6.16** Readers will skim down the list quickly, pausing only when they want to read something more closely. *Top:* When lines are too long, this forces the reader's eye across long, horizontal lines. Lists like this one also create long bands of white space. *Bottom:* A better line length. Large, white shapes no longer overpower the text.

Always start by reading the text you are designing with. It not only helps you decide what font to use, but also to identify how people might interact with it. In the case of a film series, people will most likely scan the text with a purpose: looking for a film to see on campus.

Readers will probably scan the text in one of two ways: looking at the titles to see what catches their interest, or looking at the dates to see if there are any films showing on a particular day. Either way, you need to *chunk* the information for them. Thoughtfully break it up into small pieces, so readers can glance at the first couple of words in each chunk, and then move on if they don't find what they are looking for.

Chunking is more complex that it sounds. We will break up the process and do it step-by-step over four lessons. Dividing the project into four lessons allows you to focus on specific ideas and skills.

In reality, all four parts happen simultaneously.

Designing with type is far more fluid than this project suggests. For instance, a good designer will consider vertical spacing and hierarchy at the same time, although those topics are covered in separate chapters.

Even if you are already an accomplished typographer or web designer, follow my lead and break down the process into four distinct parts. You'll find it's a challenge to change your usual methods for working with (and thinking about) type. You'll stretch your typographic muscles and become more intimately aware of the process.

## Overview of the Lesson

In this lesson, you will concentrate on honoring and promoting both horizontal and vertical scanning. You will establish a font, font size, line height, and line length.

1  Read the text you are setting, so you are familiar with all of the kinds of information people will skim and/or read.

2  Choose either Verdana or Georgia to work with. You'll have the opportunity to add another font (and to change the text font, if needed) in Part 4 of the assignment.

3  Create a sample text to experiment with. Find movies with different amounts of text: one with a short title, one with a long title, one with a short description, one with a long description, one with a short location name, and one with a long location name.

4  Quick-flow the movies you've chosen into a div, and set an appropriate size and line height. Don't worry about the other movies for now; you'll put them back in later.

5  Choose an alignment. You should use either left aligned or justified because readers will skim down the left edge of the text as they quickly read the first words in each chunk.

6  Add line breaks using p tags. All the text will look the same, but that's okay for now.

7  Adjust the width of the div to change the line length. What is the shortest line length your sample text can live in? Look at your date/time/place. Do you want those lines to break? Probably not, as this would make it more difficult to find when and where a movie is being shown.

What is the longest line length your sample text can live in? Make sure lines aren't too long to read. Also look at the ragged edge the text creates. Are the line lengths vastly different? If so, reduce the div width. Vastly different line lengths negatively affect chunking, readability, and rhythm and tension.

Extreme changes in line length create white spaces that draw the reader's eye and create unwanted visual separations within chunks of information.

8  Now it's time to decide how many columns the full text will live in (how wide your sample text divs are); how you'll use the rest of the horizontal space in the "box" holding the information; and the rhythm and tension you can create between the text, the headings, and the edge of the box. Start sketching (see Figure 6.17)!

FIGURE 6.17 Sketches using a column width—based on testing sections of the text—combined with the heading (justified, asymmetrical, right aligned, left aligned, and centered). By the end of this lesson, you'll have identified a line length and the number of columns to use. You will have sketched out multiple solutions and started building the page in HTML/CSS.

9  When you've settled on a layout idea, build your page in HTML/CSS using the entire list of films. Insert your p (text), h1 (main headline), h2 (semester), h3 (month), and h4 (title of movie) tags.

For now, set your p, h1, h2, h3, and h4 elements with exactly the same font, font size, line height, font weight, font case, and margins/padding.

You may need to adjust your line length slightly as you move forward, but you now have a general layout based on the line length your text needs.

Don't worry if your layout is not beautiful, exciting, or unique. You will modify elements, paying attention to spacing and emphasis in the next couple of lessons. You will also enhance information chunking for purposeful scanning while promoting rhythm and tension.

You have only begun the process.

## Starting the Film Series Page

In this lesson, you'll use CSS to test line length with a div, learn about `overflow:hidden`, and practice building a composition with more than one div.

In the *web_typography* folder, create a folder for the lesson. Call it *6_film_series*.

**Start the HTML File**

In your text editor, create a new document and save it as *index.html* in your *6_film_series* folder.

Copy and paste in the basic HTML syntax, add the title, and link to the CSS file:

```
<!DOCTYPE html PUBLIC "-//W3C//
    DTD XHTML 1.0 Strict//EN"
    "http://www.w3.org/TR/xhtml1/DTD
    /xhtml1-strict.dtd">
<html xmlns="http://www.w3.org/1999
    /xhtml">
<head>
```

```
<title> Lesson 6: Film Series
    (Line Length)</title>
<meta http-equiv="content-type"
    content="text/html;
    charset=utf-8" />
<link href="film_series.css"
    rel="stylesheet"
    type="text/css" />
</head>
<body>
</body>
</html>
```

Add your main_container div between the <body></body> tags:

```
<div id="main_container"></div>
```

### Start the CSS file

In your text editor, create a new document and save it as *film_series.css* in your *6_film_series* folder.

Describe the div ID for main_container

The main_container div is a white rectangle (990px wide, auto height) centered in the browser. It has some space above and below it. Write the syntax like this:

```
#main_container{
    width:990px;
    height:auto;
    margin-top:20px;
    margin-right:auto;
    margin-bottom:40px;
    margin-left:auto;
    background-color:#ffffff;
    }
```

Give the web page a gray background

To add a background color to the entire page, apply it to the body element:

```
body{
    background-color:#999999;
    }
```

View your web page

Save your HTML document, and view it in your browser. You should see a gray page, as shown in Figure 6.18. Why don't you see the main_container? Because it is set to auto height, and there isn't anything in it yet!

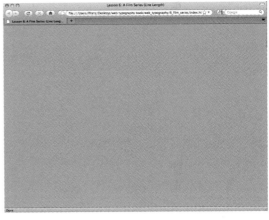

FIGURE 6.18 The main_container isn't showing up yet. You've set the height to auto, and there isn't anything in it yet (so the height is 0px).

Add sample content to test line length

In the HTML document, add a film_list_container div:

```
<div id="film_list_container">
    </div>
```

Choose four to six films to test

Choose a film with a short title, one with a long title, one with a short description, one with a long description, one with a short location name, and one with a long location name.

Copy and paste the text for the films from *6_film_series.doc* into the `film_list_container` div:

```
<div id="film_list_container">
    paste text here</div>
```

Define all titles, dates, places, descriptions, and so on as a p. The following example uses the film *Camila*:

```
<p>Camila</p>
<p>Thursday, March 26, 2009</p>
<p>11:00 AM - 1:00 PM</p>
<p>Foreign Language Lab</p>
<p>This film protests patriarchal
    terror while introducing the
    audience to Argentine values,
    concepts, social institutions,
    and culture during the dictatorial
    regime of Juan Manuel de Rosas
    (1829-1852). Camila brings a
    woman's perspective to Latin
    American history.</p>
<p>Sponsored by The Women's Studies
    Program & the Women's Resource
    Center</p>
<p>A discussion focusing on gender,
    the role of government, the
    structure of the family, and the
    role of women will follow the film.
    </p>
```

### Describe the elements in CSS

In the CSS document, type in the syntax for how each element should look.

You don't know what width the div should be yet (that's what you're testing). Nor do you know how tall it needs to be. Just start with a guess for the width, and set the height to auto:

```
#film_list_container{
    width:300px;
    height:auto;
    }
```

You don't know exactly what font size and line height you are going to use, but start by trying a standard Georgia, 13/19px. Also add a little margin so that the text doesn't completely run together:

```
p{
    font-family:georgia;
    font-size:13px;
    line-height:19px;
    text-align:left;
    margin-top:0px;
    margin-right:0px;
    margin-bottom:6px;
    margin-left:0px;
    }
```

### View your web page

Save your HTML document, and refresh your browser. You should see the white `main_container` now, with a column of text along the left edge (see Figure 6.19, top). Look closely at the sample text. Does the 300px container width work? Does the line length need to be longer or shorter (see Figure 6.19, bottom)? Change the width as needed.

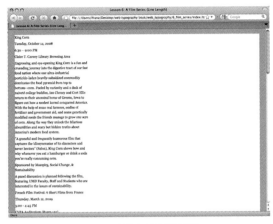

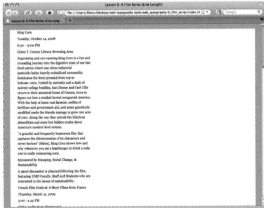

FIGURE 6.19 *Top:* The main_container has opened up to hold the film_list_container you added. Does the line length need to be longer or shorter? *Bottom:* Looking closely, it needs to be longer. This example uses the French Film Festival text, and the last names of two filmmakers are alone on a line. This creates a disparate ragged edge.

### Add a left margin to the text

Before changing the div width, you need to get the column of text off the left edge of the main container. The strong vertical line makes it difficult to focus on the ragged edge created by the text.

To do this, float the div left, and add 30px of left margin. The CSS syntax looks like the following:

```
#film_list_container{
    width:300px;
    height:auto;
    float:left;
    margin-top:0px;
    margin-right:0px;
    margin-bottom:0px;
```

```
margin-left:30px;

}
```

### View your web page

Save your HTML document and refresh your browser. Wait! What happened to the `main_container` (see Figure 6.20, top)? You can't see it anymore. This is a wonky problem with nesting floated divs inside a div with an auto height.

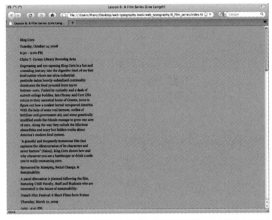

FIGURE 6.20 *Top:* The main_container is gone. The main_container's auto height ignores the floated nested div and snaps shut. To fix this, add overflow:hidden to the main_container. *Bottom:* The page after the overflow:hidden is added. The main_container is back!

The main_container's auto height is determined by what is inside the div. But the main_container div doesn't recognize floated divs within it (floated divs are out of sequence and will be ignored) and snaps shut.

So what do you do when you need to float divs (to control where they go in the composition) inside an auto height main_container?

**Add overflow:hidden;**
In the CSS file, add a property to the main_container:

```
#main_container{
    width:990px;
    height:auto;
    margin-top:20px;
    margin-right:auto;
    margin-bottom:40px;
    margin-left:auto;
    background-color:#ffffff;
    overflow:hidden;
    }
```

What does this mean? By telling the browser to look for possible overflow inside the main_container, you've forced the browser to pay attention to the floated divs inside the main_container. The main_container opens up to the full, appropriate auto height.

**View your web page**
Save your HTML document, and refresh your browser.

The main_container is back (see Figure 6.20, bottom)! Now you can experiment with the film_list_container width.

**Experiment with line lengths**
After changing the div width, write down the width that seems to work best.

How much horizontal space does that leave you inside the 990px-wide main_container? That extra horizontal space will come in handy for the left and right margins as well as any gutters if you decide to work with more than one column.

Sketch multiple solutions for the web page. Make sure you include the main heading ("Free Films on Campus") and the date ("2008–2009"). You aren't dealing with different sizes or styles of type yet, so you'll have to use contrast of space to make the main heading stand out.

Use what you learned about creating spatial tension in the last lesson—avoid repetition of form, create unequal white spaces, contrast the size of white shapes, and consider the edges— while honoring the line length your text needs.

## Building the Film Series Page

Once you've sketched out some possible solutions, pick one and build it (see Figure 6.21). You already have your HTML and CSS started. Keep working with these files.

**Add divs as needed to build the composition**
You're already using one nested div (film_list_container) in your HTML. Create, describe, and place more divs as needed (for the heading, an additional column, and so on) using the method shown in the walk-through for Lesson 5 in the preceding chapter:

• Name and describe additional divs (divs that will hold the film list should use the width that worked best when you did your testing) in CSS.

Using a border will help you see them on the page.

- Put the divs in the HTML with the `<div> </div>` tags.
- Place divs with the `float` property.
- Clear margins and padding with the universal selector.
- Put margins and padding back in as needed (to properly place the divs), making changes as needed.
- When done, remove the borders and add the content.

**FIGURE 6.21** *Top:* The page built in HTML and CSS. *Bottom:* The chosen sketch.

**Add and style the content**

Once the divs are in place

- Delete the (test) text you were using.
- Insert the entire text for the film series into the HTML.
- Insert the appropriate text between the correct `<div></div>` tags.
- Use all of the text given.
- Insert your p (text), h1 (main headline), h2 (semester), h3 (month), and h4 (title of movie) tags into the HTML.
- In the CSS, style your p, h1, h2, h3, and h4 elements with exactly the same font, font size, line height, font weight, font style, case, and margins/padding you used for the p in your test text. All the text should look exactly the same.

If you have problems building your composition or adding and describing your content, go to www. typographicwebdesign.com and browse through the FAQ/Troubleshooting section of the site. You can also view the sample HTML and CSS for this lesson to compare your syntax.

Don't worry if you don't love your layout right now. There is still a lot of work to do. For now, all the text should look exactly the same. The heading ("Free Films on Campus") is your focal point, using *contrast of space* only.

You'll add additional spacing and hierarchy in the next two lessons.

## Typographic Composition Is a Complex Process

Typographers usually do what I've broken up into four lessons all at once. When we compose a typographic page, we think about everything concurrently—line length, margins, spacing, hierarchy, creating rhythm and tension—but the process is complex, and there is a lot to explain. Your layout will seem unfinished at the end of this lesson, but you'll continue working on it in the next lesson.

## Recommended Resources

For this lesson, I recommend the following online resources:

- To download the text for this lesson, go to www.wiley.com/go/ typographicwebdesign

- To see examples of this lesson, go to www.typographicwebdesign.com

## Moving Forward

This chapter introduced you to using size, line height, line length, and alignment to create readable text. You also learned how to use `overflow:display` to open up your `main_container`.

In the next chapter, you will learn about chunking information using vertical space and proximity.

# CHAPTER 7

# Chunking Information: Vertical Spacing and Proximity

The principle of proximity is simple: We read things near each other as belonging together. For example, in a crowded room, if you see two or three people standing near each other, you might assume they are together, even if they are not engaged in conversation.

Typographically speaking, proximity works the same way. Words strung together form a sentence. Lines of text close together form a paragraph. In a list, items grouped together form a visual "chunk" of information.

Readers who are scanning with a purpose don't just scan down the text. They *jump* from section to section, looking for a specific piece of information (for example, from film title to film title).

In long or complex texts, readers *leap* from section to section, ignoring everything in between (for example, starting with "Spring 2009" when looking for a film in March). The reader will glance only at the first letter or word of each section, dismiss incorrect matches, and move on.

When working with any text, whether essay or list, simple or complex, you can help the reader by creating a system of vertical spacing. You can "chunk" the information, breaking it up into subsections or merging it together in meaningful ways, so your readers don't have to.

Proximity is a powerful principle of visual perception. When you add or remove space between lines of text, you not only make scanning information easier, but you also control the way people group (or read) text. Vertical spacing can be used to enlighten or confuse the reader (Figure 7.1).

| | |
|---|---|
| John Smith | John Smith |
| 40 years old | 40 years old |
| Jane Brown | Jane Brown |
| 24 years old | 24 years old |
| Mary Stuart | Mary Stuart |
| 65 years old | 65 years old |
| Mark Brown | Mark Brown |
| 19 years old | 19 years old |
| David Johnson | David Johnson |
| 47 years old | 47 years old |
| Ann Harris | Ann Harris |
| 6 years old | 6 years old |

FIGURE 7.1 *Left:* How old is Mark Brown? Adding vertical space "chunks" the list, so readers don't have to organize the information themselves. *Right:* Wait a minute... *How old is Mark Brown?* When you change vertical spacing, you change the way people read information. Vertical spacing can be used to enlighten or confuse the reader. So... how old *is* Mark Brown?

## Basic Separation: The Paragraph

A paragraph is a self-contained point or idea. Yet paragraphs support each other by describing something, advancing a plot, or developing an argument. As a result, paragraphs need to be visually separate from one another but still read as belonging together.

Good online paragraph spacing is 66 to 75 percent of the line height. For example, if your line height is 18px, a good paragraph spacing is 12px (18 x .66) to 14px (18 x .75, rounded up).

The `margin-bottom` shown on the top left in Figure 7.2 is set at only 25 percent of the line height. The paragraph spacing is too tight; the paragraphs start to blend together.

The `margin-bottom` shown on the bottom left in Figure 7.2 is set at 100 percent of the line height. The paragraph spacing is too loose; the paragraphs start to float away from each other.

The `margin-bottom` shown on the top right in Figure 7.2 is set at 50 percent of the line height. The paragraph spacing looks good, but that's because you are looking at text printed on the page. Paragraphs of text on the screen tend to need a little more spacing.

The `margin-bottom` shown on the bottom right in Figure 7.2 is set at 66 percent of the line height. The paragraph spacing looks good, if perhaps a little loose because you are looking at text on the printed page. The paragraph spacing will look great on the screen.

## Creating a System of Vertical Spacing

Long or complex texts need a *system* of vertical spacing. In the film series example in Chapter 6, each film has multiple elements that need to be separate from each other, yet grouped together for that film: title, date and time, place, description, a note about the film sponsor, and sometimes a note about the event.

To further complicate the matter, films must be "chunked" into months, and months must be "chunked" into semesters—so readers can jump or leap down the text as needed. For purposeful scanning, readers need to see which films belong together (all the films in March, for example), while recognizing each film as a separate event.

The principle of proximity is simple: we read things near each other as belonging together. For example, in a crowded room, if you see two or three people standing near each other, you might assume they are together, even if they are not engaged in conversation.

Typographically speaking, proximity works the same way. Words strung together form a sentence. Lines of text close together form a paragraph. In a list, items grouped together form a visual "chunk" of information.

Readers who are scanning with a purpose don't just scan down the text. They jump from section to section, looking for a specific piece of information (for example, from film title to film title).

---

The principle of proximity is simple: we read things near each other as belonging together. For example, in a crowded room, if you see two or three people standing near each other, you might assume they are together, even if they are not engaged in conversation.

Typographically speaking, proximity works the same way. Words strung together form a sentence. Lines of text close together form a paragraph. In a list, items grouped together form a visual "chunk" of information.

Readers who are scanning with a purpose don't just scan down the text. They jump from section to section, looking for a specific piece of information (for example, from film title to film title).

The principle of proximity is simple: we read things near each other as belonging together. For example, in a crowded room, if you see two or three people standing near each other, you might assume they are together, even if they are not engaged in conversation.

Typographically speaking, proximity works the same way. Words strung together form a sentence. Lines of text close together form a paragraph. In a list, items grouped together form a visual "chunk" of information.

Readers who are scanning with a purpose don't just scan down the text. They jump from section to section, looking for a specific piece of information (for example, from film title to film title).

---

The principle of proximity is simple: we read things near each other as belonging together. For example, in a crowded room, if you see two or three people standing near each other, you might assume they are together, even if they are not engaged in conversation.

Typographically speaking, proximity works the same way. Words strung together form a sentence. Lines of text close together form a paragraph. In a list, items grouped together form a visual "chunk" of information.

Readers who are scanning with a purpose don't just scan down the text. They jump from section to section, looking for a specific piece of information (for example, from film title to film title).

**FIGURE 7.2** Set paragraph spacing at 66 to 75 percent of the line height. *Top left:* When spacing is too tight, paragraphs blend together. *Bottom left*: When spacing is too loose, paragraphs float away from each other. *Top right:* This paragraph spacing looks pretty good because you're looking at it in print. It would look a little too tight onscreen. *Bottom right:* This paragraph spacing is 66 percent of the line height and will look great onscreen.

When building a system of vertical spacing, start with the line height. Make sure lines of text are properly spaced. Next, consider the elements in the basic chunk (for example, paragraph). How much space do they need to feel separate, yet related? Move out from the basic chunk using increasingly larger spaces to create each level of chunking.

To promote rhythm and tension, try to compose systems of vertical spacing around a mathematical constant. This will help you create spaces that are dissimilar (for contrast), yet have a visual relationship. The "Weekend of Workshops" list in Figure 7.3 has a 20px line height. Vertical spaces include 5px, 10px, 25px, and 35px. All spaces, including the line height, are divisible by 5.

| A Weekend of Workshops | A Weekend of Workshops |
|---|---|
| Saturday, November 2 | Saturday, November 2 |
| 9:00–11:00<br>Oak Room: Typography<br>Willow Room: Images | 9:00–11:00<br>Oak Room: Typography<br>Willow Room: Images |
| 12:00–2:00<br>Oak Room: Calligraphy<br>Birch Room: Book Binding | 12:00–2:00<br>Oak Room: Calligraphy<br>Birch Room: Book Binding |
| 3:00–5:00<br>Birch Room: Color<br>Willow Room: Embossing | 3:00–5:00<br>Birch Room: Color<br>Willow Room: Embossing |
| Sunday, November 3 | Sunday, November 3 |
| 9:00–11:00<br>Oak Room: Writing<br>Willow Room: Photography | 9:00–11:00<br>Oak Room: Writing<br>Willow Room: Photography |
| 12:00–2:00<br>Birch Room: Lettering<br>Willow Room: Drawing | 12:00–2:00<br>Birch Room: Lettering<br>Willow Room: Drawing |

FIGURE 7.3 Use as many levels of vertical spacing as the text needs. No more, no less. *Left:* This system uses two levels of vertical spacing with a lot of contrast. *Right:* A system with three levels and less contrast makes it harder to see the "chunks."

The more successful vertical spacing system shown on the left in Figure 7.3 uses only two levels of vertical spacing: 10px and 35px. The system is uncluttered and provides contrast.

The less successful vertical spacing system on the right in Figure 7.3 uses three levels of vertical spacing: 5px, 10px, and 25px. With more levels of vertical spacing and less contrast, it is harder to see the "chunks."

**Vertical Spacing and Proximity**

To summarize, we read things that are near each other as belonging together.

- The smaller the space between items, the more the items feel like they belong together.

- The larger the space between items, the more the items feel separate from each other.

- Paragraph space (`margin-bottom`) should be 66 to 75 percent of line height.

- Use as many levels of vertical spacing as the text needs—no more, no less.

- Build a system of vertical spacing using a mathematical scale. If the line height is 18px, other vertical spaces in the system might be 6, 12, 24, and 36px (all are divisible by 6).

- Chunking needs contrast. A system of vertical spacing with spaces that are too similar won't help readers.

# Lesson 7: A Film Series, Part 2

In *A Film Series, Part 1* you determined the appropriate size, line height, and line length for the text. In this lesson, you will develop a vertical spacing scale to chunk the information.

This lesson helps you achieve the following objectives:

1  Use proximity to group or separate chunks of information in text.

2  Create a vertical spacing system based on the text's line height.

3  Apply the system, paying attention to where spaces in the system need to increase or decrease. Even if you are already HTML/CSS savvy, follow the walk-through provided. I show you what a typographer looks for in the process.

## Overview of the Lesson

In this lesson, you develop a vertical spacing scale to chunk the information.

1  If possible, print out the page you built in Part 1 (Chapter 6).

2  Identify which chunks need to be grouped together, and mark them on the printout. Decide which vertical spaces need to be bigger or smaller to help separate or group information for your reader (Figure 7.4).

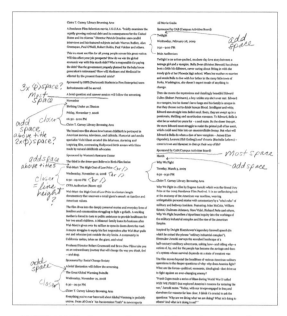

FIGURE 7.4 Mark up a printout of the web page so far. What needs to be grouped together? What spaces need to increase? What spaces need to decrease? What spaces need to be the biggest?

3  Develop a vertical spacing scale based on your line height.

4  Add top margins to your h1, h2, h3, and h4 tags to reflect your vertical space decisions. If necessary, create classes to tighten or loosen spacing on some of the <p> text.

5  Be willing to change your vertical space decisions as you progress through the system. What seemed like a good idea in theory may not work in reality. You may find the text needs more or less space within and between groupings. Stick to a mathematical scale as much as possible.

In the next chapter, you will modify elements, paying attention to emphasis. You will enhance information chunking for purposeful scanning while promoting rhythm and tension. For now, don't worry if your layout still feels unfinished.

## Developing the Vertical Spacing System

In this lesson, you use a `p.class` (add a class to the `p` element) and learn about collapsing margins. Both will help you develop your vertical spacing system. You'll modify the film series from Chapter 6, so make a copy of the last lesson's folder and name the new folder *7_film_series*. Keep it in the *web_typography* folder.

Rename the CSS file *film_series_spacing.css*. Link it to the *index.html* file by going into the HTML file and changing the syntax in the head element to the following:

```
<link href="film_series_spacing.css"
   rel="stylesheet" type="text/css" />
```

Change the title as follows:

```
<title>Lesson 7: Film Series
   (Vertical Spacing)</title>
```

### Determine and Apply Your Vertical Spacing Scale

You've already marked up on your printout what needs to be grouped together and where to add space. Now it's time to implement those decisions.

Build a scale based on your line height

In this example, assume that you have decided the best line height for your content is 19px. Nineteen is a prime number, which makes it hard to compose a mathematical scale (you can set margins at 9.5px or 4.25px, but browsers will round them up or down!). You are *not* going to change the line height because you already worked hard to determine it was best for the text, and you don't want to compromise line height (the most common vertical spacing) for the other spaces.

Round up and use 20px as your basic number and see if that works. If it doesn't, you can round down to 18px and recalculate the scale.

Using a base measurement of 20px, and knowing that you need a lot of contrast between different kinds of vertical spacing, you should probably use the following spaces:

• Between paragraphs in film descriptions, 75 percent = 15px

• Between films, a bigger space is needed, so use 45px

• Between months, an even bigger space is needed, 90px

• Between semesters, the biggest space is needed, so put your semesters in separate columns.

But this spacing system would be too big (see Figure 7.5). The lines of text would float away from each other instead of looking like chunks of information. Readers will be scanning information, not engaged in sustained reading, so chunking the information is the most important typographic objective. Try breaking the 66 to 75-percent paragraph space rule and see what happens (the beauty of CSS is that you can change it quickly and easily if you're wrong).

Camila
Thursday, March 26, 2009

11:00 AM - 1:00 PM

Foreign Language Lab

This film protests patriarchal terror while introducing the
audience to Argentine values, concepts, social institutions,
and culture during the dictatorial regime of Juan Manuel de
Rosas (1829-1852). Camila brings a woman's perspective to
Latin American history.

Sponsored by The Women's Studies Program & the
Women's Resource Center

A discussion focusing on gender, the role of government,
the structure of the family, and the role of women will
follow the film.

French Film Festival: Tell No One
Thursday, March 26, 2009

3:00 - 5:00 PM

CVPA Auditorium (Room 153)

FIGURE 7.5 A first attempt at a vertical spacing system
uses a 15px paragraph space as the smallest vertical
space. All other spaces are multiples of 15px. The
spaces are too big, and the information is not visually
chunked.

The following spaces would create a
better system:

• Between paragraphs in film descriptions, 50
percent = 10px

• Between films, a bigger space is needed, 30px

• Between months, an even bigger space is
needed, 60px

• Between semesters, the biggest space is needed,
so put your semesters in separate columns.

**Add the space into the CSS document**

Now that you've developed a vertical spacing
system, apply it in the CSS:

• Give p (paragraphs) a `margin-bottom:10px;`

• Give h4 (film titles) a `margin-top:30px;`

• Give h3 (months) a `margin-top:60px;`

*But wait!* If p has a `margin-bottom` of 10px and
h4 has a `margin-top` of 45px, won't there be
55px of space? Shouldn't you make adjustments
for two margins combining and only set your h4
`margin-top` to 35px (45px less 10px)?

Nope. Why? Collapsing margins.

### Understanding Collapsing Margins

When an element with a `margin-bottom` is
above an element with a `margin-top`, the
margins collapse, using the larger of the
two values.

This is great for web typographers! When you
establish a vertical spacing system, you don't have
to do any extra math to make sure the spaces are
correct. Just set the values exactly as you want
them, and the browser will do the work for you
(collapsing the margins so only the bigger margin
is used).

### Finesse the Vertical Spacing

The tighter vertical spacing system seems to work
(see Figure 7.6). Even though the paragraph
spacing is only 50 percent of the line height, there
is enough space to separate the blocks of text
within each film description.

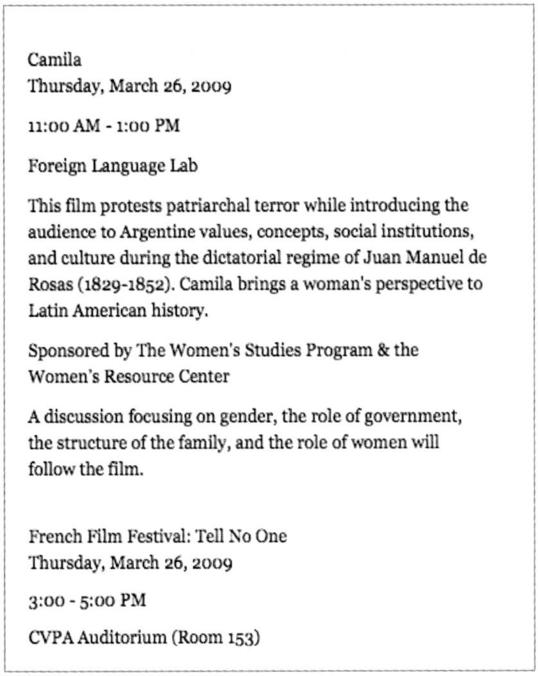

Camila
Thursday, March 26, 2009

11:00 AM - 1:00 PM

Foreign Language Lab

This film protests patriarchal terror while introducing the audience to Argentine values, concepts, social institutions, and culture during the dictatorial regime of Juan Manuel de Rosas (1829-1852). Camila brings a woman's perspective to Latin American history.

Sponsored by The Women's Studies Program & the Women's Resource Center

A discussion focusing on gender, the role of government, the structure of the family, and the role of women will follow the film.

French Film Festival: Tell No One
Thursday, March 26, 2009

3:00 - 5:00 PM

CVPA Auditorium (Room 153)

FIGURE 7.6 The paragraph spacing is fine, but it's hard to tell if the space above the film title is big enough. The film title doesn't stand out the way you want it to, and the bands of white between the date, time, and location are distracting.

But is there enough space between the films? It's hard to tell if the space above the films needs to be bigger, or if the amount of space between the date, time, and location is making the space above the films feel too small. Those extra paragraph spaces add a lot of extra white bands in the list. You're going to get rid of them and see what happens.

### Adding a class to an element

The date and time of each film are defined as `p`, but you want them to have a smaller `margin-bottom` so they will look different from the other `p` elements. You can fix this by creating a CSS class and targeting specific paragraphs.

In the CSS file, add a new element, `p.date`, and give it a `margin-bottom` of 0px. The syntax looks like this:

```
p.date {
    margin-bottom:0px;
    }
```

In the HTML file, change the `<p>` tags around the appropriate lines in the text. The date line previously looked like this:

```
<p>Thursday, March 26, 2009</p>
```

Now it looks like this:

```
<p class="date">Thursday, March 26,
    2009</p>
```

Why create a `p.class` with a 0px bottom margin instead of just using a `<br />` tag? If you use a `<br />` tag and then decide you need a small amount of space between the lines, you will have to go in and change the HTML again. By creating and applying a `p.class`, if you change your mind about the `margin-bottom`, all you have to do is change a value in the CSS. Remember, there are two more lessons on this project. As you add hierarchy and a second font in the next two chapters, you might need more space (even if you decide 0px is perfect for now). Using a `p.class` gives you more flexibility.

Why not create a class and apply it with a `<span>` tag? First, a `p.class` requires less typing. To apply a class with a `<span>` tag, the syntax would change to the following:

```
<p><span class="date">date goes here
    </span></p>
```

That's 12 more characters per change per line per film!

Second, you will only use .date with the paragraph element. Naming it p.date helps you see in an instant that the .date is applied to the p when needed.

### Finishing up

You added the p.date and the spacing is fine (see Figure 7.7). The films feel separate from each other, as do the months and the semesters. A reader can scan the list and find the film titles. Plus, the system uses a mathematical scale.

Camila
Thursday, March 26, 2009
11:00 AM - 1:00 PM
Foreign Language Lab

This film protests patriarchal terror while introducing the audience to Argentine values, concepts, social institutions, and culture during the dictatorial regime of Juan Manuel de Rosas (1829-1852). Camila brings a woman's perspective to Latin American history.

Sponsored by The Women's Studies Program & the Women's Resource Center

A discussion focusing on gender, the role of government, the structure of the family, and the role of women will follow the film.

French Film Festival: Tell No One
Thursday, March 26, 2009
3:00 - 5:00 PM
CVPA Auditorium (Room 153)

FIGURE 7.7 After you add a p.class to tighten the margin-bottom on the date and time, you can see that the space above the film title is fine.

When your vertical spacing works, you've finished the lesson. In the next chapter, you'll add hierarchy.

## Moving Forward

This chapter introduced you to using vertical space to "chunk" text. You also learned how to apply create a custom class to target a specific element.

In the next chapter, you will learn about creating and using hierarchy to further "chunk" the text.

# CHAPTER 8

# Chunking Information with Headings: Hierarchy and Similarity

The principle of similarity is simple: We read things similar to each other as belonging together. For example, in a crowded park, if you see two or three people wearing the same clothes, you might assume they are from the same club or team.

We also read things similar to each other as serving the same purpose. In a crowded store, if you see two or three people wearing the same outfit, you might assume they are employees of the store, available to help you in some way. If the employees are all busy with other patrons, you'll gaze around, looking for someone else dressed the same way.

Similarity is a fundamental element in typographic web design. In the last lesson, you used similarity to create a system of vertical spacing (all h4s had the same `margin-top`). In *A is for Alignment* in Chapter 5, the similarity between the minor counterpoints (justified, centered) created a relationship between the words (not just another layer of rhythm). In Chapter 14, you'll use similarity to indicate related information across multiple pages. In this chapter, you'll use similarity to *create a system of hierarchy*.

## Hierarchy

Complex texts have subdivisions. For example, the film series is divided into semesters, then months, and then individual films. Each division has a heading.

For readers to clearly recognize subdivisions, each heading level must feel less important than the one above it. Headline Two (h2) is subordinate to Headline One (h1), Headline Three (h3) is subordinate to Headline Two (h2), and so on (Figure 8.1).

# Headline One

Headline One is 24/40px Verdana, twice the size of the text. The size is enough to create hierarchy. Extra weight is not necessary.

## Headline Two

Headline Two is 14/20px Verdana, 2px larger than the text, font-weight:bold. Verdana's bold is heavy, and little size change is necessary.

### HEADLINE THREE

Headline Three is 11/20px Verdana, 1px smaller than the text), font-weight:bold. It is all caps (text-transform:uppercase), and has a letter-space:1px.

#### Headline Four

Headline Four is 11/20px Verdana, 1px smaller than the text. It has font-weight: bold. Verdana's bold is so heavy, it still has good contrast when 1px smaller.

A RUN-IN SIDEHEAD is 11/20px Verdana, 1px smaller than the text. It is all caps (text-transform:uppercase), and letter-space:1px.

# Headline One

Headline One is 20/40px Verdana, 8px bigger than the text. The contrast to the text is good, not to the other Headlines.

## Headline Two

Headline Two is 18/20px Verdana, 6px bigger than the text), font-weight:bold. A 2px size change from Headline One isn't enough contrast.

## Headline Three

Headline Three is 16/20px Verdana, 4px bigger than the text, font-weight:bold. The similarity between the Headlines is getting confusing. Readers need more than size contrast.

## Headline Four

Headline Four is 14/20px Verdana, 2 px bigger than the text, font-weight:bold. Verdana's bold is so heavy, it does not need to be so big at this level.

**A run-in sidehead** is 12/20px Verdana, the same size as the text. It has a font-weight:bold. Run-in sideheads can be more subtle.

FIGURE 8.1 *Left*: Each heading level is subordinate to the one above it, and contrast and similarity are woven into a system. Four sizes and two elements (bold and caps) are carefully combined to create hierarchy. *Right*: Five sizes and only one element (bold) create a system without enough contrast. It's hard to tell which level is subordinate.

Most texts will only have three levels of subdivisions (not including the overall title of the piece). Nonetheless, you should always read the text and create as many heading levels as needed (Figure 8.2).

## Hierarchy and Similarity

Apply a visual hierarchy system consistently throughout the text. This helps guide readers from section to section. A person scanning the film series page will quickly learn what a title looks like, and can jump from title to title, ignoring the other text on the screen. This is a function of similarity because all titles look the same.

Similarity also promotes contrast. When heading levels are developed with similarity in mind, they create a more effective system (Figure 8.1, left). If headings are all different from each other, it is hard to see how they are related. Hierarchy gets lost in the chaos of different fonts, font sizes, cases, styles, weights, colors, and positions (Figure 8.3, right).

---

# Spring 2009

Headline One is 26/40px Georgia, twice the size of the text. The size is enough to create hierarchy. Extra weight is not necessary.

## FEBRUARY

Headline Two is 15/20px Georgia, 2px bigger than the text. It is set all caps (text-transform:uppercase), and letter-space:1px.

### *The Future of Food*

Headline Three is 15/20px Georgia, 2px bigger than the text. It has a font-style: italic. The different forms of the italic and Roman create enough contrast for casual or sustained reading but film-goers will jump from title to title, so the headline needs to be a little bigger as well.

# Spring 2009

Headline One is 24/40px Verdana, twice the size of the text. The size is enough to create hierarchy. Extra weight is not necessary.

## FEBRUARY

Headline Two is 12/20px Verdana, the same size as the text, font-weight:bold. It is all caps (text-transform:uppercase), and has a letter-space:1px.

### The Future of Food

Headline Three is 11/20px Verdana, 1 px smaller than the text. It has a font-weight:bold. Verdana's bold is so heavy, it still has good contrast when 1px smaller than the text.

---

FIGURE 8.2 Two examples using three levels of hierarchy. *Left*: Choose styles appropriate for the content. I used italic for the third-level headings because they are titles. I'll have to keep an eye on the text, though; if I use italic in the film descriptions, I might not be able to use italic here because the contrast will be weak. *Right*: I used bold for the third-level heading instead of italic. Verdana's italic is an oblique. It is not lovely, so I try not to draw attention to it. I wouldn't use Verdana italic for a heading unless absolutely necessary.

# Headline One

Headline One is 26/40px Georgia, twice the size of the text. The size is enough to create hierarchy. Extra weight is not necessary.

## Headline Two

Headline Two is 15/20px Georgia, 2px larger than the text), font-weight:bold. Georgia's bold is very heavy, and needs little size change.

### HEADLINE THREE

Headline Three is 12/20px Georgia, 1px smaller than the text. It is all caps (text-transform:uppercase), and letter-space:1px.

*Headline Four*

Headline Four is 13/20px Georgia, same as the text. It has a font-style:italic. The different forms of the italic and Roman create contrast.

A RUN-IN SIDEHEAD is 11/20px Georgia, 2px smaller than the text. It is all caps (text-transform:uppercase), and letter-space:1px.

# Headline One

Headline One is 26/40px Georgia, twice the size of the text. The size is enough to create hierarchy. Extra weight is not necessary.

## Headline Two

Headline Two is 19/20px Georgia, 6px larger than the text, font-weight:bold. Georgia's bold is very heavy, and does not need this much of a size change.

### HEADLINE THREE

Headline Four is 17/20px Georgia, 4px bigger than the text. It is all caps (text-transform:uppercase), and letter-space:1px. The large caps are too strong.

*Headline Four*

Headline Four is 15/20px Georgia, 2px bigger than text. It has a font-style:italic. The different forms of italic and Roman create contrast.

A RUN-IN SIDEHEAD is 13/20px Georgia, the same size as the text. It is set in all caps (text-transform:uppercase), and letter-space:1px. It is too strong.

FIGURE 8.3 *Left*: Contrast and similarity are carefully woven into a system. Five sizes (to allow for subtle size changes) and three elements (bold, italic, and caps) are combined to create hierarchy. Working with so many differences is not easy, and it can backfire. *Right*: Five sizes and the same three elements create chaos.

Clear contrast helps your reader see which headlines are more important than others, and will prevent your reader from mistaking one headline for another.

---

### Hierarchy and Similarity

To summarize, when creating hierarchy

- Use as many heading levels as the text needs— no more, no less.

- Each heading level should feel subordinate to the one above it.

- Use headings in a similar manner throughout the text. Don't swap heading two and heading three halfway through.

- If heading levels are too similar to each other, hierarchy is difficult to see.

- If heading levels are all completely different from one another (with no similarities woven into the system), hierarchy is difficult to see.

---

# Lesson 8: A Film Series, Part 3

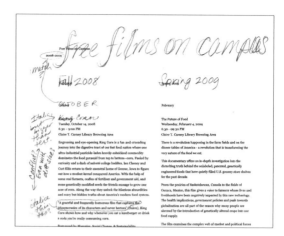

**FIGURE 8.4** Mark up a printout of the web page so far. Where are your headings? How will you handle complex descriptions (like the series of short French films all listed under one title), quotes from reviewers, and repetition of film title names in their descriptions?

This lesson helps you achieve the following objectives:

1  Create a system of headings with clear levels of hierarchy.

2  Use similarity in your system to emphasize contrasts.

3  Apply the system in a similar manner throughout the entire text. Even if you are already HTML/CSS savvy, follow the walk-through provided. I show you what a typographer looks for in the process.

4  Pay attention to where hierarchy needs to be increased or decreased as you apply the system.

## Overview of the Lesson

In this lesson, you develop a system of headings to help readers scan the text.

1  If possible, print out the page you built in Part 2 (Chapter 7).

2  Identify headings in the text (Figure 8.4).

3  Identify other areas in need of typographic work. A couple of the film descriptions have quotes. Will you use quotation marks or italicize them? One of the French Film Series titles is for a group of short films. How will you handle the titles of those films? Should they be handled in the same way as all the other titles, or would they stand out too much and feel like an individual film listing?

4  Sketch out a couple of options for creating hierarchy. Use size, case, style, weight, and/or spacing (vertical and horizontal).

5  Assign your new size, case, style, weight, and spacing (vertical and horizontal) to your h1, h2, h3, and h4 tags.

6  Create classes as needed.

You may find your vertical spacing system no longer works—you won't need as much space to create chunks. You have subdivided the text using contrasts in size, weight, and case. The extra vertical space further separates areas of text, and forces readers to work harder to scan the information.

7  Fix your vertical spacing, tightening it as needed. Continue using the mathematical scale you developed in Part 2.

Be willing to change your headings as you progress through the system. What seemed like a good idea in theory may not work in reality. You may find a heading level needs more or less hierarchy.

Remember that designing with type is far more fluid than this project suggests. Dividing the project into four lessons allows you to focus on specific ideas and skills, but in future projects you will often create and apply vertical spacing and hierarchy at the same time.

## Creating a System of Headings

In this exercise, you'll modify the film series from the last lesson, so make a copy of the last lesson's folder and name the new folder *8_film_series*. Keep it in the *web_typography* folder.

Rename the CSS file *film_series_hierarchy.css*. Link it to the *index.html* file by going into the HTML file and changing the syntax in the head element to the following:

```
<link href="film_series_hierarchy.css"
    rel="stylesheet" type="text/css" />
```

Change the title to the following:

```
<title>Lesson 8: Film Series
    (Hierarchy)</title>
```

**Determine and Apply Your System of Hierarchy**
You've already marked up on your printout where the headings are, and how you might set them.

Here's a tip: When I develop a system of hierarchy, I'll often work from the two extremes. For example, I'll set my h1 and h4 tags first, so I like the way they work in the composition (h1) and in relation to the text (h4). Then I'll set my middle levels accordingly (usually working up from the h4 tag).

**Change the h1 in the CSS. Be willing to change your idea!**
Some syntax I've alluded to throughout the chapter may come in handy:

• To italicize text, use `font-style:italic;`

• To make text all caps, use
  `text-transform:uppercase;`

• To change spacing between letters, here by 1px, use `letter-spacing:1px;`

• To tighten spacing, use
  `letter-spacing:-1px;`

• To change text color, here a dark gray, use
  `color:#333333;`

For this exercise, you'll make the h1 tag very big, taking up the whole top space, and make it italic. When text gets very big, it may feel too loose, so you might need to tighten it up a bit. You can experiment to see what works.

After testing, you should end up with something like the following for h1 (you may need to increase your header_container to make it fit):

```
h1{
    font-style:italic;
    font-size:80px;
    line-height:80px;
    }
```

**Change the h4 in the CSS**
As with the h1, make the h4 italic; I recommend italic because h4 is used for the title text. You want it bigger than the rest of the text, but not too big. Test it to see how it looks; pretend to look for a movie and scan down the page.

Hmm. After some testing, you may decide you don't like the italic: It's too hard to read while jumping from title to title. Bigger titles work better (they stand out more when you scan down the page), so you should go with a larger size instead of the italic:

```
h4{
    font-size:18px;
    margin-top:30px;
    }
```

Change h2 and h3 in CSS, and balance them with h1 and h4

You want the h2 to be stronger than the h4 you just set. Setting the semesters on separate columns means the h2 already has a strong level of hierarchy (due to contrast of space), so it will feel stronger than the h4, even when set only 33 percent bigger than the h4. Set the h4 like this:

```
h2{
    font-size:24px;
    }
```

Make the h3 all caps with loose (1px) letter-spacing; this will make the months look elegant and stand out. I personally avoid Georgia bold, which has very thick strokes. You may disagree, and choose to use Georgia bold in your version of the Film Series project. That's fine! Georgia bold is readable in headlines; sometimes, font preference is a matter of personal taste. For now, set the h4 by adding these two lines to the syntax:

```
text-transform:uppercase;
letter-spacing:1px;
```

**Go Back and Make Changes If Needed**

Here's a secret: Good web typographers (just like a good web anything) don't always know exactly how a web page is going to work before they build it. There's always something to figure out, and sometimes it takes a lot of time, patience, and attention to detail.

Finding a good system of hierarchy takes time and effort.

The months (h3) are currently all caps, with 1px letterspacing, and are the same size as the text (Figure 8.5, left). It doesn't work; the months don't stand out enough to move them above the film titles in the visual hierarchy.

You could try making the months bigger (Figure 8.5, right). But if the months get too big, they compete with the semester.

FIGURE 8.5 Finding a good hierarchy is not always easy. *Left*: February is too small. *Right*: Now it's too big, and is competing with the semester headline.

What if you make the months slightly smaller (but still bigger than the film titles), and the semesters bigger (Figure 8.6, left)? This results in a lack of contrast between the three levels; visual hierarchy is lost.

Let's start over. Months back to original size. Semesters back to original size. Try using bold with the months instead (Figure 8.6, right). Not bad, but the bold caps are sort of hard to read. (I personally don't like the way Georgia bold fills in the counterforms—aargh.)

How about instead of making the months stand out, you make the film titles "go back" so they feel subordinate?

FIGURE 8.6 We'll keep trying. *Left*: February is smaller, Spring is bigger, and the hierarchy is lost. *Right*: Everything is back to its original size, and February is bold. Not great; Georgia bold is a little hard to read because the counterforms are so small.

Try a shade of dark gray (Figure 8.7, left)... okay, that's not bad. The only problem is that now the film titles don't stand out as much when you scan down the list.

The best option is the one with the bold months (Figure 8.7, right). It's better to have too-thick letters in a heading that occurs infrequently than too-weak titles for every single film in the list.

FIGURE 8.7 Still trying to get the hierarchy right. *Left*: Everything is back to its original size and weight, but the film titles are gray so the months stand out. However, now the film titles don't stand out enough! *Right*: Go back to an earlier idea and make the months bold. The Georgia bold is not as legible, but at least the hierarchy works!

### Make adjustments to any other "headings" as needed

Think about those six short French films. Will you keep them as text with quotation marks, or do

they need to stand out more? Make and apply classes as needed.

### Update your vertical spacing system

Now that you have added visual hierarchy to your headings, you may not need as much space to chunk the information in the film list. Look carefully. Does anything feel too far away (or too close)?

### Make and apply classes if needed

Most of the spacing you set in the previous lesson still works, except for the space between the month and the film title (those two again!). The space between them makes the month "float" and undermines its hierarchy (Figure 8.8, left).

If you change the `margin-top` on the film title (h4), the space between films changes. So make a class for your h4 film title elements (for example h4.tightertop) with a smaller `margin-top` and apply it only to film titles immediately following a month (Figure 8.8, right).

FIGURE 8.8 After the headings are set, reevaluate the vertical spacing. *Left*: The margin between the month and title is too large. *Right*: You can tighten it by applying a class.

The only other spacing issue is with the lines at the end of the film description: Sometimes it's a single line ("Sponsored by..."); sometimes it's a single line followed by a couple of lines about what will happen after the film; and sometimes it's two single lines. The extra band of white space between

123

the two single lines of text is undermining the vertical space above the film title (Figure 8.9, left).

Try removing the space (Figure 8.9, right). It doesn't work; the note (about what will happen after the film) gets lost. Someone might miss out on pizza because they see the words "Sponsored by..." and ignore the rest of the text.

FIGURE 8.11 The *free films on campus* page. The hierarchy and vertical spacing system *finally* works.

Great! You're ready for the next lesson.

## Moving Forward

This chapter introduced you to using hierarchy to "chunk" text. You also learned that you need to go back and make changes (for example, to vertical space) when new design elements such as levels of hierarchy are introduced.

In the next chapter, you will learn about attending to the details (numbers and punctuation) in text. You'll also learn about using borders.

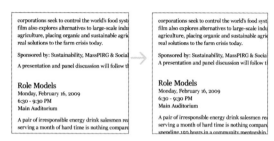

FIGURE 8.9 *Left:* The single lines at the end of the film description create bands of white space. *Right:* Removing the space doesn't work because they begin to read as a single piece of information.

Last idea, and then it's time to let it go. Tighten up the paragraph spacing. Just 1px will do it (Figure 8.10, right). It's a subtle difference, but it makes the space above the title stand out more, and the paragraphs are still fine for reading and scanning (Figure 8.11).

FIGURE 8.10 *Left*: The original spacing on the single lines. *Right*: Tightening the overall paragraph spacing reduces the white bands and does not affect chunking elsewhere.

# CHAPTER 9

# Attending to Typographic Details

At this point, you have a working film series web page from your work in the preceding chapters. It could go online as is. People can easily scan the information, stopping to read what they want or need to.

But there are things you can do to make a page more expressive, like add a second font—one with an aesthetic or emotional association, or one to improve hierarchy. And there are details you can attend to—rule lines, numbers, punctuation, acronyms, widows—to make the layout more beautiful while making the text even easier to read.

## Adding a Second Font

Try adding a second font for your main title and some of your headlines. A display font can add an aesthetic/emotional layer of meaning to your page.

A second font won't communicate, "This is an eclectic list of free films being shown on campus this year," but it might support the notion of "fun" (films are usually an extracurricular activity) or "cinema" or "eclectic" (Figure 9.1).

FIGURE 9.1 What fonts at fontsquirrel.com feel right to you? Some won't work (too heavy, too wide, not the right aesthetic), but you won't know what works until you try. Take screen shots of possible fonts and narrow down your options before moving on to HTML/CSS. *Top to Bottom:* Amadeus, EastMarket, FancyPants, Gladifilthefte, GrutchShaded, Louisianne, HamburgerHeaven, HVD Bodedo, Little Trouble Girl, and UglyQua.

It's not necessary to use the second font for every level of hierarchy. Weave it into the system, paying attention to how it works at different sizes and when it feels stronger or subordinate to the first font.

Continue thinking of the title, headlines, and text as a system. Do the sizes, weights, case, style, and positioning still work with the second font? Do you need to change the system in any way?

If the text font you've been using (Georgia or Verdana) doesn't work with the new font, change it. If you change your text font, reevaluate the line length, font size, line height, vertical spacing system, and system of hierarchy.

## Using Rule Lines

Rule lines are powerful symbols of separation. They are horizontal slices in the vertical flow of the text. The more subtle the line, the better. Use the lightest weight (1 pixel) possible, or deemphasize it with color (in our case, a shade of gray). Sometimes your text will demand more powerful rule lines, but don't make them more powerful than needed (Figure 9.2).

Use the principle of proximity. Rule lines should be closer to the information they belong with.

Use the principle of similarity. If two rule lines symbolize the same thing (start a new section), they need to look alike. If you need or want to use rule lines to mean two different things (start a new section, separate the footnotes from the text), then they need to be different. Rule lines should help clarify information for the reader, not create confusion.

---

Victoria (Rachelle Lefevre) – come to town a threaten to disrupt their way of life?

Sponsored by CAB (Campus Activities Boar

---

MARCH

Why We Fight
Tuesday, March 3, 2009
6:30–9:30 PM
Claire T. Carney Library Browsing Area

---

Victoria (Rachelle Lefevre) – come to town a threaten to disrupt their way of life?

Sponsored by CAB (Campus Activities Boar

---

MARCH

Why We Fight
Tuesday, March 3, 2009
6:30–9:30 PM
Claire T. Carney Library Browsing Area

FIGURE 9.2 *Top*: A good rule line is closer to the "chunk" it starts or ends. It is as subtle as possible. *Bottom*: A less successful rule line is too obvious, and is not connected with either "chunk" of information. It hinders the reader's vertical scanning.

Rule lines help chunk information, but don't let them become a crutch; you'll use them too much and undermine the hierarchy. Make the hierarchy work *first*, and then add rule lines where they'll serve the text.

## Numbers and Acronyms

You already know there are two kinds of numbers: lining figures (which look more like capital letters) and old-style figures (which look more like lowercase text). It is good manners to use old-style figures in text so the numbers don't YELL at the reader.

There are also two kinds of acronyms. Acronyms pronounced as a word (scuba) are set in lowercase. Acronyms pronounced as the letters (DVD) are set all caps. Acronyms can YELL, too.

If you must use lining figures or acronyms set in all caps, deemphasize their size when possible (Figures 9.3 and 9.4).

| Why We Fight is a film | Why We Fight is a film |
| Jarecki which won the | Jarecki which won the |
| at the 2005 Sundance | at the 2005 Sundance |
| It is an unflinching lo | It is an unflinching lo |
| of the American war | of the American war |

FIGURE 9.3 *Left*: Full-size lining figures stand out too much from the text. *Right*: If your font has lining figures, create and apply a class to make the numbers 1 pixel smaller than the text. If the numbers now stand out because they are smaller than the text around them, keep them the original size. The point is to help lining figures blend in, not draw attention to them.

| Why We Fight | Why We Fight |
| Tuesday, March 3, 20 | Tuesday, March 3, 20 |
| 6:30–9:30 PM | 6:30–9:30 PM |
| Claire T. Carney Libra | Claire T. Carney Libra |

FIGURE 9.4 *Left*: Full-size capitalized acronyms stand out too much from the text. *Right*: If your font has capitalized acronyms, create and apply a class to make them 1 pixel smaller than the text. If they now stand out because they are smaller than the text around them, keep them the original size. The point is to help capitalized acronyms blend in, not draw attention to them.

## Attending to Punctuation

Punctuation marks require a bit of special attention. The punctuation marks most often in need of your attention are quotation marks and the en and em dashes because they occur most often. HTML cannot render true quotation marks, en and em dashes and other special characters properly unless you insert character codes. Why? Because they are not keyboard characters; you can't just "type them in."

Special characters and punctuation marks can be added to your web page using character entities. There are two common forms of character entities: *numeric* and *semantic*. The numeric character entities have the reputation of working across more browsers (including old browsers), but I recommend using the semantic character entities (because they are easier to recognize and remember, and they work fine in contemporary browsers). I provide both forms of the character entities throughout the chapter, so you will be familiar with them when you see them in use.

### Quotation Marks

A true quotation mark is a curly quote, a mark that is as graceful as the other characters around it.

The default quotation mark in most software programs is the double prime (the symbol used when writing out a measurement in inches). The double prime, sometimes referred to as "dumb" quotes, is a pair of little vertical hashes that impede the horizontal flow of reading across a line of text (Figures 9.5 and 9.6).

127

They're all part of fearless heroine of film "Persepolis."

They're all part of fearless heroine of film "Persepolis."

FIGURE 9.5 *Left*: "Dumb" quotes. *Right*: True quotation marks (also called smart quotes) are double curly quotes (&ldquo; and &rdquo; or &#8220; and &#8221;). They are as graceful as the other characters in the text. Notice the apostrophe (&rsquo; or &#8217;).

They're all part of fearless heroine of film "Persepolis."

They're all part of fearless heroine of film "Persepolis."

FIGURE 9.6 *Left*: "Dumb" quotes. *Right*: Sans serif fonts (usually monoline) often use angled quotation marks instead of curly quotes. Notice the apostrophe.

To replace prime marks with true quotation marks, use the following code:

- Double left quotation marks
  `&ldquo;` or `&#8220;`
- Double right quotation marks
  `&rdquo;` or `&#8221;`
- Single left quotation marks
  `&lsquo;` or `&#8216;`
- Single right quotation marks (doubles as an apostrophe) `&rsquo;` or `&#8217;`

**En Dashes and Em Dashes**

The *en dash* is used to indicate a range. Think of the en dash as "between" or "to." Examples of where to use an en dash include 3–5 years, 2:30 PM–3:30 PM, and January–March (see Figure 9.7).

The default en dash in most programs is the basic hyphen. To replace a hyphen with an en dash, use the following character set:

`&ndash;` or `&#8211;`

The *em dash* is used to indicate a break in thought. It's used the way parentheses are used—when a comma is too weak, but a period is too strong. It is also used to indicate an unfinished sentence (like when a speaker has been interrupt—), or to create emphasis (see Figure 9.8).

The em dash is usually indicated by two hyphens (--). To replace two hyphens with an em dash, use the following code:

`&mdash;` or `&#8212;`

Why We Fight
Tuesday, March 3, 20
6:30-9:30 PM
Claire T. Carney Libra

Why We Fight
Tuesday, March 3, 20
6:30–9:30 PM
Claire T. Carney Libra

FIGURE 9.7 *Left*: An incorrect use of a hyphen. *Right*: An en dash (&ndash; or &#8211;) is longer than a hyphen, and half the length of an em dash. An en dash indicates a range. Here it means *from* 6:30 PM *to* 9:30 PM.

nation where one ultra subsidized commodity top to bottom--corn. F college buddies, Ian Ch

nation where one ultra subsidized commodity top to bottom—corn. F college buddies, Ian Ch

FIGURE 9.8 *Left*: An incorrect use of two hyphens. *Right*: An em dash (&mdash; or &#8212;) is twice as long as an en dash. It indicates a break in thought, an interruption, or an emphasis. Here it is used to emphasize the word *corn*.

## Avoiding Widows and Orphans

"Orphans are alone early in life; widows are alone late in life." While not a happy statement, this phrase can help you remember the difference between orphans (words or lines of text alone at the start of a column or text block) and widows (a word or words alone at the end of a column or text block).

Widows and orphans are words or lines of text left on their own, apart from the rest of the text. They disrupt the flow of reading, creating a gap in the text the reader must cross. Widows and orphans create unintended chunking. They insert extra space into a typographic design, and create emphasis (contrast of space) where you don't want it (Figure 9.9).

Orphans are words or a line of words alone at the start of a block of text. Widows are words or a line of words alone at the end of a block of text. Both disrupt the flow of reading and create unwanted emphasis. Avoid orphans and widows.

Orphans are
words or a line of words alone at the start of a block of text. Widows are words or a line of words alone at the end of a block of text. Both disrupt the flow of reading and create unwanted emphasis. Avoid orphans and widows.

FIGURE 9.9 *Top*: A properly set paragraph without a widow or orphan. *Bottom*: Widows and orphans add space and create emphasis where you don't want it.

You'll almost never need to worry about orphans and widows at the start and end of columns. Why? Because it's not good manners to set web text (prose) in more than one column.

Good web typographers don't make readers scroll down and then back up again! It's fine for the film list because people will either be looking in a specific semester (column) or glancing at titles, which they can do across columns. Multiple columns do not work for casual or sustained reading unless the text is short enough that both columns can fit without the reader needing to scroll!

The most difficult problem to avoid in web typography is the widow at the end of a paragraph.

It's impossible to completely avoid widows in web typography. Traditionally, print typographers make subtle changes to the layout: shifting type size, line length, letterspacing, line height, and column height to avoid widows.

But in web typography, we lose that control. We cannot size text in fractions of a pixel. Browsers render text with slight differences, often adjusting letter- and word spacing. Readers can change the size of the text in their browser. Content is flowed in from databases, not entered and carefully crafted by a typographer.

The best way to avoid widows is to control what you can: font size and line length. Set the font size big enough so that readers won't need to increase it on their end. Use a line length long enough to accommodate longer words. Use the *occasional* `<br />` tag to move a word or two down to the next line. If you are using more than one `<br />` tag on a page, you need to revisit your font size and line length.

And let the rest go. Don't hand-craft a rag by peppering your text with `<br   />` tags. It will backfire on you.

---

### Attending to Details

To summarize, when attending to details:

- Adding a second font might change everything in the system. Be willing and ready to make changes.

- Rule lines should be as subtle as possible for the purpose they serve, and close to the chunk they are beginning or ending.

- Rule lines with a similar purpose should look alike. Rule lines with different purposes should not look alike.

- If you must use lining figures in text, try making them smaller so they don't stand out. If the smaller size makes them stand out more, return to the original size.

- Use syntax to create curly quotes.

- Avoid widows and orphans by changing font size and line length. Don't hand-craft a rag by peppering your text with `<br   />` tags.

---

# Lesson 9: A Film Series, Part 4

In this lesson, you will learn how to add a second font, include rule lines, accommodate numbers and acronyms, tweak punctuation, and avoid widows. You will incorporate all these elements into the film series exercise from the preceding chapters. This lesson will help you achieve the following objectives:

1  Practice choosing a second font, paying attention to connotation and letter structures.

2  Practice using rule lines to separate chunks of information.

3  Practice paying attention to the details of fine typography: punctuation, numbers, acronyms, and widows.

4  Practice making changes as you add new elements to the design. A typographic layout is a system. Earlier decisions about font, size, line height, line length, vertical spacing, and heading levels might all change when you add the second font or rule lines. You need to make the necessary changes to pull everything back into a working system (Figure 9.10).

**FIGURE 9.10** Working with the text provided, Josh Terciera designed this typographic layout.

## Overview of the Lesson

In this lesson, you will attend to typographic details.

1  Choose a second font to incorporate into your design. Use @font-face or Georgia/Verdana (whichever you are not currently using). When you've added the new font, make changes so your typographic system still works.

Think back to what you learned in Chapter 2 about connotation. What meaning or feeling do you want the second font to add to the design? Think back to the discussion in Chapter 4 about choosing two fonts to work together. What kind of structural quality are you looking for in the second font? Does your choice for a second font work with the one you've been using thus far (either Georgia or Verdana)? If not, will it work if you swap your text font to the other one?

2   Add rule lines if you want to. This is not necessary. If you do add rule lines, follow the advice
given in this chapter regarding subtlety, proximity, and similarity.

3   If you are using Verdana, try making all of your
numbers 1 pixel smaller so they don't stand out
as much. If they stand out even more ("Look at
me! I'm small!"), keep them the same size as
the text.

4   Try making all of your acronyms (PM) 1 pixel
smaller so they don't stand out as much. If they
stand out even more ("Look at me! I'm small!"),
keep them the same size as the text.

5   Find all of the "dumb" quotation marks and
apostrophes and fix them.

6   Find all of the double dashes, and change them
to em dashes. Change all of the hyphens used
to mean "between" (such as the hyphens used
between two times) to en dashes.

7   Look for widows and orphans. If you have any,
try changing your line length slightly to get rid
of them. You may use one or two `<br />` tags
if necessary.

## Taking Care of the Typographic Details

In this exercise, you'll modify the film series from
the last lesson, so make a copy of the last lesson's
folder and name the new folder *9_film_series*.
Keep it in the *web_typography* folder.

Rename the CSS file *film_series_details.css*. Link it
to the *index.html* file by going into the HTML file
and changing the syntax in the head element as
follows:

```
<link href="film_series_details.css"
   rel="stylesheet" type="text/css" />
```

Change the title as follows:

```
<title>Lesson 9: Film Series
   (A Second Font and Details)
</title>
```

Create a *fonts* folder in your *9_film_series* folder.
This is where you'll keep the files for your
second font.

**Download Your Font from FontSquirrel.com**
Identify the meaning or feeling you want to help
communicate with your second font. When you're
ready, go to `fontsquirrel.com` to look for a font
that meets your needs.

### Choose your font
Test drive a variety of fonts, typing in the words
you'll use them for in the film list. Take screen
shots so you can compare and contrast the fonts
you are interested in. Look for a font that has the
right meaning/aesthetic, works with your text font
(Verdana or Georgia), and looks like it will "fit" in
the hierarchy you've established. If a font doesn't
look right to you, keep looking. Don't settle.

### Download the @font-face kit
The directions on the site are self-explanatory.
If you need additional instructions, review
"Download the @font-face kit" in Lesson 4.

### Put the EOT, TTF, SVG, WOFF, and license files in your fonts folder
Put the files in the *fonts* folder you created in *9_film_series*. Put the license file in the folder as
well. It's good to keep the license agreement with
the fonts. (Read it, too!) Leave the other files—
you won't need them in the *fonts* folder. The
*stylesheet.css* file is a valuable reference file,
and you'll use it in the next step.

**Describe @font-face in Your CSS Document**

Find the *stylesheet.css* file provided by Font Squirrel in the `@font-face` kit. Open the file in your text editor. Find and copy the following syntax:

```
@font-face{
    font-family:
        'GrutchShadedRegular';
    src:url('GrutchShaded-webfont
        .eot');
    src:url('GrutchShaded-webfont
        .eot?iefix') format('eot'),
        url('GrutchShaded-webfont.woff')
            format('woff'),
        url('GrutchShaded-webfont.ttf')
            format('truetype'),
        url('GrutchShaded-webfont
            .svg#webfontsya16SUC')
            format('svg');
    font-weight:normal;
    font-style:normal;
    }
```

Open your CSS file for this lesson (*film_series_details.css*), and paste the syntax at the top of the file.

This syntax is not going to work... yet. You need to tell the various browsers to find the files they need in the *fonts* folder. Thus you need to add `fonts/` to all of the URLs, like so:

```
@font-face{
    font-family:
        'GrutchShadedRegular';
    src:url('fonts/GrutchShaded-webfont
        .eot');
    src:url('fonts/GrutchShaded-webfont
        .eot?iefix') format('eot'),
```

```
        url('fonts/GrutchShaded-webfont
            .woff') format('woff'),
        url('fonts/GrutchShaded-webfont
            .ttf') format('truetype'),
        url('fonts/GrutchShaded-webfont
            .svg#webfontsya16SUC')
            format('svg');
    font-weight:normal;
    font-style:normal;
    }
```

**Reminders about the syntax**

In the syntax, I used the font *GrutchShaded Regular*. Use your own font information wherever I used information specific to GrutchShaded.

This syntax is always available in the *stylesheet.css* file provided by Font Squirrel. Now that you know what to look for, I highly recommend that you copy and paste it to avoid errors.

If you choose to type in the syntax, remember that indented lines belong together on a single line, and do not add spaces before periods (.) or forward slashes (/). Thus the following syntax would be typed in as a single line, with no space between `webfont` and `.ttf`:

```
url('fonts/GrutchShaded-webfont
    .ttf') format('truetype'),
```

**Use the font-family name in your h1 selector**

You've named the `font-family` and told browsers where to find the font, so now you're ready to use it.

Change your `h1` (or whatever tag you are using the second font for) `font-family` syntax to include the new font. The `h1 font-family` has been Georgia up to now in my example. I'll add GrutchShaded to my `font-family` options:

```
h1{
    font-family:
    GrutchShadedRegular, georgia;
    }
```

### Build and test a font stack

Notice that I added `GrutchShadedRegular`, but kept Georgia as an alternate, separating the fonts with a comma.

You did this in the bibliography lesson in Chapter 4, and it bears repeating: Always build font stacks. It keeps your websites from defaulting to Times or Arial, and ensures a fallback if your desired font is not available for whatever reason.

You should also test your font stack by purposely removing your first choice from the stack during the design process—see what the page would look like if it defaulted to the second font. Fonts have different widths, bowls, thicks, and thins. Build your font stack so the next font in the stack works, too!

### Provide copyright information

Use a comment to identify any fonts linked in your file. Most EULAs (End User License Agreement) require that you provide the copyright information.

Providing copyright information also helps web typographers identify and find good fonts! You'll appreciate it when others do it in their CSS.

The syntax below is only slightly modified from the copyright comment at FontSquirrel. Again, read the EULA to see what you are expected to include for each font.

```
/*
 * GrutchShadedRegular is copyrighted
   by the vendor listed below.
 *
 * @vendor:      Steeve Gruson
 * @licenseurl: http://www.
   fontsquirrel.com/license
   /GrutchShaded
 *
 */
```

### Identify What Needs to Change

Before you added the second font, you had a working Film Series web page with readable text and a carefully considered composition. But when you added the second font, it probably affected the readability of the headline as well as the overall composition. You need to make some changes.

Your design is different from mine, so I can't tell you exactly how to refine your composition, but I can show you how I refined mine. This will help you see the process, and give you tips on how to approach different problems.

In my example, I'm using my second font in my `h1`, so I'll start there. `GrutchShaded regular` is wider than Georgia italic and breaks the main heading onto two lines (Figure 9.11). I have a decision to make. Should I make the main heading smaller so it will fit on one line again? Do I leave it big and make adjustments to the composition?

GrutchShaded regular needs to be big for two reasons: one, to show off the texture of the marks, and two, because it is not an elegant font. It should feel a little clunky.

I'm not going to change the `h1` (yet) but I do need to change the divs. The larger heading is messing things up (my main heading is overlapping "Fall 2008"). Plus, the new font is inspiring me… because it needs to be clunky, I think I'm going to set it asymmetrically instead of left aligned.

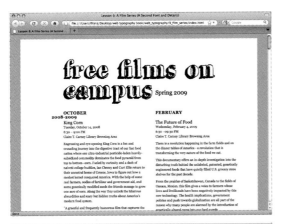

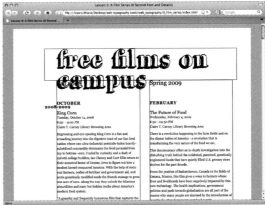

FIGURE 9.11 *Top*: The new font is wider, so the main heading no longer fits on one line. It overflows the div and covers the Fall 2008 heading. The question is, do I make the main heading smaller or break it onto two lines and fix the div? GrutchShaded regular is sort of clunky. It won't work as well small. I'll keep it on two lines and make changes to the composition as needed. *Bottom*: The original main heading in Georgia italic.

### Put borders back on your divs to help you see them

I know I need to change my divs. Headings shouldn't be overlapping, and I want to make my main heading asymmetrical. It's easier to see what I'm doing if I can see the borders of my divs. I'll add a 1px solid #000000 (black) border back on each div (Figure 9.12).

FIGURE 9.12 *Top*: My main heading is so big it's going outside its div. I need to change the div so the main heading fits. *Bottom*: I change the placement and width of the div, as well as the h1.class, so the main heading is asymmetrical with a sense of depth. I remove 2008–2009 and use GrutchShaded regular to associate the semesters with the main heading.

### Make changes to hierarchy and vertical space as needed

Once the second font is in, you'll probably need to make changes to your hierarchy and vertical spacing system (Figures 9.13 and 9.14). A typographic composition is a system; when one element changes, the others respond to the change. Use what you've learned in the previous lessons to look for areas that need to be changed.

**FIGURE 9.13** *Top:* When I remove the div borders, the semesters feel like they belong in the main heading. Nor do I like the lining figures for 2008 and 2009. *Bottom:* I change the semesters back to Georgia. I also add a rule line above the months to help chunk the films by month.

**FIGURE 9.14** *Top:* I try making the background black (films are shown in the dark). The film list doesn't work with white on black because it's almost impossible to read. *Bottom:* I keep the text in white boxes, and add padding inside the divs so the text isn't right up against the black line. This helps keep the text readable. The black background makes the film titles feel less important, so I make them a little bigger.

### Add rule lines if you need to

To add rule lines, use the `border` property.

So far, I've been adding a border to all four sides of divs. It's possible to add a border to a single side of an element.

To add a rule line above a heading, add a `border-top`. My months are described with the following syntax:

```
h3{
    font-weight:bold;
    text-transform:uppercase;
    margin-top:46px;
    font-size:17px;
    letter-spacing:1px;
    border-top:1px solid #000000;
    padding-top:4px;
    }
```

The syntax for the border is in bold. Notice I've added a line for `padding-top`, too. The `padding-top` code adds a little space above the heading, inserting space between the rule line (`border-top`) and the month.

Notice I've also removed 4px from the `margin-top`. Adding the padding increased the vertical space by 4px. I didn't want the extra space, so I removed it from the margin.

I used similar syntax to create the white dotted line on the left edge:

```
#main_container{
    width:990px;
    height:auto;
    margin-top:20px;
```

```
    margin-right:auto;
    margin-bottom:40px;
    margin-left:auto;
    border-left:dotted 10px #ffffff;
    }
```

### Deemphasize numbers and acronyms

Now that the heading with the new font is fixed, it's time to attend to the typographic details. How you style numbers and acronyms will differ based on whether you are using Verdana or Georgia for your text. Again, your design is different from mine, so I can't tell you exactly how to refine the numbers and acronyms, but I can show you how I refined mine.

I'm using Georgia, so my numbers are okay. But I still need to go in and fix the acronyms (PM, PIRG, SIFE, CAB, CVPA).

*Note:* You'll notice there are a lot of acronyms in the text. Your readers probably won't recognize most of them (for example, CVPA stands for College of Visual and Performing Arts). You can help solve this problem using the <acronym> tag around your acronyms. I'm not using it in this chapter because I want you to practice controlling type even when there is not a tag available. But you'll learn more about the <acronym> tag and how to use it in the lesson for Chapter 10.

For this lesson, fix numbers and acronyms by creating a class in the CSS file with a font size 1 pixel smaller than the text (p):

```
.acronyms{
    font-size:12px;
    }
```

137

In the HTML file, insert the following tag before each number or acronym:

```
<span class="acronyms">
```

Then add the closing tag after each number or acronym:

```
</span>
```

### Find and change hyphens used for film times

In a range of time, the proper punctuation is an en dash. Find and replace the hyphens used in the film times with en dashes:

```
&ndash;
```

### Find and change double hyphens used within the text

To suggest a break in narrative, the proper punctuation is an em dash. Find and replace all double hyphens with em dashes:

```
&mdash;
```

### Find and fix apostrophes

Proper apostrophes are "curly." Find and replace all prime marks with curly versions:

```
&rsquo;
```

### Find and fix quotation marks

Proper quotation marks are "curly." Find and replace all double prime marks, or "dumb" quotation marks, with the following codes as appropriate:

- Left double quotation marks `&ldquo;`
- Right double quotation marks `&rdquo;`
- Left single quotation marks `&lsquo;`
- Right single quotation marks `&rsquo;`

### Find and remove unnecessary punctuation

If you've italicized any titles (such as the six short films from France in the film descriptions), remove the quotation marks around them.

### Fix widows

The occasional widow is fine, especially if the word alone on the last line is long. But sometimes a widow feels odd (like when a filmmaker's last name is alone on a line, for example) and can be fixed easily (see Figure 9.15).

To fix the occasional widow, create a line break by inserting a `<br />` tag.

**Double-check Your Work**

You've taken care of a lot of typographic details in this lesson. Take the time to go back and double-check your work. Did you catch everything? Is there anything you need to change (Figure 9.16)?

Congratulations! You have finished the *Free Films on Campus* project.

## Taking Root

Thursday, April 2, 2009

7:00–9:00 PM

Frederick Douglass Unity House

PBS film preview: "Taking Root" by Lisa Merton & Alan Dater

How does the simplest act of planting trees lead to winnin the Nobel Peace Prize? Ask Wangari Maathai of Kenya. In 1977, she suggested rural women plant trees to address problems stemming from a degraded environment. Under her leadership, their tree-planting grew into a nationwide movement to safeguard the environment, defend human rights and promote democracy... and brought Maathai the

## Taking Root

Thursday, April 2, 2009

7:00–9:00 PM

Frederick Douglass Unity House

PBS film preview: "Taking Root" by Lisa Merton & Alan Dater

How does the simplest act of planting trees lead to winnin the Nobel Peace Prize? Ask Wangari Maathai of Kenya. In 1977, she suggested rural women plant trees to address problems stemming from a degraded environment. Under her leadership, their tree-planting grew into a nationwide movement to safeguard the environment, defend human rights and promote democracy... and brought Maathai the

FIGURE 9.15 *Top:* A filmmaker's last name is alone on a line, separated from his film, and creating a large vertical space within the chunk. *Bottom:* The widow is fixed with a <br /> tag. Peppering the text with <br /> tags invites trouble. Don't do it. If a reader increases or decreases text size in his browser, the ragged edge will go crazy. Instead, use <br /> tags sparingly and where they'll do the most good. If you need to use more than one <br /> tag per page, you are using too many!

FIGURE 9.16 *Top:* One last change. The black background was overwhelming, so I changed the background color to #372f2d. The new color is still dark but not so intense. It also adds warmth to the composition. If you want to try a different color, use the Hues Hub web page (see "Recommended Resources") to find the syntax for your CSS file. *Bottom:* The page with a black background.

**Recommended Resources**

For this lesson, I recommend the following online resources:

- To choose and download fonts, go to www.fontsquirrel.com

- To choose a color, go to the Hues Hub at www.december.com/html/spec/colorhues.html

- To find out more about em and en dashes, go to www.alistapart.com/articles/emen/

- To find the syntax for more special characters and punctuation, go to digitalmediaminute.com/reference/entity/index.php

- To learn more about the acronym tag, go to diveintoaccessibility.org/day_17_defining_acronyms.html

- To see examples of this lesson, go to www.typographicwebdesign.com

## Moving Forward

This chapter introduced you to some of the details a web typographer needs to attend to: adding a second font, working with rule lines, deemphasizing numbers and abbreviations, and fixing punctuation.

In the next chapter, you will learn about using tables to lay out tabular data.

# Tabular Information

*Good typographic answers are not elicited by asking questions such as "How can I cram this number of characters into that amount of space?"*

ROBERT BRINGHURST, THE ELEMENTS OF TYPOGRAPHIC STYLE (1997)

# CHAPTER 10

# A Typographic Approach to Tabular Information

Readers don't just read text; they read numerical data. They don't always scan down a column; sometimes they need to scan across a line. Sometimes, readers need to scan both down *and* across to find the information they seek. Thus, attending to the typography in tabular information is as important (if not more important!) as setting text. As always, you need to pay attention to legibility, proximity, similarity, and how people read.

## Legibility

First and foremost, you need to maintain legibility within tables. Avoid setting text too small to read, using condensed fonts (counterforms get lost and legibility is undermined), and tightening letterspacing.

Getting text to fit in a table doesn't matter if people can't read the information!

## Proximity

Items that are closer together are seen as belonging together. Items that are farther apart are seen as being separate from each other. Whitespace is your friend. Don't give it up to fit more information in.

More space between columns urges readers to read down. Why? The columns seem separate from each other. Readers don't know to "jump the gap" between columns. The (tighter) information in each column seems to belong together (Figure 10.1, top).

What if the table is meant to be read across, not down? Tighter space between columns combined with more space between rows of data turns columns into a table. The improved horizontal flow encourages people to read across (Figure 10.1, bottom).

| | Monday | Tuesday | Wednesday | Thursday | Friday | Saturday |
|---|---|---|---|---|---|---|
| Tykes | 1:00–1:40 | 2:00–2:40 | 9:00–9:40 | 2:00–2:40 | 1:00–1:40 | 9:00–9:40 |
| Preschool | 9:00–9:40 | 1:00–1:40 | 2:00–2:40 | 9:00–9:40 | 9:00–9:40 | 9:00–9:40 |
| Beginner | 3:00–3:50 | 4:00–4:50 | 5:00–5:50 | 4:00–4:50 | 3:00–3:50 | 1:00–1:50 |
| Intermediate | 4:00–5:15 | 5:00–6:15 | 4:00–5:15 | 5:00–6:15 | 4:00–5:15 | 2:00–3:15 |
| Advanced | 5:00–6:15 | 6:30–7:45 | 3:00–4:15 | 6:30–7:45 | 5:00–6:15 | 3:00–4:15 |

| | **Monday** | **Tuesday** | **Wednesday** | **Thursday** | **Friday** | **Saturday** |
|---|---|---|---|---|---|---|
| **Tykes** | 1:00–1:40 | 2:00–2:40 | 9:00–9:40 | 2:00–2:40 | 1:00–1:40 | 9:00–9:40 |
| **Preschool** | 9:00–9:40 | 1:00–1:40 | 2:00–2:40 | 9:00–9:40 | 9:00–9:40 | 9:00–9:40 |
| **Beginner** | 3:00–3:50 | 4:00–4:50 | 5:00–5:50 | 4:00–4:50 | 3:00–3:50 | 1:00–1:50 |
| **Intermediate** | 4:00–5:15 | 5:00–6:15 | 4:00–5:15 | 5:00–6:15 | 4:00–5:15 | 2:00–3:15 |
| **Advanced** | 5:00–6:15 | 6:30–7:45 | 3:00–4:15 | 6:30–7:45 | 5:00–6:15 | 3:00–4:15 |

FIGURE 10.1 *Top*: Space can be used to separate and bind information into "chunks." Spaces in the top table suggest information should be read down the columns. Yet, to find useful information, readers must read across rows. *Bottom*: Tighter space between columns and more space between rows can help facilitate reading.

## Similarity

Items that are similar are seen as having a similar meaning or purpose. Items that are dissimilar are seen as having different meanings or purposes.

Use similarity to create contrast between headings and data (Figure 10.2). Headings should be consistent with each other yet different from the data (otherwise, they may blend in).

Consistency goes beyond font, weight, and style. Keep alignment and size consistent as well. If you are tempted to decrease the font size of a heading to help it fit into a table, remember the importance of similarity and find another solution.

## How People Read

Knowing how people read helps when setting tabular data. Understanding how people scan across rows and down columns of information helps determine where to apply rule lines and how to align numbers.

### Rule Lines

We are suggestible creatures. We will follow a line along its path. Rule lines or other dividers (extra space, bands of color behind data), if necessary, should follow the flow of the information—and thus help direct the flow of the reader.

| Classes | Monday | Tuesday | Wednesday | Thursday | Friday | Saturday |
|---|---|---|---|---|---|---|
| Tykes | 1:00–1:40 | 2:00–2:40 | 9:00–9:40 | 2:00–2:40 | 1:00–1:40 | 9:00–9:40 |
| **Preschool** | 9:00–9:40 | 1:00–1:40 | 2:00–2:40 | 9:00–9:40 | 9:00–9:40 | 9:00–9:40 |
| Beginner | 3:00–3:50 | 4:00–4:50 | 5:00–5:50 | 4:00–4:50 | 3:00–3:50 | 1:00–1:50 |
| **Intermediate** | 4:00–5:15 | 5:00–6:15 | 4:00–5:15 | 5:00–6:15 | 4:00–5:15 | 2:00–3:15 |
| Advanced | 5:00–6:15 | 6:30–7:45 | 3:00–4:15 | 6:30–7:45 | 5:00–6:15 | 3:00–4:15 |

| | *Monday* | *Tuesday* | *Wednesday* | *Thursday* | *Friday* | *Saturday* |
|---|---|---|---|---|---|---|
| **Tykes** | 1:00–1:40 | 2:00–2:40 | 9:00–9:40 | 2:00–2:40 | 1:00–1:40 | 9:00–9:40 |
| **Preschool** | 9:00–9:40 | 1:00–1:40 | 2:00–2:40 | 9:00–9:40 | 9:00–9:40 | 9:00–9:40 |
| **Beginner** | 3:00–3:50 | 4:00–4:50 | 5:00–5:50 | 4:00–4:50 | 3:00–3:50 | 1:00–1:50 |
| **Intermediate** | 4:00–5:15 | 5:00–6:15 | 4:00–5:15 | 5:00–6:15 | 4:00–5:15 | 2:00–3:15 |
| **Advanced** | 5:00–6:15 | 6:30–7:45 | 3:00–4:15 | 6:30–7:45 | 5:00–6:15 | 3:00–4:15 |

FIGURE 10.2 *Top*: Similarity between weekdays and data makes the top headings disappear. A lack of similarity between the levels of study makes it difficult to see they are all left headings. Instead, we start to read: Classes, Preschool, Intermediate. *Bottom:* Creating contrast between weekdays and data—and similarity between levels of study—improves hierarchy.

Use as few rule lines or other dividers as possible. Let the tabular *information* be the most important element (Figure 10.3).

A border (rule line) around the outside of a table usually doesn't serve a function for reading. Such a border says, "Hello, I am a table." But text arrangement and margins of space around the table already serve that function.

## Numbers

Align numbers on the decimal (align-right), so the numerical columns (hundreds, tens, ones) line up. Numbers have meaning based on their position in a column (Figure 10.4). This principle must be recognized and attended to whenever possible (aligning numbers on the decimal will not work in every situation... do your best).

| | Monday | Tuesday | Wednesday | Thursday | Friday | Saturday |
|---|---|---|---|---|---|---|
| **Tykes** | 1:00–1:40 | 2:00–2:40 | 9:00–9:40 | 2:00–2:40 | 1:00–1:40 | 9:00–9:40 |
| **Preschool** | 9:00–9:40 | 1:00–1:40 | 2:00–2:40 | 9:00–9:40 | 9:00–9:40 | 9:00–9:40 |
| **Beginner** | 3:00–3:50 | 4:00–4:50 | 5:00–5:50 | 4:00–4:50 | 3:00–3:50 | 1:00–1:50 |
| **Intermediate** | 4:00–5:15 | 5:00–6:15 | 4:00–5:15 | 5:00–6:15 | 4:00–5:15 | 2:00–3:15 |
| **Advanced** | 5:00–6:15 | 6:30–7:45 | 3:00–4:15 | 6:30–7:45 | 5:00–6:15 | 3:00–4:15 |

| | Monday | Tuesday | Wednesday | Thursday | Friday | Saturday |
|---|---|---|---|---|---|---|
| **Tykes** | 1:00–1:40 | 2:00–2:40 | 9:00–9:40 | 2:00–2:40 | 1:00–1:40 | 9:00–9:40 |
| **Preschool** | 9:00–9:40 | 1:00–1:40 | 2:00–2:40 | 9:00–9:40 | 9:00–9:40 | 9:00–9:40 |
| **Beginner** | 3:00–3:50 | 4:00–4:50 | 5:00–5:50 | 4:00–4:50 | 3:00–3:50 | 1:00–1:50 |
| **Intermediate** | 4:00–5:15 | 5:00–6:15 | 4:00–5:15 | 5:00–6:15 | 4:00–5:15 | 2:00–3:15 |
| **Advanced** | 5:00–6:15 | 6:30–7:45 | 3:00–4:15 | 6:30–7:45 | 5:00–6:15 | 3:00–4:15 |

FIGURE 10.3 *Top*: A table with too many rule lines. Rule lines do not help with flow or chunking. They clutter the data. *Bottom*: Rule lines follow the flow of information, leading people to read across rows. Rule lines are subtle and are only used to separate the five levels of study.

| ($) | (F°) | ($) | (F°) |
|---|---|---|---|
| 1,000.00 | 100.2 | 1,000.00 | 100.2 |
| 12.50 | 102.5 | 12.50 | 102.5 |
| 500.25 | 50.3 | 500.25 | 50.3 |
| 25.75 | 25.7 | 25.75 | 25.7 |
| 100.00 | 100.0 | 100.00 | 100.0 |

FIGURE 10.4 Numbers have meaning based on their position in a column. *Left*: Improperly aligned numbers. *Right*: Properly aligned numbers.

## Setting Tabular Data

To summarize, when setting tabular data:

• Maintain legibility. Do not resort to small sizes, condensed typefaces, or tight letterspacing to cram in information.

• Use vertical and horizontal space to organize information into meaningful chunks. Be mindful; don't force readers to "jump the gap."

• Maintain reading flow. Run rule lines and other guides in the direction data is read.

• Use as few rule lines and borders as possible. Let the information stand out.

• Align numbers on the punctuation (decimal, colon) whenever possible, so columns (tens, ones) stay consistent.

# Lesson 10: A Ferry Schedule for Martha's Vineyard

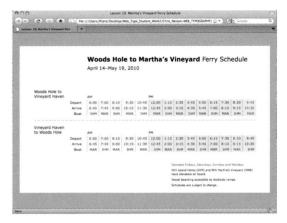

FIGURE 10.5 Working with the text provided, Chris Nelson designed the above Ferry Schedule.

This lesson helps you achieve the following objectives:

1  Make complex information more usable. Pay attention to how people read the information.

2  Use proximity to group or separate chunks of information in a table.

3  Use rule lines sparingly, and in the same direction as the reading flow.

4  Respect the numerical data, aligning it on the punctuation.

5  Pay attention to the typographic details (for example, abbreviations).

6  Pay attention to the "boring" text. Numbers and charts aren't sexy, but are important to your readers (and when done well, they are beautiful).

7  Write syntax for tables in HTML.

## Overview of the Lesson

Working with the content from *10_ferryschedule. doc*, design a table (columns, rows) to help readers find out when ferries are leaving and/or arriving at Woods Hole and Martha's Vineyard (Figure 10.5).

As with the previous lessons, start by understanding what the content needs in order to be easily read.

1  Read the text. Familiarize yourself with the kinds of information in the table.

2  Think about how people will use the information. Imagine you want to spend the day at Martha's Vineyard. How do you use the chart? Speak aloud as you use the chart. Ask others to do the same. What information do people look for first? Second? Do people read down or across?

3  Sketch out a couple of quick solutions for the chart. Visualize reading direction and hierarchy for the table. Visualize a composition for the entire page. Remember to create a focal point, a strong vertical line, and spatial tension.

4  Choose either Verdana or Georgia to work with.

5  Create your composition with multiple divs.

6  In one div, create a table to hold the data.

7  Adjust the font size as well as the size and padding of the cells to promote reading and create chunks.

8  Add rule lines or shading as needed to promote reading.

9  Put additional information in the other divs, using h1, p, classes, and so on to carefully set headings and text. Use a second font if you want to for your main heading.

## Incorporating Tables with <table><tr><td>

In the *web_typography* folder, create a folder for the lesson. Call it *10_ferryschedule*.

Create a new folder in the *10_ferryschedule* folder called *fonts*. Font files (should you choose to use a second font for your main heading) will go here.

### Start the HTML File

In your text editor, create a new document and save it as *index.html* in your *10_ferryschedule* folder.

Copy and paste in the basic HTML syntax, title, and link to the CSS file:

```
<!DOCTYPE html PUBLIC "-//W3C//DTD
    XHTML 1.0 Strict//EN"
    "http://www.w3.org/TR/xhtml1
    /DTD/xhtml1-strict.dtd">
<html xmlns="http://www.w3.org/1999
    /xhtml">
<head>
<title>Lesson 10: Martha&rsquo;s
    Vineyard Ferry Schedule</title>
<meta http-equiv="content-type"
    content="text
    /html;charset=utf-8" />
<link href="ferryschedule.css"
    rel="stylesheet" type="text/css" />
</head>
```

```
<body>
</body>
</html>
```

Add your `main_container` div between the `<body></body>` tags:

```
<div id="main_container"></div>
```

### Start the CSS file

In your text editor, create a new document and save it as *ferryschedule.css* in your *10_ferryschedule* folder.

Describe the div ID for `main_container`.

The `main_container` div is a white rectangle (990px wide, auto height) centered in the browser. It has some space above and below it. Write the syntax as follows:

```
#main_container{
    width:990px;
    height:auto;
    margin-top:20px;
    margin-right:auto;
    margin-left:auto;
    background-color:#ffffff;
    overflow:hidden;
    }
```

Give the web page a gray background:

```
body{
    background-color:#999999;
    }
```

### Build the Ferry Schedule Page

After you've sketched out some possible solutions, pick one and build it. You already have your HTML and CSS files started. Keep working with these files.

**Add divs as needed to build the composition**

• Create, describe, and place nested divs as needed to hold the heading, the table, and the "small print" information. Use the method shown in Chapter 5. Name and describe divs (make the `table_container` div `width:950px` for now—you can change it as needed) in CSS. Using a border will help you see the divs on the page.

• Put the divs in the HTML with the `<div></div>` tags.

• Place divs with the `float` property.

• Clear margins and padding with the universal selector.

• Put margins and padding back in as needed (to properly place the divs), making changes as needed.

• Remove the borders and add the content.

You can change div size and placement later as needed.

**Add the nontabular content**

Once the divs are in place, insert the text for the heading into the HTML. Insert it between the correct `<div></div>` tags. Use all of the text given.

Do the same for the "small print" information.

Just keep it there for now. You'll design the nontabular information after you get the table working.

**View your web page**

Save your HTML document and view it in your browser. You should see a white `main_container` on a gray background, three divs with black borders (so you can see them), and text in the `heading_container` and the

`smalltext_container`. You don't exactly know the size and placement of the divs yet. You'll figure that out based on the table. For now, it's an estimate of where things might go (Figure 10.6).

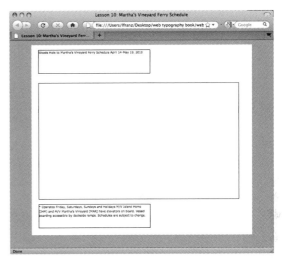

FIGURE 10.6 You don't know exactly where the divs will end up until you design the table. For now, the composition is an estimate of how elements might work together. As always, be willing to make changes as the typography progresses.

**Build the Table**

A table is a complex creature. While readers will see only columns and rows, browsers read individual cells. The three tags used to build a table are `<table>`, `<tr>`, and `<td>`.

**Use <table> tags to show where a table starts and ends**

To insert the table, add the following syntax into your HTML inside your `table_container` div:

```
<table></table>
```

**Use <tr> tags to designate the rows of the table**

To get started, put a couple of rows inside your table. Your HTML syntax should look like the following (rows are in bold):

```
<table>
<tr></tr>
<tr></tr>
<tr></tr>
</table>
```

**Use <td> tags to designate cells within the rows**
The browser does not read columns; it reads cells within each row. When you describe cells so they line up one above the other, visual columns emerge.

There are five columns in the table we are designing, so we'll put five cells in each row. Your HTML syntax should look like the following (cells are in bold):

```
<table>
<tr>
    <td></td>
    <td></td>
    <td></td>
    <td></td>
    <td></td>
</tr>
<tr>
    <td></td>
    <td></td>
    <td></td>
    <td></td>
    <td></td>
</tr>
<tr>
    <td></td>
    <td></td>
    <td></td>
    <td></td>
    <td></td>
</tr>
</table>
```

*Note:* I put an extra space between each row to help me visually organize them. This is not necessary.

---

### Tables Are for Data
If you think working with divs is challenging, we used to lay out web pages with tables. Yes, back when dinosaurs roamed the earth, we'd type in <tr> and <td> until our eyes crossed.

Never use tables for page layout. CSS is more fluid and accessible. Tables are for data.

---

**View your web page**
Save your HTML document, and view it in your browser. You can't see the table. Why? The cells are all empty. Let's put in some content and view it again.

**Add some content**
Copy and paste the content for each of the five columns into the first three rows of the table. Your HTML now looks like the following code (added content in bold):

```
<table>
<tr>
    <td>Depart Woods Hole</td>
    <td>Arrive Vineyard Haven</td>
    <td>Vessel</td>
    <td>Depart Vineyard Haven</td>
    <td>Arrive Woods Hole</td>
</tr>
<tr>
    <td></td>
    <td></td>
    <td>Mar</td>
    <td>6:00 am</td>
    <td>6:45 am</td>
```

```
</tr>
<tr>
    <td>6:00 am</td>
    <td>6:45 am</td>
    <td>ihm</td>
    <td>7:00 am</td>
    <td>7:45 am</td>
</tr>
</table>
```

### View your web page

Save your HTML document and view it in your browser. The content is there, but yikes! Row 1 is all one long line of text, and the rest of the content feels scattered (Figure 10.7, top).

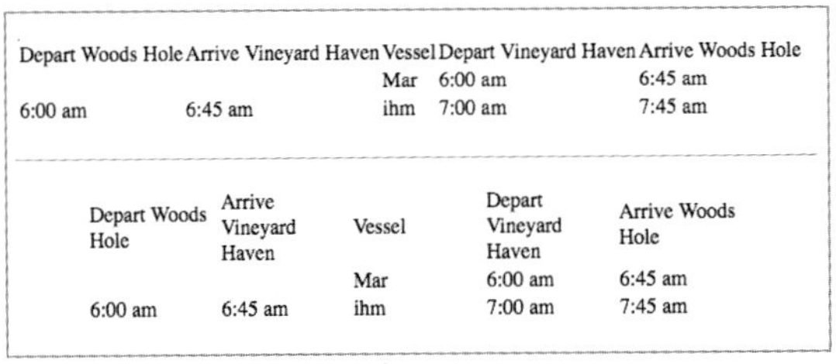

FIGURE 10.7 *Top*: The content is there, but it's not organized. Everything in the top row runs together. *Bottom*: You can create visual "columns" by controlling the cell widths. Here, all the cells are the same width, which doesn't work.

### Create "columns" by controlling <td> (cell) width

You need to control the width of the cells to create columns. You don't know what width each cell needs to be yet. (As in the film series lessons, width depends on content!)

Start by making all the cells the same size. In your CSS file, define the cells like so:

```
td{
    width:100px;
}
```

### View your web page

Save your HTML document, and view it in your browser. Making the cells all the same size is not going to work (it rarely does).

### Set your text, so you know what you're working with

Some columns are too wide, while some are too narrow (see Figure 10.7, bottom). You'll have to create styles for the cells so different "columns" are different widths.

First, though, set your text so you are designing the space (columns) appropriate to what the text needs. After some testing, I found Verdana 13/20px to feel most comfortable. This is a little larger than I usually use, so it makes scanning the numbers a little easier.

I usually prefer Georgia's numbers in text. But Verdana's slightly heavier monoline numbers, combined with the slightly looser character spacing, feels more comfortable to me. Also, from the text provided, it looks like you will need a main heading, a subheading, and perhaps some small footnote text at the end. Verdana can handle all of these things well.

Try setting the text to Verdana, 13/20px. If you think Georgia's numbers are more readable, or you prefer a different size or line height, feel free to set your text accordingly.

You are going to be creating a lot of classes in this file. To avoid confusion, set the font information right in the `td` element:

```
td{
    width:100px;
    font-family:verdana;
    font-weight:normal;
    font-size:13px;
    line-height:19px;
    }
```

### View your web page

Save your HTML document and view it in your browser. It looks better already, but you still need to adjust the widths of the columns/cells. You'll do that with classes.

### Create an appropriate column/cell width

Start by fixing the Vessel column. Because columns are actually individual cells, you need to fix the corresponding cell in each row. The Vessel column is made up of the third cell in each row.

In your HTML, change the opening tag for the third cell in each row to the following:

```
<td class="vessel">
```

For example, the third cell in the second row now reads (added class in bold)

```
<td class="vessel">Mar</td>
```

In your CSS, create and describe the "vessel" class:

```
td.vessel{
    width:60px;
    }
```

### View your web page

Save your HTML document and view it in your browser. Much better (Figure 10.8)!

Figure 10.8 *Top*: Columns must be wide enough to accommodate information, but narrow enough to promote horizontal scanning. Don't make your readers jump the gap! *Bottom*: The Vessel column is narrower, but we need to build the rest of the table in order to find the perfect width for each column.

### Build the rest of the table

Setting an appropriate column width depends on how much space the information in each column needs. You need to see how the data fits in the table.

The first step to finding the best column widths is to build the rest of the table. You'll need 16 rows, each with five cells. Put each piece of content into its correct cell. Make sure to apply the `class="vessel"` to the third cell of each row.

### Identify the Problems

Analyze the table. It needs a lot of work. Identify the problems, so you can fix them one at a time (Figure 10.9).

| Depart Woods Hole | Arrive Vineyard Haven | Vessel | Depart Vineyard Haven | Arrive Woods Hole |
|---|---|---|---|---|
|  |  | Mar | 6:00 am | 6:45 am |
| 6:00 am | 6:45 am | ihm | 7:00 am | 7:45 am |
| 7:00 am | 7:45 am | mar | 8:15 am | 9:00 am |
| 8:15 am | 9:00 am | ihm | 9:30 am | 10:15 am |
| 9:30 am | 10:15 am | mar | 10:45 am | 11:30 am |
| 10:45 am | 11:30 am | ihm | 12:00 pm | 12:45 pm |
| 12:00 pm | 12:45 pm | mar | 1:15 pm | 2:00 pm |
| 1:15 pm | 2:00 pm | ihm | 2:30 pm | 3:15 pm |
| 2:30 pm | 3:15 pm | mar | 3:45 pm | 4:30 pm |
| 3:45 pm | 4:30 pm | ihm | 5:00 pm | 5:45 pm |
| 5:00 pm | 5:45 pm | mar | 6:15 pm | 7:00 pm |
| 6:15 pm | 7:00 pm | ihm | 7:30 pm | 8:15 pm |
| 7:30 pm | 8:15 pm | mar | *8:30 pm | *9:15 pm |
| 8:30 pm | 9:15 pm | ihm | 9:45 pm | 10:30 pm |
| *9:45 pm | *10:30 pm | mar |  |  |

FIGURE 10.9 Identify the problems and tackle them one by one.

- Column headers look exactly like the content. You need to create hierarchy.

- Column headers lack similarity. They have one, two, or three lines of text, and do not line up on their baselines.

- The data reads like five vertical lists. Readers need to scan across. You need to narrow columns and increase line height. Possibly add subtle rule lines.

- The acronyms look like words. They need to be set in caps, and text size reduced, or maybe you need to increase the heading size so the caps and numbers won't yell.

- The numerical columns (tens, ones) are mixed up. Numbers should be right aligned, so the punctuation lines up better.

### Use a heading tag to create hierarchy

Decide how you want to create hierarchy in your layout, and style your headings. I recommend using h3 for your column headings because they are not the main title of the page. Save h1 and h2 to use for the main heading and dates above the table.

### Make the column headings similar

Use <br /> tags to break the columns into multiple lines of text as needed. If column headings have the same number of lines (three), and take up a similar width, they will look more alike. This will help the column width as well. Narrower column headers mean narrower columns.

The headings aren't aligned on the baseline. That's because the td defaults to a centered vertical alignment. To baseline align the column headings, change the vertical alignment to top or bottom. I prefer bottom, so the one-line heading (Vessel) is closer to the data. Add the bolded syntax to your td element (additions in bold):

```
td{
    width:100px;
    font-family:verdana;
    font-weight:normal;
    font-size:13px;
    line-height:19px;
    vertical-align:bottom;
}
```

153

This line moves the Vessel column heading down to the same bottom line as the other column headings. It doesn't affect the data in the rest of table because everything else is only one line.

### View your web page

Save your HTML document and view it in your browser. Make sure your headings work (Figure 10.10).

FIGURE 10.10 *Top*: Column headers take up one, two, and three lines, and they don't stand out from the data. *Bottom*: Create hierarchy between column headings and the data. I've made my headings bold and 1px bigger. Create similarity between headings so they are recognized as serving the same purpose. I split my headings, using bold for places, and normal weight for "Depart," "Arrive," and "Vessel." This helps the places stand out.

### Change reading flow from vertical to horizontal

Tighten up the column spacing by changing the `td` and `td.vessel` widths. You'll be able to make them a little narrower now that the column headings are on three lines.

### Add vertical spacing between the rows of data

Do this by adding padding to the cells (as shown in bold):

```
td{
    width:95px;
    font-family:verdana;
    font-weight:normal;
    font-size:13px;
    line-height:19px;
    vertical-align:bottom;
    padding-top:4px;
    padding-bottom:4px;
}
```

### Add rules to emphasize the horizontal flow of the data

Add a border to the top of your cells. Make the border subtle (border syntax in bold):

```
td{
    width:95px;
    font-family:verdana;
    font-weight:normal;
    font-size:13px;
    line-height:19px;
    vertical-align:bottom;
    padding-top:4px;
    padding-bottom:4px;
    border-top:1px solid #999999;
}
```

### View your web page

Save your HTML document and view it in your browser (Figure 10.11). You don't want the rule at the top of the table (above headings). It's unnecessary. Create a class for the top row of cells to get rid of that border. You may need to create a special `td.header_vessel` class. You will take care of that in a minute. Let's move on and fix numbers and acronyms first.

### Capitalize acronyms that are pronounced as letters

MAR, IHM, AM, and PM are all pronounced by saying the letters in the acronym (rather than pronouncing them as a single word, as with *scuba*). Thus, they should be capitalized.

In Chapter 9, you fixed the acronyms in the Film Series by creating and applying a class. Do the same here to get your acronyms started:

```
.abbrev{
    text-transform:uppercase;
    letter-spacing:1px;
    font-size:12px;
    }
```

The class worked for the AM and PM, but not for the vessels. The acronyms for the vessels don't have enough presence; they need to be a little bigger. Correct this by adding more syntax directly into your `td.vessel` class:

```
td.vessel{
    width:63px;
    padding-right:0px;
    text-transform:uppercase;
    letter-spacing:1px;
    }
```

| Depart Woods Hole | Arrive Vineyard Haven | Vessel | Depart Vineyard Haven | Arrive Woods Hole |
|---|---|---|---|---|
| | | Mar | 6:00 am | 6:45 am |
| 6:00 am | 6:45 am | ihm | 7:00 am | 7:45 am |
| 7:00 am | 7:45 am | mar | 8:15 am | 9:00 am |
| 8:15 am | 9:00 am | ihm | 9:30 am | 10:15 am |
| 9:30 am | 10:15 am | mar | 10:45 am | 11:30 am |
| 10:45 am | 11:30 am | ihm | 12:00 pm | 12:45 pm |
| 12:00 pm | 12:45 pm | mar | 1:15 pm | 2:00 pm |
| 1:15 pm | 2:00 pm | ihm | 2:30 pm | 3:15 pm |
| 2:30 pm | 3:15 pm | mar | 3:45 pm | 4:30 pm |
| 3:45 pm | 4:30 pm | ihm | 5:00 pm | 5:45 pm |
| 5:00 pm | 5:45 pm | mar | 6:15 pm | 7:00 pm |
| 6:15 pm | 7:00 pm | ihm | 7:30 pm | 8:15 pm |
| 7:30 pm | 8:15 pm | mar | *8:30 pm | *9:15 pm |
| 8:30 pm | 9:15 pm | ihm | 9:45 pm | 10:30 pm |
| *9:45 pm | *10:30 pm | mar | | |

| Depart Woods Hole | Arrive Vineyard Haven | Vessel | Depart Vineyard Haven | Arrive Woods Hole |
|---|---|---|---|---|
| | | Mar | 6:00 am | 6:45 am |
| 6:00 am | 6:45 am | ihm | 7:00 am | 7:45 am |
| 7:00 am | 7:45 am | mar | 8:15 am | 9:00 am |
| 8:15 am | 9:00 am | ihm | 9:30 am | 10:15 am |
| 9:30 am | 10:15 am | mar | 10:45 am | 11:30 am |
| 10:45 am | 11:30 am | ihm | 12:00 pm | 12:45 pm |
| 12:00 pm | 12:45 pm | mar | 1:15 pm | 2:00 pm |
| 1:15 pm | 2:00 pm | ihm | 2:30 pm | 3:15 pm |
| 2:30 pm | 3:15 pm | mar | 3:45 pm | 4:30 pm |
| 3:45 pm | 4:30 pm | ihm | 5:00 pm | 5:45 pm |
| 5:00 pm | 5:45 pm | mar | 6:15 pm | 7:00 pm |
| 6:15 pm | 7:00 pm | ihm | 7:30 pm | 8:15 pm |
| 7:30 pm | 8:15 pm | mar | *8:30 pm | *9:15 pm |
| 8:30 pm | 9:15 pm | ihm | 9:45 pm | 10:30 pm |

**FIGURE 10.11** *Top*: The data reads as five distinct columns. *Bottom*: Adding padding and subtle rule lines increases the horizontal flow of the table. The rule line above the heading is not necessary. You will remove that later. Making slight changes in column width also improves the horizontal flow. Spaces between columns will continue to improve as you fix number alignment and acronyms.

## View your web page

Save your HTML document, and view it in your browser. The acronyms look good, except "Vessel" is now "VESSEL." You'll fix that shortly when you create the `td.header_vessel` class.

## Define the vessel acronyms

Make the information in the table more meaningful for readers: Define the vessel acronyms by applying the `<acronym>` tag.

When you apply the `<acronym>` tag, it reveals what the acronym stands for when a reader hovers over it. This isn't strictly necessary for acronyms like AM and PM, but will help readers who don't know (and don't read the small print) that MAR is actually an abbreviation for a vessel named *Martha's Vineyard* and IHM is an abbreviation for a vessel named *Island Home*. We'll treat them like acronyms because they are pronounced by saying each letter.

In your CSS, add the `acronym` element:

```
acronym{
    }
```

Because the vessel names are already styled using the `td.vessel` class, you don't have to style them here. I tend to insert the element in the CSS anyway; the system feels incomplete if I don't. In the future, if it works for your project, you do *not* have to apply both a class and the `<acronym>` element to style your acronyms. In fact, while it's difficult to ascertain from such a complex lesson, it's best to style your text with as few classes and elements as possible.

In this lesson, you styled the acronyms with a class because you're only going to apply the `<acronym>` tags twice on the page.

Add the tag around the first occurrence of each vessel name in your HTML, like so:

```
<acronym>mar</acronym>
```

and

```
<acronym>ihm</acronym>
```

To activate the definitions for each acronym, provide the appropriate titles in your HTML:

```
<acronym title="Martha's
    Vineyard">mar</acronym>
```

```
<acronym title="Island
    Home">ihm</acronym>
```

I recommend adding the `<acronym>` tags to the first instance of each acronym only. Why? Because the default styling for `<acronym>` in most browsers is a dotted underline. The dotted underline is great because it tells readers to interact with the acronym—to hover over it to read the definition—so you don't want to remove it. But too many dotted underlines can clutter up the tabular data and make it more difficult to scan.

You can modify the dotted underline in your CSS if you want to. In the following code, the dotted underline is set to a medium gray so it doesn't stand out as much on the page:

```
acronym{
    border-bottom:1px dotted #666666;
    }
```

156

### View your web page

Save your HTML document, and view it in your browser. The first occurrence of MAR and IHM have a dotted underline. If you roll over them, the name of the corresponding vessel appears.

### Align columns of numbers correctly

The numbers are currently `align-left`, which makes them more difficult to read. (If a 9 is in the tens column, does it still mean 9?)

There isn't a way (yet) to align numbers on the punctuation (decimal, colon). The best you can do is `align-right` the text. Do this in the `td` element:

```
td{
    width:95px;
    font-family:verdana;
    font-weight:normal;
    font-size:13px;
    line-height:19px;
    vertical-align:bottom;
    padding-top:4px;
    padding-bottom:4px;
    border-top:1px solid #999999;
    text-align:right;
}
```

## Identify New Problems

View your page in the browser to analyze the table again. It still needs work. Identify the new problems, so you can fix them one at a time (Figure 10.12).

"Vessel" is "VESSEL" and is aligned left. To fix this problem, create and apply a new `td.header_vessel` class.

The list of vessels looks odd right aligned. Center them in the `td.vessel` element.

The columns look odd as well. The spacing between the columns is a little worse after the `align-right`. The Vessel column is particularly bad (look at the headings). Fix the `td` and `td.vessel` widths. *Note:* I find they work better with slightly narrower `td` widths and some `padding-right`.

The rule lines above the headings need to be removed. Do this with two classes: `td.header` and the previously created `td.header_vessel`.

Finally, the `table_container` needs to be changed to fit the table inside it.

## Rework the Composition around the Table

Use what you've learned in previous chapters to re-arrange the composition around the table (Figure 10.13). Here are some typographic issues to attend to:

- Create hierarchy between the main heading and the date.

- Use a comfortable line length and paragraph spacing to carefully set the small text. Include a text-indent (like you used in the Bibliography in Chapter 3) to "hang" the asterisk.

- Use an en dash between the dates.

- Align the main heading and small text to vertical and horizontal lines created in the table.

| Depart Woods Hole | Arrive Vineyard Haven | VESSEL | Depart Vineyard Haven | Arrive Woods Hole |
|---|---|---|---|---|
|  |  | MAR | 6:00 AM | 6:45 AM |
| 6:00 AM | 6:45 AM | IHM | 7:00 AM | 7:45 AM |
| 7:00 AM | 7:45 AM | MAR | 8:15 AM | 9:00 AM |
| 8:15 AM | 9:00 AM | IHM | 9:30 AM | 10:15 am |
| 9:30 AM | 10:15 AM | MAR | 10:45 AM | 11:30 AM |
| 10:45 AM | 11:30 AM | IHM | 12:00 PM | 12:45 PM |
| 12:00 PM | 12:45 PM | MAR | 1:15 PM | 2:00 PM |
| 1:15 PM | 2:00 PM | IHM | 2:30 PM | 3:15 PM |
| 2:30 PM | 3:15 PM | MAR | 3:45 PM | 4:30 PM |
| 3:45 PM | 4:30 PM | IHM | 5:00 PM | 5:45 PM |
| 5:00 PM | 5:45 PM | MAR | 6:15 PM | 7:00 PM |
| 6:15 PM | 7:00 PM | IHM | 7:30 PM | 8:15 PM |
| 7:30 PM | 8:15 PM | MAR | *8:30 PM | *9:15 PM |
| 8:30 PM | 9:15 PM | IHM | 9:45 PM | 10:30 PM |
| *9:45 PM | *10:30 PM | MAR |  |  |

| Depart Woods Hole | Arrive Vineyard Haven | Vessel | Depart Vineyard Haven | Arrive Woods Hole |
|---|---|---|---|---|
|  |  | MAR | 6:00 AM | 6:45 AM |
| 6:00 AM | 6:45 AM | IHM | 7:00 AM | 7:45 AM |
| 7:00 AM | 7:45 AM | MAR | 8:15 AM | 9:00 AM |
| 8:15 AM | 9:00 AM | IHM | 9:30 AM | 10:15 am |
| 9:30 AM | 10:15 AM | MAR | 10:45 AM | 11:30 AM |
| 10:45 AM | 11:30 AM | IHM | 12:00 PM | 12:45 PM |
| 12:00 PM | 12:45 PM | MAR | 1:15 PM | 2:00 PM |
| 1:15 PM | 2:00 PM | IHM | 2:30 PM | 3:15 PM |
| 2:30 PM | 3:15 PM | MAR | 3:45 PM | 4:30 PM |
| 3:45 PM | 4:30 PM | IHM | 5:00 PM | 5:45 PM |
| 5:00 PM | 5:45 PM | MAR | 6:15 PM | 7:00 PM |
| 6:15 PM | 7:00 PM | IHM | 7:30 PM | 8:15 PM |
| 7:30 PM | 8:15 PM | MAR | *8:30 PM | *9:15 PM |
| 8:30 PM | 9:15 PM | IHM | 9:45 PM | 10:30 PM |
| *9:45 PM | *10:30 PM | MAR |  |  |

FIGURE 10.12 Always step back and analyze work after making changes. Find what needs to be fixed. *Top*: As the table improves, new problems emerge—extra rule lines, poor spacing, odd alignment, and an all-capped heading. *Bottom*: The table after these problems are fixed.

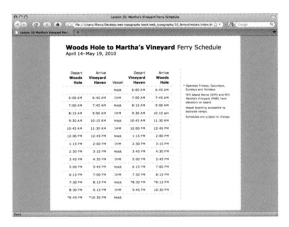

FIGURE 10.13 After the table is done, re-arrange the heading and small text around it. Details to attend to include an en dash in the date, and "hanging" the asterisk (to create a clean, strong vertical line on the small text) with a text-indent. You are welcome to use a second font for the main heading (I chose not to), and to use a background color. Keep color subtle. Bright colors make it difficult to focus on details (like tabular information).

Congratulations. You are ready to move on to the next section!

## Recommended Resources

For this lesson, I recommend the following online resources:

- To download the text for this lesson, go to `www.wiley.com/go/typographic webdesign`

- To see student examples of the lesson, go to `typographicwebdesign.com`

- To choose a color, visit `www.december.com/html/spec/ colorhues.html`

## Moving Forward

This chapter introduced you to setting tabular information with a typographic approach. You applied the concepts of legibility, proximity, and similarity to numerical data. In addition, you learned about making text more meaningful by defining acronyms with the `<acronym>` tag.

In the next chapter, you will learn more about how people read.

# Making Type Work: Casual and Sustained Reading

*See [the grid system] as a
way of providing distinct
articulation to the different
voices expressed within the
text through both color and
position on the page.*

JOHN KANE, A TYPE PRIMER (2003)

# CHAPTER 11

# How We Read, Part 2

Readable text allows a person to move easily through a passage, whether they are skimming a list or engaged in casual or sustained reading.

In deference to our readers, we have already explored aspects of legibility (how to choose a font) and readability (how to use a good line length, line height, font size, and alignment to promote horizontal and vertical scanning).

Now, we'll look at the impact of case, style, weight, and color on otherwise-legible fonts. You'll remember from earlier that *we read word shapes*. You'll also remember that legibility depends on two elements: the *strokes of the letters*, and the *spaces in and around the letters*. If we lose word shapes, strokes, or spaces, then legibility is compromised, and reading becomes arduous.

Yet texts often contain more than one "voice." A single text may have an introduction, captions for images, pull quotes, lists, and finally, the main story or main body of text. Much like a system of headings, parts of a text need different treatment; they need to look and feel different from each other so that readers will understand their role in relation to other elements on the page. You'll often use case, style, weight, and color to create multiple voices (for example, "I'm a caption, not part of the main text, that's why I'm italic" or "I'm an important quote from the article, and you should read me first, that's why I'm big"). But passages of text require more reading than headings do. The trick is to balance creating multiple voices with maintaining readability.

## Case

Type set in all capital letters (caps) loses legibility (Figure 11.1). Word shapes, often defined by ascenders and descenders, get lost. Readers have to slow down to recognize individual letters, and have difficulty processing more than one word at a time.

Word shapes, defined by ascenders and descenders, get lost when text is set in all caps. Use all caps sparingly. It is most appropriate for a short passage, a single thought, or even a single word.

WORD SHAPES, DEFINED BY ASCENDERS AND DESCENDERS, GET LOST WHEN TEXT IS SET IN ALL CAPS. USE ALL CAPS SPARINGLY. IT IS MOST APPROPRIATE FOR A SHORT PASSAGE, A SINGLE THOUGHT, OR EVEN A SINGLE WORD.

FIGURE 11.1 *Top:* Text is more legible when set with upper- and lowercase characters. *Bottom:* A paragraph set in all caps becomes a decorative element. It no longer invites people to read the text.

When a single word is set in all caps, it feels powerful and important. When a word or two within a body of text is set in all caps, it feels to the reader like shouting. When an entire body of text is set in all caps, it becomes a texture, a decorative element. Use all caps sparingly. It is most appropriate for a short passage, a single thought, or even a single sentence.

## Style

Type set in italics (or oblique) can lose legibility (Figure 11.2). Word shapes shift as sans serif fonts slant over to one side. Spacing within and between letters gets lost as serif fonts tend to get narrower and closer together in their italic form. Readers have to slow down to process the word shapes, and have difficulty taking in more than one word at a time.

Not all italics are the same; some are more readable than others (Figure 11.2, bottom). When setting a passage of text in italic, choose a font that retains some of its openness.

Type set in italics can lose legibility. Word shapes shift as sans serif fonts slant over to one side. Spacing within and between letters gets lost as serif fonts tend to get narrower and closer together in their italic form.

*Type set in italics can lose legibility. Word shapes shift as sans serif fonts slant over to one side. Spacing within and between letters gets lost as serif fonts tend to get narrower and closer together in their italic form.*

*Type set in italics can lose legibility. Word shapes shift as sans serif fonts slant over to one side. Spacing within and between letters gets lost as serif fonts tend to get narrower and closer together in their italic form.*

FIGURE 11.2 *Top:* Text is more legible when set in normal style. *Middle:* Italics change the word shapes and force readers to slow down. Use italics for short-to-medium passages within a text. *Bottom:* Beware! Not all italics are created equal. Some lovely italics, such as Serif Beta 12 italic, are too narrow and less legible on screen.

Setting text as italic does not affect legibility as powerfully as setting text in all caps. While I wouldn't recommend setting an entire text as italic (roman forms are far easier to read), it can be appropriate for short-to-medium passages within a text.

## Weight

Text set in bold (even a well-designed bold) loses legibility (Figure 11.3). Spacing within and between letters gets lost as strokes get thicker and take up more space. Readers have to slow down to process letters (is that an *e*, an *s*, or an *a*?), and have difficulty taking in more than one word at a time.

Text set in bold loses legibility. Spacing within and between letters gets lost as strokes get thicker and take up more space. Readers have to slow down to process letters and have difficulty taking in more than one word at a time.

**Text set in bold loses legibility. Spacing within and between letters gets lost as strokes get thicker and take up more space. Readers have to slow down to process letters and have difficulty taking in more than one word at a time.**

FIGURE 11.3 *Top:* Text is more legible when set in normal weight. *Bottom:* Bold text works for emphasis, but a paragraph set in bold is harder to read. It becomes a dark field of texture punctuated by word spaces.

When a few words are set in bold, they feel important. They create hierarchy and draw the reader's eye. When an entire body of text is set in bold, it becomes a dark field of texture, punctuated by the white word spaces. Use bold sparingly. It is most appropriate for a short passage, a single thought, or even a single sentence.

## Color

Type set in color can lose legibility if the text color is too similar to the background color. It can also lose readability (the reading experience becomes uncomfortable) if the text is too bright, or "vibrates" with the background color.

Not all colors are equal; some are more appropriate than others for text. When setting a passage in color, avoid colors that are too light (Figure 11.4)—when you squint, can you still see it? Also avoid colors that are too bright (Figure 11.5)—does the color jump out too much? Do the letters sparkle or hurt your eyes? Finally, avoid using the combinations yellow plus purple, red plus green, and blue plus orange for background and text colors (Figure 11.6). These color combinations vibrate, making text harder to read.

Not all colors are the same, some are more appropriate than others for text. When setting a passage in color, avoid colors that are too light — when you squint, can you still see it?

Not all colors are the same, some are more appropriate than others for text. When setting a passage in color, avoid colors that are too light — when you squint, can you still see it?

FIGURE 11.4 *Top:* Use colors dark enough to define the text. *Bottom:* The text is too light too read.

Not all colors are the same, some are more appropriate than others for text. When setting a passage in color, avoid colors that are too bright — does the color jump out too much? Do the letters sparkle or make your eyes hurt?

Not all colors are the same, some are more appropriate than others for text. When setting a passage in color, avoid colors that are too bright — does the color jump out too much? Do the letters sparkle or make your eyes hurt?

**FIGURE 11.5** *Top:* Use colors dull enough to engage readers. *Bottom:* The text is too bright to read comfortably. It becomes a decorative element.

Not all colors are the same, some are more appropriate than others for text. When setting a passage in color, avoid using yellow+purple, red+green, and blue+orange for background and text colors. These color combinations vibrate, making text harder to read.

Not all colors are the same, some are more appropriate than others for text. When setting a passage in color, avoid using yellow+purple, red+green, and blue+orange for background and text colors. These color combinations vibrate, making text harder to read.

**FIGURE 11.6** *Top:* Use color combinations that don't vibrate. This combination uses contrast (dark text on a light background) and dull colors (neither color is painfully bright). It does not use colors that vibrate. *Bottom:* Text in a bright blue plus orange combination will vibrate even more on the screen.

Setting text in color doesn't have to affect legibility or readability if done right. In fact, color can be used in very subtle ways, almost imperceptible to the reader. Using a very dark, dull brown for text can make a page feel warm (Figure 11.7). Using a very dark gray can make reading a little easier (it reduces that "sparkle" or unpleasant glare caused by the contrast between black and white).

Setting text in color doesn't have to affect legibility at all if done right. In fact, using a very dark, dull brown for text can make a page feel warm.

Setting text in color doesn't have to affect legibility at all if done right. In fact, using a dark gray can make reading a little easier, reducing sparkle caused by the contrast between black and white on the screen.

**FIGURE 11.7** *Top:* A very dark, dull color can add a subtle tone or feeling to a web page. Brown adds warmth. *Bottom:* A dark gray softens the text.

Using color in text can visually connect the words to images on the page, help divide a page into multiple voices, or let readers know where to click. The trick is to use colors that create a comfortable reading experience.

### Creating Readable Text

To summarize, reading large amounts of text is easier when it uses:

- Lowercase letters (not all caps)
- A font style that is normal, not italic (`font-style:normal;`)
- A font weight that is normal, not bold (`font-weight:normal;`)
- A color with enough value (dark/light) contrast to keep it from blending into the background.

## Creating Multiple Voices

Similar to a system of headings, parts of a text need to feel different from each other to the reader, yet work together in a system. Unlike a system of headings, parts of a text do not need a strong sense of hierarchy. In fact, trying to create too much hierarchy between elements on the page can make it difficult to read the text.

### Common Elements in a Text

Identifying the elements in the text you are working with is part of the design process. These are some common elements to look for:

- An introduction by the author or editor
- Captions for images or diagrams
- An aside or sidebar to introduce the reader to related information
- The body text itself, which may be expository or instructional
- Lists of items or steps within the text
- The navigation

### Multiple Voices Help Define Elements

Theoretically, all the elements in a text could be set exactly the same way in a single column. But this approach would force readers to work to find the elements they are most interested in.

When each element has its own voice, readers can quickly see what to read if they want to learn more about the image, what to ignore if they aren't interested, and where to click if they want to move around within a site (Figure 11.8).

FIGURE 11.8 *Left:* Even at this very small size, we can "read" a logo, a navigation bar, text, captions, and pullquotes. Design by Meighan Tague (Fall, 2009). *Right:* Without unique voices, the content all "reads" the same.

### Voice Is Also about the Feeling of the Site

The elements in a text can work together to evoke an overall feeling. If the site should feel more elegant, classic, or traditional (or clean, geometric, contemporary), then work toward that goal with every element. Revisit Chapter 2 ("Aesthetics and Emotions: Does the Font Convey the Right Message?") for a refresher on how case, style, and fonts can create a feeling. If you are looking for inspiration, try jumping ahead to Chapters 16 ("The Traditional Page") and 17 ("The Modernist Page").

---

### Creating Multiple Voices

To summarize, create a system of voices that:

- Are different enough to help readers identify different elements on the page.

- Are similar enough to allow elements to work together as a whole.

- Create an overall feeling. (What should the site convey in support of the text?)

- Maintain legibility.

---

# Lesson 11: A Recipe, Part 1

Like the film series in Part 2, this is an assignment in four parts.

In this part, you'll identify all the elements in a text, and find the font, size, line height, line length, case, style, weight, and color appropriate for each element. You'll create each element in its own div, letting the divs flow down the page in a single column (Figure 11.9).

Don't worry yet about where on the page each element will go. While typographers usually consider placement while setting text, *I am purposely separating the two.* I want you to clearly experience creating a grid from text elements in the next lesson.

Like the Film Series project in Chapters 6–9, the recipe project is divided into four lessons; this allows you to focus on specific ideas and skills. Designing with type is far more fluid than these segregated lessons suggest. For instance, a good designer will test ideas (systems) across multiple pages from the beginning to make sure they'll work, but I've left it for the very last lesson.

Even if you are already an accomplished typographer or web designer, breaking down the process into four distinct parts challenges you to change your usual methods for working with (and thinking about) type. You'll stretch your typographic muscles and become more intimately aware of your process.

**FIGURE 11.9** By the end of this lesson, you'll have a column of divs (each with an element in it), like this example by Chris Nelson.

This lesson helps you achieve the following objectives:

1   Practice identifying different parts or elements in a text.

2   Practice choosing a font, font size, line height, line length, alignment, case, style, weight, and color to:

   • Create a voice for each element

   • Promote comfortable reading

   • Make the elements work together as a system

3   Write syntax in HTML and CSS to insert an image, apply color to text, and create a list. Even if you are already HTML/CSS savvy, follow the walk-through provided. I show you what a typographer looks for in the process.

## Overview of the Lesson

Always start by understanding your client's message and the text you'll be working with.

1   Read the client profiles available from this book's download files at www.wiley.com/go/typographicwebdesign. Choose whether your client is John Smith (the owner of a successful bistro who describes his French cooking as "classic, quality, but with warmth") or Jane Smith (the owner of a local restaurant and catering company who describes her environmentally aware approach to cooking as "fresh, local, simple, delicious, sustaining").

2   Read the text you are setting, also available from this book's download files at www.wiley.com/go/typographicwebdesign. Identify the different elements in the text, such as captions, lists, memories, and so on.

3   Choose either Verdana or Georgia as your font.

4   Place the site logo, image, and text elements into a web page. Set the text so each element has its own voice, but works with the other elements to create an overall voice for the site.

## Incorporating Color, Images, and Lists

In the *web_typography* folder, create a folder for the lesson and call it *11_recipe*.

Create a new folder in the *11_recipe* folder called *images*. Put your two images (*11_crust.jpg* and *11_logo.gif*) here.

### Start the HTML File

In your text editor, create a new document and save it as *index.html* in your *11_recipe* folder.

Copy and paste in the basic HTML syntax, title, and link to the CSS file:

```
<!DOCTYPE html PUBLIC "-//W3C//DTD
    XHTML 1.0 Strict//EN"
    "http://www.w3.org/TR/xhtml1/DTD
    /xhtml1-strict.dtd">
<html xmlns="http://www.w3.org/1999
    /xhtml">
<head>
<title> Lesson 11: Recipe
    (Establishing Voices)</title>
<meta http-equiv="content-type"
    content="text
    /html;charset=utf-8" />
<link href="recipe_voice.css"
    rel="stylesheet" type="text/css" />
</head>
<body>
</body>
</html>
```

Add your `main_container` div between the
`<body></body>` tags:

```
<div id="main_container"></div>
```

**Start the CSS File**

In your text editor, create a new document and
save it as *recipe_voice.css* in your *11_recipe* folder.

Describe the div ID for main_container"

The `main_container` div is a white rectangle
(990px wide, auto height for now—you can change
this later) centered in the browser. It has some
space above and below it. It has an auto height,
and will have divs floated inside. To force the div
open, you need to include an `overflow:hidden`
property. Write the syntax like this:

```
#main_container{
    width:990px;
    height:auto;
    margin-top:20px;
    margin-right:auto;
    margin-bottom:40px;
    margin-left:auto;
    background-color:#ffffff;
    overflow:hidden;
    }
```

Give the web page a gray background

To add a background color to the entire page,
apply it to the `body` element:

```
body{
    background-color:#999999;
    }
```

**Start Putting in the Content**

Before you do this step, read the text and identify
the different elements in the text. Is there a
caption? A list? An introduction? A main text?

Create a div for each element you place. This
allows you to easily manage line length for the
text for each element. Remember, line length
affects readability. Don't worry; you will consolidate most of these divs later in the process.

In your CSS file, create divs for each element

Here are the elements I've identified, reading the
text document from start to finish:

```
#memory_container{
    }
#recipe_name_container{
    }
#ingredients_container{
    }
#directions_container{
    }
#image_container{
    }
#caption_container{
    }
#main_navigation_container{
    }
#section_links_container{
    }
#copyright_container{
    }
#designer_container{
    }
#advertisement_pbs_container{
    }
#advertisement_book_container{
    }
#advertisement_restaurant_container{
    }
```

And, there is at least one last div you need that is
not in the text document:

```
#logo_container{
    }
```

When you create the grid in Chapter 12, you will remove most of these divs. For now, keep each element separate, so all text is treated according to its own needs.

In your HTML file, insert all the divs, one after another

For example, the syntax for the first three divs is:

```
<div id="memory_container"></div>
<div id="recipe_name_container"></div>
<div id="ingredients_container"></div>
```

Paste the text into the proper divs

Copy the text from the file provided at make sure to paste the correct content within each div—that is, between the <div id...> and </div> tags.

Insert the image and logo into their proper divs

Between the appropriate div tags, use this syntax:

```
<img src="images/11_crust.jpg">
```

You've just told the browser to use the image source *11_crust.jpg* found in the folder *images*.

Now try putting in the syntax for the logo on your own. (You only need to change the name of the file you are telling the browser to access.)

View your web page

Save your HTML document, and view it in your browser. Wow! This page needs a lot of work (Figure 11.10). Next, you will break down the steps and do them one by one.

FIGURE 11.10 Wow. That's a lot of text. That's okay, though; chunking it will help you see the elements. Just follow the steps one by one.

## Break Up the Text So You Can See the Elements

Right now, the only elements that stand out are the picture and the logo. It's hard to see where text elements start and end, much less design them.

Move all elements away from each other

Separating the elements will help you see the text better. You're not going to set margins on headings and paragraphs yet, so just add margins to all of the divs instead of using a universal selector.

Adding the following syntax to each div will add a 50-pixel margin on all four sides:

```
margin:50px;
```

*Note:* There is a shorthand method to add margins to every div at once (div{margin:50px;}), but we're not going to use it here. If you are new to

HTML and CSS, shorthand methods are harder to keep track of because they break up element styling to different areas of the CSS. If you are experienced with writing HTML and CSS, feel free to use any shorthand methods you know.

Unfortunately, a `margin-top` will not show up on your top div because one div is nested in another div and not floated. If you want some space above the top div, add some `padding-top` to your `main_container`.

## Chunk the Information

Now that there is some space between the blocks of text, it's time to add some headings.

### Identify and apply headings and p tags

You'll notice there is a list in the text (ingredients), as well as lists for the `main_navigation` and `section_links`. Leave the lists for now; you'll take care of them after inserting the h and p tags.

Ask yourself: what is the:

- Main heading (h1) for this page?
- Second-level heading (h2)?
- Third-level heading (h3)?
- Fourth-level heading (h4)?

Once you've identified the headings and hierarchy, apply the tags to the appropriate text.

Referring to the text document for guidance if needed, add p tags to break up the text into paragraphs. The text is beginning to take shape (Figure 11.11).

FIGURE 11.11 Once p, h1, h2, h3, and h4 tags are added, the text begins to take shape. However, line lengths are still way too long!

## Create and Define the Ingredient List

There are at least three lists on this page: the ingredients, the main navigation, and the section links.

Theoretically, each list can be set using a `p` tag or a class applied to a `p` tag, but it is good to know how to use the list tags in HTML. The list tags give you another tool in your typographic toolbox. In addition, using list syntax tells text-based browsers, browsers with CSS turned off, and other devices that the information is a list—not just lines of text. This improves the accessibility of your typographic websites.

### Create a simple list for the ingredients

The syntax for a list is `<ol></ol>` for an *ordered list* (a list with numbers) or `<ul></ul>` for an *unordered list* (a list without numbers).

The syntax for a *line item* in either list is `<li></li>`.

Because the list of ingredients is not ordered, use the `<ul></ul>` tags around the text (in the HTML). Define each line item with the `<li></li>` tags, and remove the bullets that came from the text document:

```
<ul>
    <li>2/12 cups all-purpose flour,
        plus extra for rolling</li>
    <li>16 Tbsp (2 sticks) unsalted
        butter, very-cold, cut into
        1/2 inch cubes</li>
    <li>1 teaspoon salt</li>
    <li>1 teaspoon sugar (increase to
        1 1/2 teaspoons if for a sweet
        recipe)</li>
    <li>4 to 8 tablespoons ice water
        </li>
</ul>
```

### View your web page

Save your HTML document, and refresh your browser. The ingredients appear as a list. Even

though you deleted the bullets, each line item has a bullet (Figure 11.12, top). Why?

FIGURE 11.12 *Top:* Even though you removed the bullets from the HTML, the list has bullets. The default for unordered lists is round bullets. These can be changed or removed. *Bottom:* The list after the bullets and left margin have been removed.

This is because unordered lists have round bullets by default. The bullets can be changed to square bullets or even removed. The bullets automatically hang outside the left alignment, which is a good thing. This preserves the strong vertical line of the list. But you can control your list.

### Modify the list in CSS

In the CSS document, create an ID for the list. Why? Because you will potentially use three lists on this page, and they will not all look the same, so you need to name each list.

Creating an ID for a list is just like creating an ID for a container or any other element. Use the following syntax:

```
#ingredient_list{
    margin-left:0px;
    padding-left:0px;
    }
```

This syntax will move the line items over to align with the heading.

To modify the line items themselves (remove bullets, add space between items, and so on), you need to describe the `li` element as well:

```
#ingredient_list li{
    list-style:none;
    }
```

This syntax sets the bullet style to `none` for the line items in the `ingredient_list`.

For the changes to work, you need to define the list as `ingredient_list` in the HTML document.

**Define the ingredient_list in the HTML document**
Using an ID for a list is just like using an ID for a container:

```
<ul id="ingredient_list">
    <li>2/12 cups all-purpose flour,
        plus extra for rolling</li>
    <li>16 Tbsp (2 sticks) unsalted
        butter, very-cold, cut into
        1/2 inch cubes</li>
    <li>1 teaspoon salt</li>
    <li>1 teaspoon sugar (increase to
        1 1/2 teaspoons if for a sweet
        recipe)</li>
    <li>4 to 8 tablespoons ice water
        </li>
</ul>
```

**View your web page**
Save your HTML document and refresh your browser. The list is now flush left with the heading and no longer has bullets (Figure 11.12, bottom).

**Make the Ingredients Div Narrower**
The list of ingredients has long and short line lengths.

You need to even up the line length a little. This is not always a requirement, but creates a more pleasing list. Plus, I want to show you how to approach a list with some multi-line items.

Change the width of the ingredients_container:

```
#ingredients_container{
    margin:50px;
    width:240px;
    }
```

**View your web page**
Ugh. What once was a list now looks like a paragraph of text (Figure 11.13, top). How do you make it look like a list again?

**FIGURE 11.13** *Top:* With a shorter line length, the list looks like a paragraph with an obvious ragged edge. *Bottom:* Adding space between line items helps.

**Option one: Add space between line items**
Adding space between line items visually chunks the list using a vertical spacing system. Multiple lines of text in an item will continue to stay close together; space is only added between the line items.

In the CSS, add a `margin-bottom` to the `li` syntax (additions in bold):

```
#ingredient_list li{
    list-style:none;
    margin-bottom:10px;
    }
```

### View your web page

Save your HTML document and refresh your browser. The ingredients are a list again (Figure 11.13, bottom), separated by spaces.

### Option two: Add bullets to the line items

Adding a bullet to each line item will help the reader clearly see the separate items. Bullets tend to get in the way of rhythm and tension, though. They may stand out a bit too much, drawing the reader's eye away from the content.

In the CSS, add the bullets to the `li` syntax and change the `margin-bottom` to 0:

```
#ingredient_list li{
    list-style:disk;
    margin-bottom:0px;
    }
```

### View your web page

Save your HTML document, and refresh your browser. The ingredients are a list, each item marked with a bullet (Figure 11.14, top). It's not great, though. The bullets feel a bit heavy, and there isn't enough separation between the items.

### Add some space back in between line items

You won't need as much space to visually separate the items because the bullet does some of the work. You might try changing to `margin-bottom:6px;`.

**Ingredients**

- 2/12 cups all-purpose flour, plus extra for rolling
- 16 Tbsp (2 sticks) unsalted butter, very-cold, cut into 1/2 inch cubes
- 1 teaspoon salt
- 1 teaspoon sugar (increase to 1 1/2 teaspoons if for a sweet recipe)
- 4 to 8 tablespoons ice water

**Ingredients**

- 2/12 cups all-purpose flour, plus extra for rolling
- 16 Tbsp (2 sticks) unsalted butter, very-cold, cut into 1/2 inch cubes
- 1 teaspoon salt
- 1 teaspoon sugar (increase to 1 1/2 teaspoons if for a sweet recipe)
- 4 to 8 tablespoons ice water

**FIGURE 11.14** *Top:* Putting bullets back in isn't enough to indicate list items with multi-lines, and the bullets stand out too much. *Bottom:* Add space between the items and make the bullets lighter.

### Change the color of the bullets

Lists are flexible creatures, and with time and attention you can learn to manipulate them in various ways. You can even use your own choice of image for bullets, if you prefer.

As a typographer, I prefer to use the text and characters given to me in the syntax as much as possible. You can change the color of the bullets in CSS. You just need to add a `span` to the text. Here's how it works.

First, identify the color you want to use and add it to the CSS syntax (use medium gray for now, because you haven't developed a color palette yet):

```
#ingredient_list li{
    list-style:disk;
    margin-bottom:6px;
    color:#666666;
    }
```

Unfortunately, this turns the entire list (including the text) medium gray. To fix this, you need to tell the browser to make the text black again. Create a `.list_text` class in the CSS:

```
.list_text{
   color:#000000;
   }
```

Now apply it to each line item in the HTML:

```
<li><span class="list_text">
   1 teaspoon salt</span></li>
```

### View your web page

Save your HTML document, and refresh your browser. The bullets are lighter, the text is black, and the items have more separation (Figure 11.14, bottom).

### Create and Define the Main Navigation List

A list of links is a list, whether it runs across or down a page. If you think you want your main navigation to run across the page, you can still use an unordered list.

### Create the main_navigation_list in your CSS document

Start by setting the `margin-left` to 0 and removing the bullets, just like you did for the last list:

```
#main_navigation_list{
   margin-left:0px;
   padding-left:0px;
   }
```

```
#main_navigation_list li{
   list-style:none;
   }
```

### Define the list and line items in your HTML document

Once again, you'll create an unordered list:

```
<ul id="main_navigation_list">
   <li>Crusts</li>
   <li>Fruit Fillings</li>
   <li>Custard and Pudding Fillings
      </li>
   <li>Savory Fillings</li>
   <li>About the Author</li>
</ul>
```

If you were to view the list in your browser now, it would look very much like the ingredients list. But you are going to make some changes.

### Make the list run across the page in a single row

To keep the list from going down in a column, insert the following syntax in the `li` element (in bold):

```
#main_navigation_list li{
   list-style:none;
   display:inline;
   }
```

### View your web page

Save your HTML document, and refresh your browser. The main navigation list `li` runs across the page and is starting to look like a navigation bar (Figure 11.15, top).

Crusts Fruit Fillings Custard and Pudding Fillings Savory Fillings About the Author

Crusts    Fruit Fillings    Custard and Pudding Fillings    Savory Fillings    About the Author

FIGURE 11.15 *Top:* Using display:inline makes a list of items collapse and run "in-line" as paragraph text, here neatly collapsing into a single row. *Bottom:* Add some padding and rule lines, and you have the start of a navigation bar.

### Fix the spacing between the items

Add padding to the `li` element (in bold):

```
#main_navigation_list li{
    list-style:none;
    display:inline;
    padding-right:20px;
    }
```

### Add rule lines

Use `border-top` and `border-bottom` to add rule lines. Add padding to position the list items and the rule lines where you want them (additions in bold):

```
#main_navigation_list{
    margin-left:0px;
    padding-left:15px;
    margin-right:230px;
    padding-top:5px;
    padding-bottom:5px;
    border-top:1px solid #999999;
    border-bottom:1px solid #999999;
    }
#main_navigation_list li{
    list-style: none;
    padding-right:20px;
    display:inline;
    }
```

The preceding syntax adds space to the left of the first item, shortens the list on the right side, and adds space above and below the row of items. It also adds a solid-gray rule line above and below the row of items to create what looks like a navigation bar—without working links, of course (Figure 11.15, bottom).

### Add a background color to each item

Use `background-color` to add a background color to each item, and remove the rule lines.

```
#main_navigation_list{
    margin-left:0px;
    }
#main_navigation_list li{
    list-style: none;
    padding-top:10px;
    padding-right:15px;
    padding-bottom:10px;
    padding-left:15px;
    background-color:#cccccc;
    display:inline;
    }
```

The preceding syntax adds space around each item and gives each item a background color. This is another way to create what looks like a navigation bar, again, without working links (Figure 11.16, top). If you set the type, it will look even better (Figure 11.16, bottom).

| Crusts | Fruit Fillings | Custard and Pudding Fillings | Savory Fillings | About the Author |

| CRUSTS | FRUIT FILLINGS | CUSTARD AND PUDDING FILLINGS | SAVORY FILLINGS | ABOUT THE AUTHOR |

FIGURE 11.16 *Top:* Modify the padding and add a background color to mimic a navigation bar. *Bottom:* Set your type. Your final navigation bar does not have to look like this—but practice making it work anyway.

Finally, you can modify the type

Type in lists can be styled using the same syntax you use for p tags, h1 tags, and so on:

```
#main_navigation_list li{
    list-style:none;
    padding-top:10px;
    padding-right:15px;
    padding-bottom:10px;
    padding-left:15px;
    background:#cccccc;
    display:inline;
    font-family:georgia;
    font-size:13px;
    line-height:14px;
    text-transform:uppercase;
    letter-spacing:1px;
}
```

## Set Each Text Element in Its Own Voice

Using what you already know about setting text so it is legible and readable (while creating hier-archy), style your p, h1, h2, h3, and h4 elements. Create classes as needed to accommodate text elements.

Style the ingredients list, the main navigation list, and the section links list, too.

While styling the elements in the text, try to create a look and feel that is appropriate for the client and their approach to cooking. In Chapter 2, you learned about the way we "read" serif fonts, sans serif fonts, capitalized letters, lowercase letters, and italicized text. How can you use this knowledge to help the text subtly communicate either "French cooking that is classic, quality, but with warmth" or "environmentally aware cooking that is fresh, local, simple, delicious, sustaining?"

In addition, identify which elements need to have their own voice. Should the memory of the great-grandmother churning her butter every Thursday be styled the same way as the directions ("Cut the sticks of butter into 1/2-inch cubes and place in the freezer for at least 15 minutes")? Subtle styling changes between elements will help them have their own voice on the page. But keep an underlying consistency; the voices need to work together as a system.

Don't worry yet about moving the elements around on the page. You'll do that in the next chapter. Focus on creating readable text with a good size, line height, and line length.

Find the perfect line length for each element

Although it's extra work, I had you place each element in its own div for a reason: to find the best line length for each element. Font, size, length of paragraph, and length of list items all affect line length.

Will the headline be long (on a single line) or short (break up into two lines of text)? What line length does the memory (the story about the chef's great-grandmother) need to read comfortably? What line length do the directions need to read comfortably? The ingredients? Each section may or may not work at the same line length.

Explore good line length by individually setting the width for each div. You will consolidate most of these divs in the next chapter, and some of your line lengths may be modified in the process. But this chapter is about finding the perfect target setting for each element. Take the time to do this step. It will help you lay out your page based on *what the text needs*—not based on filling up the page!

## Choosing and applying color to text

When choosing color, I highly recommend referencing the images used on the page. The images will be part of the color palette, so they are a good place to start.

Test and use colors from the charts at the Hues Hub (`december.com/html/spec/colorhues.html`), choosing colors that feel like they are in the photo or can work with the photo. Be willing to test multiple colors. Do not settle.

If you'd like the colors in an image identified automatically, try using `whatsitscolor.com`. The site does a pretty good job of identifying the dominant colors in an uploaded image. It will also provide you with an average of the dominant colors as well as a complimentary color (to use for contrast).

Once you've chosen a color, use the hexadecimal code in your CSS syntax. For example, if your text is dark gray, use the following syntax:

```
p{
    color:#666666;
    }
```

When you are done, you'll have the text set for a web page. Each element will have its own voice, yet work together to communicate the feeling of the site as determined by the client's approach to cooking. The text is legible and readable, there is hierarchy within the text, and the colors work together in a system (Figure 11.17).

In the next chapter, you'll develop the grid.

FIGURE 11.17 When you are done, you'll have set the text for the web page. You'll develop a grid in the next lesson. For now, focus on legibility, readability, hierarchy, and voice.

---

**Recommended Resources**

For this chapter, I recommend the following online resources:

- To read about the two client profiles (John Smith and Jane Smith), and to download the text for this chapter go to `www.wiley.com/go/typographicwebdesign`

- To see examples of this lesson go to `typographicwebdesign.com`

- To learn more methods for designing links with lists, I recommend Listamatic: `css.maxdesign.com.au/listamatic/`

- To pick colors for your layout, I recommend visiting the Hues Hub at `december.com/html/spec/colorhues.html`

- To automatically analyze the colors in an image, I recommend `whatsitscolor.com`

---

## Moving Forward

This chapter introduced you to maintaining readability by paying attention to how you use case, style, weight, and color. Case, style, weight, and color are imperative for creating multiple voices on the page. The chapter also introduced you to using lists.

In the next chapter, you will learn about establishing a grid to place the various elements on the page.

# CHAPTER 12

# Expressing Structure and Rhythm: The Grid

Grids are systems of horizontal and vertical lines used to organize information on a page. A grid system is usually applied across multiple pages.

You've already created simple grids on single pages. Look back at the page you designed for the lesson *A is for Alignment* in Chapter 5. In order to create rhythm and tension, you considered the relationship between multiple elements, created a strong vertical line, created a focal point, acknowledged the horizontal repetition of lines of text, and paid attention to the relationships between the elements on the page and edges of the page itself. These are exactly the things we think about when creating a grid (Figure 12.1, top).

Now look back at the Film Series you designed in Chapters 6 through 9. Again, you considered the relationship between multiple elements and the edge of the page. In addition, you paid attention to vertical spacing and line length (column width)—the vertical and horizontal spaces—which are two basic elements in designing a grid.

## The Modular Grid and Text

When learning (or teaching) about how to use a grid, we often start with a modular grid exercise. The modular grid is usually based on an equal number of columns and rows (Figure 12.1, bottom).

Students apply a small amount of text to the grid; the objective is to create multiple, varied solutions. This sensitizes students to the possibilities of the grid—to the idea that the typographer decides where to put elements on the grid.

But when working with large amounts of text, modular grids rarely work. If you find you cannot work within a strict modular grid, do not despair. Grids should be organic and respond to the needs of the text you are working with.

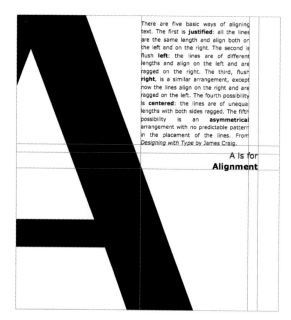

FIGURE 12.1 *Top:* When you pay attention to relationships between elements and create a strong vertical line, a grid starts to develop. Composition by Chris Nelson. *Bottom:* The modular grid is usually based on an equal number of columns and rows. Here, the white spaces become too regular and the composition has less tension than the one above.

## Web Grids and Reading

Figure 12.2 shows a common web "grid" used to show how content can be laid out on a web page. This layout is a practical approach. Most web pages need a top header/navigation bar and a footer. They also need a left or right column (or both) for navigation or support content.

A problem arises if you assume the template is the only possible design. Margins do not have to be equal all the way around. Content does not have to take up the entire width of a browser. The left and right columns do not have to be equal.

Line length affects the readability of the text. In Figure 12.3, the center column of the grid is too wide. Column widths—whether for navigation, main text, or an aside—should acknowledge what the text needs. To respect your readers and honor the content, you must negotiate space and content (Figure 12.4).

FIGURE 12.2 A practical web template is not the same as a grid, and should not be used for laying out text.

FIGURE 12.3 When the Film Series is applied to a web template, the line length gets too long. Equal left and right spaces undermine rhythm and tension.

FIGURE 12.4 Developing a grid based on line length, vertical spacing, and the relationship between elements creates a more readable text and a composition with more rhythm and tension. Film Series by Chris Nelson.

## Grid Templates Aren't "One Size Fits All"

Templates are available to streamline creating a grid. Most notable are Blueprint (www.blueprintcss.org/) and the 960 Grid System (www.designinfluences.com/fluid960gs/).

Templates offer a variety of solutions: Fewer columns make a more traditional layout, while more columns mean more flexibility. But templates are not "one size fits all," and they are not organic. They don't know if you are working with a narrow or wide font, small or large text, a list, prose, or a lot of images. They often dictate how much space you are allowed to put between elements, and how much space you are allowed to fill.

If you want to use a template in the future, go for it. But if you find your content doesn't fit in a template, and if you find you're not satisfied and are doing a lot of math ("What if I use more or fewer columns?" "What if I use a wider or narrower container div?"), then put aside the template and build your own grid.

Over time, as you become more familiar with HTML, CSS, and working with type, I recommend using percentage-based grids like the Perfect Percentage Grid system (www.jetscram.com/ppgrid/). For now, you'll focus on controlling your layout with pixels.

## How to Establish a Grid

Lay out the elements and move them around to discover the grid they need. Arrange them so they feel like individual parts of a whole. Web grids rely primarily on columns because readers scroll down long texts. To make the composition most pleasing, strive for rhythm and tension. Rhythm and tension can be subtle (the space between the edge of the text and the edge of the page; the way the h2s and links create counterpoints to the text) and still be successful.

### Start with What Your Text Needs

Set your text first (like you did in the last lesson). If you try to work with text elements before establishing size, line height, and line length, the grid won't work. It's like shopping for a refrigerator without measuring the space in your kitchen.

After you have the text set, you can move the pieces around, as described in the next sections.

### Physically Move Things Around

Print out a page with your text elements. Draw a long, blank browser. Cut up the elements (Figure 12.5) and move them around until they create a strong vertical line, horizontal relationships between elements, a focal point, and spatial tension in the white space. Document layouts with a photocopier, camera, or scanner (Figure 12.6). Try dozens of ideas. Work quickly; don't worry about perfection.

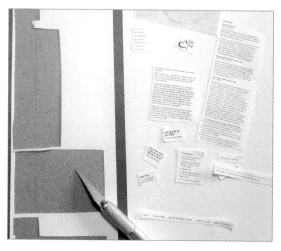

FIGURE 12.5 Cut up your long column of web type so each element (list, caption, memory, and so on) is on its own piece of paper.

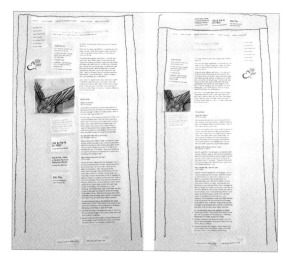

FIGURE 12.6 Arrange the paper scraps in a hand-drawn border. Document your explorations with a scanner, photocopier, or digital camera. Work quickly; don't worry about perfection.

## Use Image Software to Move Things Around

If you don't have a printer (or scissors, or tape, or even just the inclination to use your hands), create an image file of a blank browser. Cut and paste screenshots of the text and image elements on to different layers. Move them around until they create a strong vertical line, horizontal relationships between elements, a focal point, and spatial tension in the white space. Document layouts with screen shots or save multiple versions of the file (Figures 12.7 and 12.8).

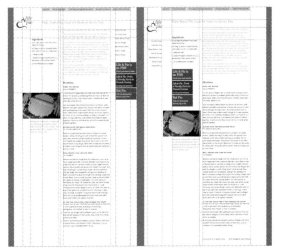

FIGURE 12.8 *Left:* The section links work when on the right side, too. This layout could work, but to me, the elements feel scattered around the page, and the image might be too big. *Right:* This is the best one yet. The image is smaller. When I draw in "grid" lines, I can see this layout is more cohesive than the others. However, the image should shift over so it is on the grid. This will help the rhythm and tension on the page because it will improve the vertical lines.

## Be Willing to Make Modifications

As you move things around, you'll realize that something doesn't work (a color, a font size, a div width). Be willing to modify the text and image elements. You may have to settle for a less-than-perfect line length now and again, but at least you'll have started with the reader in mind (not the width of the browser).

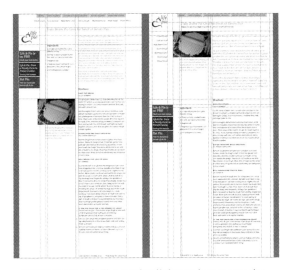

FIGURE 12.7 *Left:* The section links get lost across the top, and the ads are too prominent. Elements do not feel cohesive. *Right:* Moving the section links to the left under the logo works much better. But the image isn't in the right place. It should be with the directions, as it shows a step in the recipe.

### Hand-Color Your Best Solutions

Whether you've documented your exploration with a camera, a scanner, or by saving multiple versions in the image software of your choice, print out the pictures so you can see all of them at once. Lay out the multiple versions and edit down to the best solutions. I recommend pulling out some color pencils and hand-coloring the layouts to explore possible color palettes (Figure 12.9). Again, try dozens of ideas. Work quickly; don't worry about perfection.

## Sketching Is More Important than Ever

Why is sketching more important than ever? *When you're trying to lay out elements, you're looking at syntax.* It helps to work out the composition in advance. I recommend finding the grid by hand whenever possible. It allows you to develop more ideas in a shorter amount of time than sketching with image software. In addition, sketches done by hand feel impermanent; it's okay to try new ideas and make mistakes when sketches take only a couple of minutes and can be thrown into the recycling bin.

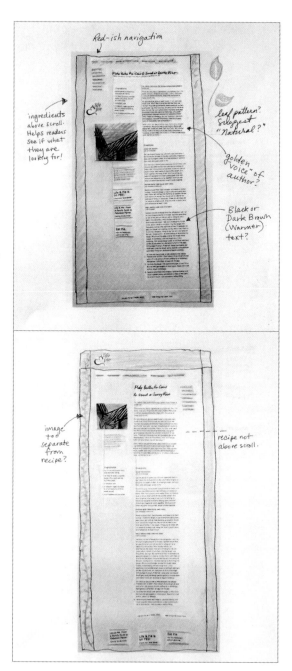

**FIGURE 12.9** Edit down your best explorations. Hand-color the layouts to explore color palettes. Make notes to yourself about what is working and what isn't.

### The Grid

Grids are systems of horizontal and vertical lines. To summarize:

- Grids organize information on a page.

- Grid systems are applied across pages.

- Grids should be organic and respond to the needs of the text.

- Web grids rely primarily on columns because readers scroll down long texts.

- Line length affects readability. Base column width on text, not available space.

- To discover a grid, move elements around on a page. Document possible solutions.

- When discovering the grid, work with text already set to a possible font, size, and so on.

- Continue to strive for a strong vertical line, a focal point, horizontal relationships between elements, and thoughtful relationships between elements on the page and the edge of the page itself.

# Lesson 12: A Recipe, Part 2

In this lesson, you'll build upon the work you did in the last lesson. You'll discover the grid, and then build the page by nesting divs inside of one another (Figure 12.10). Finally, you'll remove the divs you created in the last lesson from your HTML and CSS files.

The process of building this page, as outlined in the lesson, has more steps than are strictly necessary. Typographers usually consider placement while setting text, but *I purposely separated the two*. I want you to clearly experience creating a grid from the text elements you set in the previous lesson.

This lesson helps you achieve the following objectives:

1   Practice discovering a grid by moving around the elements on a page.

2   Practice the process of design—trying multiple solutions, documenting solutions, allowing yourself to try things you know won't work.

3   Refine your grid based on the needs of the text on the page.

4   Build the grid (and thus the page) using nested divs. Even if you're already HTML/CSS savvy, follow the walk-through provided. I show you what a typographer looks for in the process.

FIGURE 12.10 By the end of this lesson, you'll have a grid built in HTML and CSS, like this example by Chris Nelson.

## Overview of the Lesson

When developing a grid for a web page, start by setting your text to the correct size, line height, and line length. Properly set text elements are the building blocks for your layout.

### Discover the Grid and Document the Process

Working with the text elements you created in the last lesson, cut up the elements and discover their grid.

You can work with paper printouts, scissors/blade, and tape. Or you can work with imaging software, cutting and pasting each element onto its own layer. Either way, document your process. This will help you keep track of what you have already tried. It will also allow you to walk away from the project and return with a fresh eye. Having multiple ideas to review can inspire a greater variety of possible solutions.

Be willing to try things you know won't work. Sometimes, moving things around without pre-conceived limits will lead to a new way of looking at the elements.

Don't worry about taking up the whole width of the browser. You can make your `main_container` narrower. In fact, I recommend using a width of 990px for the main container throughout this book, but I have built sites using 970px, and a very common `main_container` width is only 960px.

### Build the Grid

Finally, build the grid and page using nested divs. Don't worry about getting the navigation and links working. You'll create those next.

## Creating Complex Columns by Nesting Divs

In this example, you'll modify the recipe from the last lesson, so make a copy of the last lesson's folder and name the new folder *12_recipe*. Keep it in the *web_typography* folder.

Rename the CSS file *recipe_grid.css*. Link it to the *index.html* file by going into the HTML file and changing the syntax in the `head` element to the following:

```
<link href="recipe_grid.css"
    rel="stylesheet" type="text/css" />
```

Change the title to the following:

```
<title>Lesson 12: Recipe
    (Grid)</title>
```

### Pick the Layout You Want to Build

By now, you should have multiple solutions for a layout. Pick the one that works the best: Line lengths are good for reading, there's a strong vertical line (elements are lined up and create a vertical line via continuation), and there's spatial tension between elements and the edge of the page. Overlay a grid of equal units to help you figure out size and placement of elements (Figure 12.11).

which will live *across* columns (Figure 12.12). This will help you figure out what containers you need to make to hold other containers (Figures 12.13 to 12.17). I refer to the containers that make up the basic structure of the site as *structural divs* and containers that nest inside other containers as *nested divs* for the remainder of this lesson.

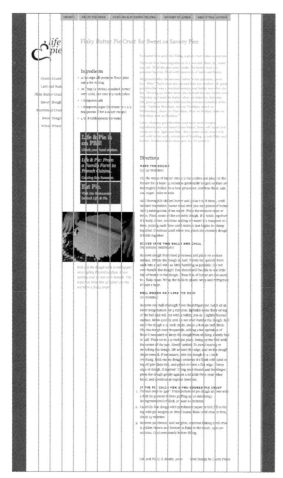

FIGURE 12.11 A grid overlay divides the composition into equal 50px units. Use a grid to estimate size and placement of elements; this is especially helpful when working with mock-ups that aren't the actual size.

## Figure Out the Columns and Rows

You'll need to build a structure in which to place the elements—the content. You'll do this by nesting divs inside of larger divs. Start by identifying which elements will live in columns, and

FIGURE 12.12 Identify where columns are, and what elements won't fit in a single column. This will help you figure out how to build the site.

**FIGURE 12.13** My design starts with three structural divs: a top row, a left column, and a right column.

**FIGURE 12.14** Nested in the right column are three more divs: a top row, a left column, and a right column.

**FIGURE 12.15** Pages can get complex. This page, by Chris Nelson, starts with five structural divs: three rows, a left column, and a right column.

FIGURE 12.16 When creating a complex page, think of packing boxes inside of boxes so items don't shift during transit. Here, nested divs are in blue.

FIGURE 12.17 More divs (violet) are nested inside the nested divs. I recommend giving divs a background color. It will help you see the page you are building!

## Get Organized: Notations in CSS

As you build a complex page, your CSS syntax will get longer. You'll have syntax for divs that structure the page, syntax for the text elements that create hierarchy, and syntax for the classes that describe subtle shifts in the system. Making good type decisions often means taking care of subtle details with classes. Now is the time to get organized and start using CSS comments!

As the CSS becomes more complex, use notation marks to organize the syntax. Anything within the /* and */ characters will be ignored by browsers.

In your CSS file, mark sections of syntax for links, structural layout, and elements. Create headings like the one below to separate chunks of syntax.

```
/* ------- STRUCTURAL LAYOUT -------*/
```

The hyphens are not necessary, but they create stronger visual breaks in the CSS, which will help you quickly scan your syntax.

Because anything between the /* and */ characters will be ignored by browsers, notation marks are also a great way to turn styling "off" and "on" in your CSS. You can use them to turn a div background color off and on when you need to (Figure 12.18).

```
#left_column{
float:left;
width:310px;
height:auto;
display:inline;
/*background-color:#9CC9A9;*/
    }

#text_column{
float:left;
width:380px;
height:auto;
margin-left:20px;
display:inline;
/*background-color:#D8DBBD;*/
    }

/* ----------- recipe name ----------------- */
h1{
font-size:26px;
line-height:24px;
padding-left:75px;
color:#BFA640;
}

/* ----------- memory ----------------- */
p.memory{
font-size:16px;
line-height:22px;
margin-bottom:12px;
color:#B29E4D;
}
```

FIGURE 12.18 Use notation to organize your CSS syntax and to turn styling off and on. In this example, the div background colors are turned into notation, and no longer show up in the browser.

## Notations in HTML

The `<!--` and `-->` characters for separating sections of the HTML syntax work in a similar manner. I tend to use them less often, but they can be helpful to chunk sections of a site. HTML syntax is also used to call attention to particular syntax on the page. Web designers working in teams use notation to mark syntax for other team members (also known as *commenting* or *documenting* code).

Use notation in CSS and HTML to make your job easier. It takes a few minutes to organize syntax and create "headings," but you'll be able to find a specific section of syntax in a file later, and you'll be able to pass files back and forth with a colleague. Commenting also allows you to better understand the structure of your work when you revisit it later.

## Build the Underlying Page Structure

This part of the lesson is more complex than previous lessons because you are nesting divs. But everything you do in this lesson is built upon something you've done before. You're using the same syntax and techniques you used in *A is for Alignment* and in the Film Series project. You're just using them in a new way.

Your design is different from mine, so I can't tell you exactly how to build your page, but I can show you how I built mine. This will help you see the process—it will give you tips on how to approach your page structure, and how to control your elements within the divs. First, we'll start with an overview of the process.

### Make changes to text elements based on sketching

When sketching solutions, you may have modified some elements.

For example, in Chapter 11, I set the memory text bigger than the directions. But when I started laying out the elements, I realized the memory text was too big (it took up too much space on the page). In my sketches, I quickly reduced the memory text so I could work with it. Now I need to go back and change the memory text in the CSS so it is the correct size and column width.

For another example, in Chapter 11, I set my section links list to be aligned left. While sketching, I realized I want them aligned right. I'll need to make that change in the CSS, too.

Identify what changes you made to your elements during your sketching process, and make them in your CSS now, before you start building the structure. Color changes can wait until later.

### Make changes to images based on sketching

You'll definitely have to make one change: the image size. In the sketching process, you found the best size and placement for the image.

Using imaging software, resize the image to the correct size. Make sure your image remains at 72 ppi and that you save it as a JPEG file. *Always fix the size of an image before placing it into the web page.* Unless you are designing a scalable web site, placing big images and reducing them in CSS slows down the site with unnecessary data. Small images enlarged in CSS result in poor-quality images.

You may crop the image (cutting off parts of it), either to change the shape of the image box or to focus on an aspect of the image. For this content, that's fine. The recipe and the memories are the main content; the image is secondary. If you ever design a site with images as the primary content—such as a site for a photographer—refrain from cropping unless you have explicit permission.

Honor the image as you would honor the text. Avoid arbitrarily cropping an image to create a grid. If you find yourself chopping off parts of people's heads or hands—or eliminating important aspects of an image so you can make it fit—it's time to reevaluate how the image fits in the grid (Figure 12.19).

FIGURE 12.19 Top: The cook has hands, and the image is more active. Bottom: Without hands in the picture, the rolling pin could simply be resting on the dough. Avoid arbitrarily cropping images. If you start chopping off people's heads and hands to make an image fit, it's time to reevaluate your grid.

1  Name and describe the structural divs in CSS.

2  Put the divs in the HTML with the `<div></div>` **tags**.

3  Place divs with the `float` property.

4  Clear margins and padding with the universal selector if you haven't already done so.

5  Put margins and padding back in as needed (to properly place the divs), making changes as needed.

I highly recommend giving each structural div a light background color. This will help you see them, to help you make adjustments as you build the composition.

I recommend using a background color rather than a border. Borders add pixels to the widths of the divs. In more complex compositions like this one, the extra pixels create complications when it's time to remove them.

### How I Built My Underlying Page Structure

Again, your design is different from mine, but walking you through my example should give you insight into how to proceed. I followed the steps recommended in the preceding section. I started by modifying both my text elements and my image based on my sketching process. Then I tackled the structural divs.

### I figured out what structural divs I needed

My design (Figure 12.13) needs a container across the top to hold the navigation links (a `header_container`). It also needs a left container to hold the logo and links for the current section (a `section_nav_container`). Finally, my design needs a right container to hold three nested divs (a `content_container`).

Inside the right container, which I've called `content_container` because it holds all my actual content, I need to nest three more containers (Figure 12.14). Why? Because the recipe title isn't in a single column; it spans across two columns. I need to put the title in a container that spans two containers forming the two columns. If I try to put these three containers in without nesting them inside another container, it's much more difficult to get the composition to work. Browsers will try to place these containers by following the rule: Place floated containers in a row until there is no more room, and then start the next row. Thus, the title will show up correctly (next to the section navigation), but the columns may show up in a row *below* the section navigation!

With time, practice, and experience, you can use additional syntax to place content perfectly without so many divs. But if you are just starting out, I recommend using nested divs. You can see them in context as you build the composition. As you gain experience and confidence in working with HTML and CSS, explore positioning content with less divs. An excellent article to get you started is "Divitis: What it is and How to Avoid It" at `apaddedcell.com/div-itis`.

Inside the right container, my design needs a nested container across the top to hold the recipe title (a `recipe_title_container`). It also needs a nested left container to hold the content in the left column: the ingredients, ads, picture, and caption (a `left_column`). Finally, my design needs a nested right container to hold the content in the right column: the memory text, the recipe instructions, and the copyright information (a `text_column`).

**A note about naming divs:** In this project, I am breaking a rule about naming divs. You shouldn't use words like "left" or "right" in div names. As a website grows or gets reorganized, you might need to change where the divs live. And it would be very confusing to have your `left_column` div on the right side of your web page! But because I'm showing you something complex, I think the simple term `left_column` is helpful here. So I'm breaking the rules and using it as a div name for this project.

### I used a grid overlay to estimate the size of each structural div

My chosen sketch was made by cutting and pasting elements onto layers in Photoshop. To create a grid overlay, I drew lines over the design at 50px intervals (Figure 12.11). This helped me see how big my divs needed to be. I ended up with the following seven divs with the following measurements (note that there is a left margin on the `text_container` that separates the two columns):

```
#main_container {
    width:950px;
    height:auto;
    margin-top:0px;
    margin-right:auto;
    margin-left:auto;
    padding-bottom:20px;
    overflow:hidden;
    }
#header_container {
    width:860px;
    height:90px;
    float:left;
    }
#section_nav_container {
    width:150px;
    height:auto;
```

```
    float:left;
    }
#content_container {
    width:710px;
    height:auto;
    float:left;
    }
#recipe_title_container {
    width:710px;
    height:65px;
    float:left;
    }
#left_column {
    width:310px;
    height:auto;
    float:left;
    }
#text_column {
    width:380px;
    height:auto;
    margin-left:20px;
    float:left;
    }
```

### I put the divs into my HTML

I put my new divs in at the very top of my HTML page. I didn't worry about the content yet. I put my structural divs in first, and then nested other structural divs in where I needed them. Nesting divs is a matter of putting divs inside of other divs, like so:

```
<div id="main_container">
  <div id="header_container">
    Top navigation bar goes here.
    </div>
  <div id="section_nav_container">
    Logo and section links go here.
    </div>
  <div id="content_container">
    <div id="recipe_title_container">
```

```
      Recipe title goes here.
      </div>
    <div id="left_column">
      Ingredients and other
     elements go here.
      </div>
    <div id="text_column">
      Memory and directions go here.
      </div>
  </div>
</div>
```

### I added color to my divs, and viewed my web page

Adding background colors to divs helps you see what's going on while you're building a complex structure (Figures 12.20 and 12.21). This structure was simple enough for me to do all at once. But when a structure feels complicated to me, I will view the page multiple times as I build it. That way, I can catch mistakes as I make them.

If your structure feels complicated, I recommend you do the same. Mistakes are easier to catch and fix if you view the page at every step.

**FIGURE 12.20** Building a page can be easier if you insert the basic structural divs first. Notice they have background color. It can also help to write in the HTML what each div will hold. Because you are building the structure at the top of an existing page, you might see some of your existing HTML below the new structure. That's fine; you'll delete it soon.

FIGURE 12.21 After your basic structure is working, you can nest divs as needed.

When you're finished, you should have a structure in which to insert your content.

## Place Content in the Structural Divs

In the HTML, cut and paste the correct content into the structural divs (Figure 12.22).

Do *not* include the original divs you set up in the last lesson. You are going to delete those. Only copy and paste the content and any tags you used to define the content (ul, h1, h2, p, and so on). Paste the content inside structural div tags, in the order it should appear.

For example, in my syntax, the following code:

```
<div id="header_container">
    Top navigation bar goes here.
    </div>
```

becomes this:

```
<div id="header_container">
    <ul id="main_navigation_list">
    <li>Crusts</li>
    <li>Fruit Fillings</li>
    <li>Custard & Pudding Fillings</li>
    <li>Savory Fillings</li>
    <li>About the Author</li>
    </ul>
</div>
```

FIGURE 12.22 The content has been cut from the old divs and pasted into the new divs. The old divs were left at the bottom of the HTML syntax. They'll be deleted.

### View your web page... often!

Adding so much content at once into your structure can be complicated. If you accidentally paste something into the wrong div, or even into an element tag, the results can look a little weird. I highly recommend you view the page multiple times as you build it. Mistakes are easier to catch and fix if you view the page at every step.

When you're finished, you should have a page structure with all of your content in place. The content won't look right yet. That's okay; you'll fix it.

### Delete old divs

After you move the content up into the new structure, your HTML page will still contain the old divs—the ones you used in the last lesson to set your line length. You don't need these divs anymore. Go ahead and delete them all. You may even have a second `main_container` in there that holds all the old divs. If you do, delete it.

You can also delete the IDs for the old divs from your CSS file. You won't be using them again.

### Refine Placement of Content

As always, review your layout, note what needs to change, and tackle the changes one by one.

You can move things up, down, left, and right by using margins, padding, and floats. If necessary, you can change the widths of divs.

Refining your content placement may be more complex here than in previous lessons because you may have many different kinds of element tags (`h1`, `h2`, `p`, `ul`, `li`) in a single div. But everything you do in this lesson is built upon something you've done before. You're using the same syntax and techniques you used in the Film Series project. You're just using them in a new way.

Using floats, padding, and margins, you should be able to get your elements to do what you want, although you might have to make some classes to

do it. If you find you can't get an element to position correctly, I have two suggestions. First, Google the problem; you now have enough experience with HTML and CSS to understand a discussion online. Second, you may need to create a special div to wrap an element. Wrapping an element in its own div can give you more control. On simple pages, this isn't necessary, but on more complex pages, you may need the occasional extra div.

Again, your design is different from mine, but walking you through my example should give you insight into how to proceed.

### How I Refined My Content

As recommended earlier, I started by noting what needed to change, and tackled the changes one by one. I started from the top of the page, and worked my way down. As each area of the page was fixed, I turned off the div background colors.

### I shifted the main navigation links to the right

In my design, the main navigation links should be aligned with the right edge of the content. When I flowed them in, they were aligned to the left edge. I fixed this by adding a `float:right;` to the `#main_navigation_list` (Figure 12.23).  Floats can be added to other elements, not just divs. The syntax looks like this:

```
#main_navigation_list{
    float:right;
    }
```

### I shifted the logo to the right

In my design, the right edge of the logo should be aligned to the right edge of the section links below it. I fixed this by creating a class called `logo`, floating it right, and applying the class to the logo image in my HTML (Figure 12.23). The CSS syntax looks like this:

```
.logo{
    float:right;
    }
```

The HTML syntax looks like this:

```
<img src="images/11_logo.gif"
    class="logo">
```

### I shifted the section links down

In my design, the section links should be lower on the page than they are when just pasted into the div. I lowered them by adding a `float:right;` to the list and then adding a top margin equal to the top of the list (Figure 12.23). Why did I float the list? Because I floated the logo, I had "taken it out of the flow" of the elements in the div. In order to force the list to recognize the bottom edge of the logo, I had to float the list, too. The CSS syntax looks like this:

```
#section_links_list{
    float:right;
    margin-top:40px;
    text-align:right;
    }
```

### I shifted the recipe title and ingredients list over

In my design, the recipe title and the ingredients are lined up on their left edge. They are also positioned farther away from the logo and section links. I moved them over by adding a left padding of 75px to both the h1 and the `#ingredient_list` (Figure 12.24). The CSS syntax looks like this:

```
h1{
    font-size:26px;
    line-height:24px;
    color:#BFA640;
    padding-left:75px;
    }
```

```
#ingredient_list{
    padding-left:75px;
    }
```

FIGURE 12.23 The ul for the top navigation is now float:right. The logo and section links ul are also float:right. Space has been added above the section links ul with a margin. As each area of the page is fixed, I turn the div background colors off.

**I shifted the ingredients heading and text over**
When I moved the ingredients list over, the heading and the text that says, "Makes enough for 2 single-crust pies…," needed to move over as well. The heading is an h2. The text is a p. I didn't want to add a 75px left padding to every single h2 and paragraph on the page, so I made classes and applied them in the HTML (Figure 12.24). Here's the CSS syntax:

```
h2.ingredients{
    padding-left:75px;
    }
p.ingredients{
    padding-left:75px;
    }
```

The HTML syntax looks like this:

```
<h2 class="ingredients">Ingredients
    </h2>
<p class="ingredients">Makes enough
    for 2 single-crust pies or 1
    double-crust fold-over pie.</p>
```

**I shifted the ingredients heading and text down**
In my design, the ingredients are lower on the page than they are when just pasted into the div. I want the top of the section links to line up with the top of the ingredients list (Figure 12.24). This will create a horizontal line, which will help create tension in the page layout. I also need a little vertical space between the bottom of the ingredients list and the "Makes enough for 2 single-crust pies…" text. I had already created and applied classes for the ingredients h2 and the ingredients p, so I simply added some top padding to each. The CSS syntax looks like this:

```
h2.ingredients{
    padding-left:75px;
```

```
    padding-top:52px;
    }
p.ingredients{
    padding-left:75px;
    padding-top:15px;
    }
```

**I positioned the ads and the image**
In my design, the ads line up with the ingredients list, so they needed to be moved over 75px. They also have space between them, so they needed top and bottom margins added. I added more space to the top of the first ad and the bottom of the last ad than I did between the ads. This helped group the ads so they didn't feel too close to the ingredients above them or to the image below them (Figure 12.24). Here's the CSS syntax:

```
#advertisement_pbs_container{
    margin-left:75px;
    margin-top:40px;
    width:155px;
    height:75px;
    padding:7px;
    background:#364C63;
    }
#advertisement_book_container{
    margin-left:75px;
    margin-top:10px;
    width:155px;
    height:90px;
    padding:7px;
    background:#423624;
    }
#advertisement_restaurant_container{
    margin-left:75px;
    margin-top:10px;
    margin-bottom:50px;
    width:155px;
    height:75px;
```

```
padding:7px;
background:#364C63;
}
```

### I moved the caption over and down

In my design, the caption is lined up with the ingredients list, has a shorter line length, and isn't so close to the bottom of the image. I fixed this by adding 75px of space to the left of the caption and 10px of space above the caption. I was already using a class called `caption` for the caption text, so I simply added the new spacing to the class (Figure 12.24). The CSS syntax looks like this:

```
.caption{
    padding-left:75px;
    padding-top:10px;
    font-style:italic;
    color:#B29E4D;
    }
```

### I fixed the spacing on the h2 and the copyright text

I want more space above the "Directions" h2 (Figure 12.25) than there is when the content is just pasted into the div. I fixed this problem by adding top padding to the h2. The CSS syntax looks like this:

```
h2{
    font-size:18px;
    line-height:22px;
    padding-top:30px;
    padding-bottom:6px;
    color:#423624;
    }
```

**FIGURE 12.24** The h1, ingredients, ads, image, and caption are all in their right places, thanks to adding margin and padding where needed. Notice how the top line of the ingredients list lines up with the top section link. This helps create a subtle horizontal line that increases rhythm and tension. Typographers often let the h2 pop up above the horizon of the text.

There should also be more space above the copyright notice, and a bit of space between the notice and the "Designed by" text right next to it (Figure 12.25). I fixed these problems by creating and applying classes to the copyright notice and the "Designed by" text. The CSS syntax looks like this:

```
p.footer{
    padding-top:30px;
    }
.design{
    padding-left:10px;
    }
```

The HTML syntax looks like this:

```
<p class="footer">Life & Pie &copy;
2010, J. Smith <span
class="design">Web Design by
Laura Franz</span></p>
```

## Fixing the "Double-Margin" Bug

This book is about typography, not debugging HTML and CSS to work across platforms. However, I'd be remiss if I didn't mention the "double-margin" bug.

Internet Explorer doubles the measurement of the margin on the same side a div is floated. That is, if a div is floated left and has a left margin, the measurement of the left margin is doubled in Internet Explorer only.

This can wreak havoc with your layout in Internet Explorer. The quickest fix to this bug is to add the following (in CSS) to each floated div:

```
display:inline;
```

FIGURE 12.25 The last div was the easiest. I added space above the h2 and the copyright information.

I've added it to my structural divs throughout this chapter. For example:

```
#text_column {
    width:380px;
    margin-left:20px;
    height:auto;
    float:left;
    display:inline;
    }
```

Another fix would be to use padding inside the structural divs instead of using margins outside of them, or to skip the `margin-left` altogether and just float the right-hand div to the right. But the way I've shown you is fine and will work. As you become more familiar with HTML and CSS, you will find the method that works best for you.

**Finishing Up**

If you haven't already done so, fix the characters in your text. Fix curly quotes (`&ldquo;` and `&rdquo;` for double curly quotes, and `&lsquo;` and `&rsquo;` for single curly quotes), apostrophes (`&rsquo;`), and em (`&mdash;`) and en (`&ndash;`) dashes. You will also find a degree symbol (`&deg;`), a copyright symbol (`&copy;`), and an ampersand (the "and sign" in the "Custard & Pudding Fillings" link) (`&amp;`) that need to be fixed.

When the page is laid out according to your grid, you're ready to refine your system of links (and make them work!). We'll do this in the next lesson.

But first, congratulations are in order! You have built a complex structure of divs. Every web page is different, and you'll learn something new every time you design a solution to a new problem—but you now have a solid foundation on which to build your knowledge.

---

**Recommended Resources**

For this lesson, I recommend the following online resources:

- To learn about Blueprint, a popular grid system for the web, go to www.blueprintcss.org/
- To learn about the 960 Grid System, another popular grid system, go to www.designinfluences.com/fluid960gs/
- When you're ready to learn about how to use a percentage-based grid, go to www.jetscram.com/ppgrid/
- To learn more about the Modernist modular grid, go to www.thegridsystem.org/
- To read about how to reduce the number of divs in your future compositions, go to apaddedcell.com/div-itis
- To find character entities for symbols, go to w3schools.com/tags/ref_entities.asp w3schools.com/tags/ref_symbols.asp

---

## Moving Forward

This chapter introduced you to finding and building a grid based on the needs of the text. The chapter also introduced you to nesting divs and positioning multiple elements in a div.

In the next chapter, you will learn about establishing a system of links.

# CHAPTER 13

# Helping Readers Move through the Site: Navigation

Navigation has a voice on the page. It says, "Click on me and I'll take you where you want to go."

It says other things, too: "You are here," and "These are places you have been." It says, "Here are some places in the same area of the site you can go to," and "Here are different areas of the site you can go to."

When a reader rolls over a link, it gives feedback: "You have engaged me—I am ready to take you where you want to go."

When a reader clicks on a link, it gives additional feedback: "Interaction successful—prepare to go to a new place."

When done well, navigation communicates to readers on many levels.

## Navigation Is Text and Needs to Be Readable

Readers scan navigation elements quickly. You should help them by setting the links (size, line height, line length, alignment, case, style, weight, and color) to promote readability.

More like headings than prose, links can withstand caps, italics, and display fonts. However, the more links you have, the more the reader will have to scan, and the more readable you should make the navigation (Figure 13.1). A handful of links is manageable when set in all caps or center aligned. If the reader has to parse a dozen links, you can provide word shapes and a left edge to help.

## If You Click on Me, I'll Take You Places

Links need to feel different from the rest of the text—they need to have a different voice. Placing navigation bars and lists of links apart from areas of text helps communicate this difference. But links are in the text as well. Inline links need to be set apart in other ways: color, style, size, case, or weight. When using one of these characteristics for links, don't use it for other text. Using the characteristic that means "I'm clickable" on nonlinks creates confusion (Figure 13.2).

| AREAS OF STUDY | AREAS OF STUDY |
|---|---|
| 2D STUDIES | ART EDUCATION |
| 3D STUDIES | ART HISTORY |
| ART EDUCATION | CERAMICS |
| ART HISTORY | DIGITAL MEDIA |
| MUSIC | DRAWING |
| VISUAL DESIGN | GRAPHIC DESIGN |
| | ILLUSTRATION |
| | JEWELRY/METALS |
| | MUSIC |
| | PAINTING |
| | PHOTOGRAPHY |
| | PRINTMAKING |
| | SCULPTURE |
| | TEXTILE DESIGN |
| | TYPOGRAPHY |
| | WOOD |

FIGURE 13.1 *Left:* A handful of links set in all caps and centered is easy to scan. *Right:* A long list of links gets hard to read. Providing word shapes with lowercase letters and a left-aligned edge would help readers scan the list.

FIGURE 13.2 *Top:* It looks like there are many links in the text, but there is only one link in the first paragraph. Using the characteristic (red) that means "I'm clickable" on nonlinks creates confusion. *Bottom:* The red has been removed. Readers can see what is clickable and what isn't.

## You Are Here

Knowing where they are in the site helps orient readers to other places they want to visit. This guidance is especially important in a site with complex navigation.

Use contrast (change in color, case, size, or background color) to indicate where in the list of links the reader is in the site (Figure 13.3).

If you do not want to orient readers through changes in the navigation, make sure the heading for each page uses the same wording as the corresponding navigation link. Matching headings and navigation links (wording) helps readers orient themselves in a site.

FIGURE 13.3 *Top:* Meighan Tague uses color to say, "You are here." *Bottom:* The navigation system without the color.

## Oh, the Places You Can Go

In a complex site, readers navigate within, and move between, sections of the site. Think of a multi-story building: a visitor can go into rooms on the same floor or move between floors as needed.

Visiting a new section of a site (or a new floor of a building) means leaving one category of information for another, and is a significant jump within a site. Readers need to know what links will take them where.

Use vertical spacing, proximity, hierarchy, and similarity to create navigation links that "chunk" the site for your readers. Set navigation links leading to other sections differently from navigation links within a section (Figure 13.4).

| | |
|---|---|
| Foundations Program | **Foundations Program** |
| Art Education | **Art Education** |
| Art Education BFA \| MAE | Art Education BFA \| MAE |
| Art History | |
| Art History BA | **Art History** |
| Artisanry | Art History BA |
| Ceramics BFA \| MFA | |
| Jewelry/Metals BFA \| MFA | **Artisanry** |
| Textile Design/Fiber Arts | Ceramics BFA \| MFA |
| BFA \| MFA | Jewelry/Metals BFA \| MFA |
| Wood/Furniture MFA | Textile Design/Fiber Arts |
| Certificate Program | BFA \| MFA |
| Fine Arts | Wood/Furniture MFA |
| Drawing MFA | Certificate Program |
| Painting/2D BFA \| MFA | |
| Printmaking MFA | **Fine Arts** |
| Sculpture/3D BFA \| MFA | Drawing MFA |
| Certificate Program | Painting/2D BFA \| MFA |
| Visual Design | Printmaking MFA |
| Digital Media BFA \| MFA | Sculpture/3D BFA \| MFA |
| Graphic Design BFA \| MFA | Certificate Program |
| Illustration BFA \| MFA | |
| Photography BFA \| MFA | **Visual Design** |
| Typography MFA | Digital Media BFA \| MFA |
| Graduate Certificate: Web | Graphic Design BFA \| MFA |
| and Interaction Design | Illustration BFA \| MFA |
| Music | Photography BFA \| MFA |
| Music BA | Typography MFA |
| | Graduate Certificate: Web |
| | and Interaction Design |
| | |
| | **Music** |
| | Music BA |

FIGURE 13.4 *Left:* All links look the same. Where will they take your reader? *Right:* Visual chunking helps readers form a mental model of the site.

If all navigation links look alike, then scanning and chunking become more difficult. Think back to the film series assignments. The visual "chunking" truly occurred when hierarchy was added—before then, it was difficult to see the list chunked by semester and month.

Visual chunking helps readers form a mental model of the site.

## You've Been There Already

Knowing where they have been also helps readers orient themselves on a website. Readers are looking for something. What link might help them find it? Which links have they already tried?

Showing readers where they have been is especially important with inline links (links within text). A reader may be able to keep track of the links they've visited in a navigation bar, but inline links often use different wording (never, of course, "Click here") or link to external pages (Figure 13.5).

Visited links are often indicated with a color change. A duller or lighter color will still say "link," but with less emphasis.

## Your Wish Is My Command

Links can respond—changing color, case, size, weight, style, background color, or underline—when readers roll over or click on them. This inter-activity reinforces that a link is a portal to more content, and readers will be taken to another place (Figure 13.6).

**Additional Pages and Resources**
National Association for Community Mediation
www.nafcm.org

Mediate.com
www.mediate.com

Public Conversations Project
www.publicconversations.org/pcp/index.php

Conflict Resolution Info Source
crinfo.org

Uniform Mediation Act
pon.harvard.edu/guests/uma

**Additional Pages and Resources**
National Association for Community Mediation
www.nafcm.org

Mediate.com
www.mediate.com

Public Conversations Project
www.publicconversations.org/pcp/index.php

Conflict Resolution Info Source
crinfo.org

Uniform Mediation Act
pon.harvard.edu/guests/uma

FIGURE 13.5 *Top:* All the links look the same. *Bottom:* Color can be used to say, "You've been there already."

The trick (usually) is to keep it subtle, especially when changing a typographic element (size, weight, case, and style).

If an interaction makes other words in the text move over or down to the next line, then find another solution. The movement of the other words in the text will draw the reader's eye and undermine the interactivity of the link (Figure 13.7).

In "A Natural History of Typography" (1992), J Abbott Miller and Ellen Lupton write, "What sort of semiotic system is typography?"

In "A Natural History of Typography" (1992), J Abbott Miller and Ellen Lupton write, "What sort of semiotic system is typography?"

Figure 13.6 Interactivity reinforces links as portals. *Top:* The original link state. *Bottom:* The link changes color when a reader hovers over it.

In "A Natural History of Typography" (1992), J Abbott Miller and Ellen Lupton write, "What sort of semiotic system is typography?"

In **"A Natural History of Typography"** (1992), J Abbott Miller and Ellen Lupton write, "What sort of semiotic system is typography?"

FIGURE 13.7 Keep changes on hover subtle. If words move, it will distract the reader from the link. *Top:* The original link state. *Bottom:* The link becomes bold when a reader hovers over it. Notice how some words get bumped down to the next line. This is not good practice.

## Creating Helpful Navigation

To summarize, navigation is most helpful when:

- Links are readable.
- Links are easily identified because they look different from the rest of the text.
- Contrast is used to show readers where they are in the site.
- Navigation links are "chunked" to help readers form a mental model of the site.
- Subtle contrast is used to show readers what links they have already tried.
- Subtle contrast is used to create interactions with the links.

# Lesson 13: A Recipe, Part 3

You've already incorporated the navigation into your grid. Now it's time to make sure your typographic choices help readers move through the site. By the end of this lesson, you'll have created a working navigation system (Figure 13.8).

FIGURE 13.8 By the end of this lesson, you'll have a working navigation system like in this example by Chris Nelson. Notice the link color change (a:hover) for "sweet dough."

This lesson helps you achieve the following objectives:

1  Practice applying the rules for good typography to text-based navigation.

2  Practice the process of design: Try developing multiple solutions to the navigation system. Be willing to sketch ideas on paper! The system is complex and difficult to visualize.

3  Refine your navigation based on helping readers navigate the site.

4  Make a system of links work using link syntax and pseudo-class selectors.

Even if you are already HTML/CSS savvy, follow the walk-through provided. I show you what a typographer looks for in the process.

## Overview of the Lesson

Analyze your navigation system. Are the links readable? If not, how can you make them more readable? Do other text elements on the page look similar to the links? If so, how can you change the elements so the links are unique? Have you chunked the navigation to help readers form a mental model of the site?

Does your navigation show readers where they are in the site? If not, how can you use typography (in the navigation, in the recipe title) to help orient your readers? How will this system work across multiple pages?

Finally, think about how the links will change as the reader moves through the site. What will a link look like after it's been visited? What will it look like when your reader rolls over it? When they click on it? Changes can be indicated typographically or by color, but they should be subtle. Don't let the experience of interacting with the links overwhelm the text.

Use printouts, paper, and pencil as needed to help you pin down your ideas quickly and easily. Because a navigation system is so complex, I recommend printing out your current page and marking up where you need to make changes before making them in the CSS. Sketching is also helpful.

It is difficult to visualize a full navigation system all at once. Parts of the system become apparent only when interacted with, or after a reader has left and returned to a page.

## Link Syntax and Pseudo-Class Selectors

In this lesson, you'll modify the recipe from the last lesson, so make a copy of the last lesson's folder and name the new folder *13_recipe*. Keep it in the *web_typography* folder.

Rename the CSS file *recipe_navigation.css*. Link it to the *index.html* file by going into the HTML file and changing the syntax in the `head` element to the following:

```
<link href="recipe_navigation.css"
    rel="stylesheet" type="text/css" />
```

Change the title as shown:

```
<title>Lesson 13: Recipe
    (Navigation)</title>
```

### Getting Started: Download Some Pages to Link To

I find it helpful to have pages to link to when I'm building a navigation system. It allows me to experience how the links will actually work.

I've made four simple pages for you to link to in this lesson. They represent the three additional recipes you will set in the next lesson—Allie's Meat Pasties, Apple Pie, and Chess Pie—and a page to use as a placeholder.

Once you've downloaded the files from the book's companion website at www.wiley.com/go/ typographicwebdesign, put them in the *13_recipe* folder.

### Adding the Link Syntax: Main Navigation

There are three kinds of links on the recipe page: the main navigation, the section links, and the ads. A fourth kind of link might show up in later recipes: the inline link. For this project, each kind of link will need four states: link, visited, hover (rollover), and active (click).

You can start with any group of links. In this lesson, you'll start with the main navigation.

#### Add the main navigation link syntax in the HTML document

The link syntax is made with the anchor tag, like so:

```
<a href="nameofpage.html"></a>
```

What does this mean? It means to create an anchor (an `a` tag) to the hypertext reference (`href`) called "nameofpage.html." The link syntax goes around the text link:

```
<a href="apple.html">Fruit
    Fillings</a>
```

The preceding line tells the browser, "Create a link that reads *Fruit Fillings*, which points to the page `apple.html`."

In your HTML document, add the link syntax for the links in the main navigation. You don't have an HTML document to link to for "About the Author" so just use `fpo.html` (*fpo* stands for "for placement only") as a placeholder. When you're done, the syntax will read:

```
<ul id="main_navigation_list">
    <li>Crusts</li>
    <li><a href="apple.html">Fruit
        Fillings</a></li>
    <li><a href="chess.html">Custard
        &amp; Pudding Fillings</a></li>
    <li><a href="pasties.html">Savory
        Fillings</a></li>
    <li><a href="fpo.html">About the
        Author</a></li>
</ul>
```

213

Notice "Crusts" doesn't have any link syntax around it. Why? Because your page is already in the "Crusts" section of the site. Leave this for now; you'll come back to it later.

### View your web page

Save your HTML document, and view it in your browser. Yikes. That's what links look like by default (Figure 13.9). You're going to fix them in CSS.

FIGURE 13.9 By default, links are bright blue and underlined. Visited links are bright purple and underlined. In my design, the links are too big because I set the font size to 14px with the universal selector.

### Add the link syntax in CSS

You will attend to four states for each link: link, visited, hover (rollover), and active (click). Three of these states have default descriptions.

By default, unvisited links are bright blue and underlined. Visited links are bright purple and underlined. Active (clicked) links are bright red, underlined, and have a dotted outline.

Hover (rollover) links do not have a unique state unless you describe one.

The syntax for describing a link in CSS is as follows:

```
a:link{}
a:visited{}
a:hover{}
a:active{}
```

The link states must be in this order for everything to work! (An easy way to remember their order is to remember the words LoVe HAte.)

This syntax looks different from anything you've done thus far. You've used `p.class`, but not a `p:class`. You use a colon here because you are using what's called a *pseudo-class selector*. A pseudo-class acts like a class, but isn't one because it's predetermined (for instance, you don't "make up" the name for the class, the name is already established). Link pseudo-class selectors are associated with actions (such as a mouse hover or a click). Unlike classes, pseudo-classes are already recognized by the browsers and have unique functions assigned to them.

For example, `:hover` is a pseudo-class that can be used with any element and describes what should happen to that element when the mouse hovers over it.

If this makes your head hurt, that's okay. Just use these four pseudo-class selectors with the anchor selector (a) to describe how links should behave and look.

## A Fifth Link State

There is a fifth link state that I don't cover in this book: focus. The default property for focus works fine for the examples here, and I want to get you up and running with your links so I've chosen not to cover it in the lesson. But I'd be remiss if I didn't mention it.

The focus state shows nonmouse users where their keyboard focus is. That is, focus shows what link a nonmouse user is at as they tab through links on a page, or what box they're in when filling out a web-based form. Because the focus state has a default `outline` (a dotted line around the link), you do *not* have to worry about the focus state unless you are an advanced HTML and CSS user, you are using reset stylesheets, and you are zeroing the `outline` property. For more information on the focus state and accessibility, see www.456bereastreet.com/archive/201004/whenever_you_use_hover_also_use_focus/.

### Describe the links in CSS

When you designed your main navigation, you described the "links" (they weren't real links yet) in your `li` element. Now that you're making real links, you need to move most of the styling out of the `li` and into the pseudo-classes.

First, identify what styling remains constant between the four link states. For example, in my design, all four states are Georgia, 11/28px, uppercase, with 1px of letterspacing. Theoretically, I could keep font, size, line height, case, and letterspacing in my `li` element, and it would work across all four states. Then I would add unique changes to the individual pseudo-classes.

But that won't work in my design. I've used the universal selector (*) to set all text elements to 14/20px Georgia. I don't have to set the font family for the pseudo-classes, but I do have to set the font size and line height for all of them. Otherwise, they will use the font size and line height set in the universal selector.

In my design, I can only set the case and letter-spacing in the `li` element. All other styling will have to be set in the four pseudo-classes.

Thus, for my design, the syntax for the `li` and the `link` pseudo-classes end up looking like this:

```
li{
    font-size:11px;
    line-height:28px;
    list-style: none;
    text-transform:uppercase;
    letter-spacing:1px;
    display:inline;
    }

a:link{
    font-size:11px;
    line-height:28px;
    color:#000000;
    text-decoration:none;
```

```
padding-top:8px;
padding-right:10px;
padding-bottom:7px;
padding-left:10px;
background-color:#a3b2c2;
}
```

Notice that `color` and `text-decoration` are set in the pseudo-class selector. That's because links have default colors and underlines. You have to override them. Notice I've also set my padding and background color in the pseudo-class selector. That's because in my design, the background color changes between states. If your background color remains constant in all four states, then you can set your padding and background color in the `li` element.

### View your web page

Save your HTML document, and refresh your browser. The links should look like those you designed (Figure 13.10). "Crusts" may not, because it's not a link. You'll fix this later.

FIGURE 13.10 The links now look the way I want them to. *Crusts* no longer has a background because the background color is set in the a:link, not the li—and *Crusts* isn't a link.

### Add Interactivity to the Main Navigation Links

The hover, active, and visited states allow readers to interact with the links you design.

### Describe the :hover pseudo-class

What will your main navigation links look like when your reader rolls over them? Mine will primarily remain the same, changing only the background color:

```
a:hover{
    font-size:11px;
    line-height:28px;
    color:#000000;
    text-decoration:none;
    padding-top:8px;
    padding-right:10px;
    padding-bottom:7px;
    padding-left:10px;
    background-color:#e3e6e8;
}
```

### View your web page

Save your HTML document, and refresh your browser. Roll over one of the links to see your hover state.

### Describe the :active pseudo-class

What will your main navigation links look like when your reader clicks on them? Mine will primarily remain the same as the `:hover` state, only adding an underline:

```
a:active{
    font-size:11px;
    line-height:28px;
    color:#000000;
    text-decoration:underline;
    padding-top:8px;
    padding-right:10px;
```

```
padding-bottom:7px;
padding-left:10px;
background-color:#e3e6e8;
}
```

### Describe the :visited pseudo-class

What will your main navigation links look like after your reader has visited them? Mine will remain the same as the unvisited links. I don't think my readers need to know if they've visited the main sections of the site. It will be more helpful to them to know which specific recipes they have visited. I'll attend to that when we do the section links.

You are adding the syntax in the order in which a reader will interact with the links you design for them. *This is not the correct order for the syntax to work.* Add the `a:visited` *before* the `:hover` and `:active` syntax (remember, "LoVe HAte"):

```
a:visited{
    font-size:11px;
    line-height:28px;
    color:#000000;
    text-decoration:none;
    padding-top:8px;
    padding-right:10px;
    padding-bottom:7px;
    padding-left:10px;
    background-color:#a3b2c2;
}
```

### Create and Describe a "You Are Here" Class

The main navigation now looks like you want it to; however, "Crusts" doesn't because it's not a link. What do you want the "you are here" item to look like?

I want mine to have a white background, with a dotted border to the left and right that is the color of the link background. The dotted left and right border will help define the item. I've chosen not to use a bottom border so the background color will flow into the background color of the recipe page.

### Create and define a class in CSS for the line item

My class looks like this:

```
li.youarehere_main{
    padding-top:8px;
    padding-right:10px;
    padding-bottom:7px;
    padding-left:10px;
    border-left:1px dotted #a3b2c2;
    border-right:1px dotted #a3b2c2;
}
```

### Add the class in the HTML

Add the class within the `li` tag, as shown:

```
<ul id="main_navigation_list">
    <li class="youarehere_main">
        Crusts</li>
    <li><a href="apple.html">Fruit
        Fillings</a></li>
    <li><a href="chess.html">Custard
        &amp; Pudding Fillings<a></li>
    <li><a href="pasties.html">Savory
        Fillings</a></li>
    <li><a href="fpo.html">About the
        Author</a></li>
</ul>
```

### View your web page

Save your HTML document, and refresh your browser. The main navigation links are done (Figure 13.11). Next you'll do the section links.

FIGURE 13.11 With a "you are here" class applied to Crusts, the main navigation links are complete. I decided not to use a bottom border on Crusts so the background color of the "you are here" element would flow into the background color of the recipe.

## Adding the Link Syntax: Section Links

Your web page has more than one set of links. It's time to get the section links working.

### Add the section links syntax in the HTML document

In your HTML document, add the link syntax for the links in the section links. You don't have an HTML document to link to for any of the links, so just use `fpo.html` as a placeholder. You'll better experience the visited links if you add a unique word to each `fpo.html`—for example, try using `fpo_crumb.html`. When you're done, the syntax should read:

```
<ul id="section_links_list">
    <li>Butter Crust</li>
    <li><a href="fpo_crumb.html">Crumb
        Crusts</a></li>
    <li><a href="fpo_lard.html">Lard
        and Suet</a></li>
    <li><a href="fpo_savory.html">
        Savory Dough</a></li>
    <li><a href="fpo_shortbread.html">
```

```
        Shortbread Crust</a><li>
    <li><a href="fpo_sweet.html">Sweet
        Dough</a></li>
    <li><a href="fpo_wheat.html">Whole
        Wheat</a></li>
</ul>
```

Notice that "Butter Crust" doesn't have any link syntax around it. Why? Because you are already in that recipe. Leave it for now; you'll come back to it later.

### View your web page

Save your HTML document, and view it in your browser. Yikes. The section links look like the main navigation links (Figure 13.12, top)! Why? Because you've only got one kind of link described in the CSS. All links will look the same unless you set up multiple formats for the links. You're going to fix that next.

### Designate the existing pseudo-classes for main navigation links only

The pseudo-classes you set up should only be used for the main navigation links, not for every link on the page.

Put `#main_navigation_list` in front of the pseudo-classes. This tells the browser to use the pseudo-classes described only for links in the list you've called `#main_navigation_list`. All other links will use different pseudo-classes.

For example, the syntax for my main navigation `a:link` now reads as follows:

```
#main_navigation_list a:link{
    font-size:11px;
    line-height:28px;
    color:#000000;
```

```
text-decoration:none;
padding-top:8px;
padding-right:10px;
padding-bottom:7px;
padding-left:10px;
background-color:#a3b2c2;
}
```

FIGURE 13.12 *Top:* All the links look the same. You can fix this by designating where certain pseudo-classes should be used. *Bottom:* After adding #main_naviga-tion_list to the pseudo-classes, the section links return to a default state and are ready to be styled.

Make sure you do this for all four main navigation pseudo-classes!

### View your web page again

Save your HTML document, and view it in your browser. The main navigation links still look right, and the section links default to underlined blue and purple (Figure 13.12, bottom). Good. Next, you need to define the pseudo-classes for the section links.

### Describe the section links in CSS

Describe the section links like you did the links for the main navigation. This time, make it clear in the CSS that the pseudo-classes are for the section links only—put the name of the list in front of the pseudo-classes:

```
#section_links_list a:link{}
#section_links_list a:visited{}
#section_links_list a:hover{}
#section_links_list a:active{}
```

First, identify what styling remains constant between the four link states. For example, in my design, all four states are Georgia, 14/32px. The font and size are already set in the universal selector, so I don't have to style them. I do have to style the line height, and I can do that in the `li` element. The padding remains constant across all four states, but I'm using a background color that changes. So I need to set my padding in pseudo-class selectors. If your background color doesn't change, you can set your padding in the `li` element. Remember, because of default colors and underlines, you need to set `color` and `text-decoration` in your pseudo-class selectors.

For my design, the syntax for the `li` and the `link` pseudo-class ends up looking like this:

```
#section_links_list li{
    list-style: none;
    color:#364C63;
    line-height:32px;
    }
```

```
#section_links_list a:link{
    padding-top:3px;
    padding-right:1px;
    padding-bottom:3px;
    padding-left:1px;
    text-decoration:none;
    color:#364c63;
    }
```

### View your web page

Save your HTML document, and view it in your browser. The section links should look the way you want them to. Now it's time to add interactivity.

### Add Interactivity to the Section Links

The hover, active, and visited states allow readers to interact with the links you design.

### Describe the :hover pseudo-class

What will your section links look like when your reader rolls over them? Mine will primarily remain the same, changing only the background color:

```
#section_links_list a:hover{
    padding-top:3px;
    padding-right:1px;
    padding-bottom:3px;
    padding-left:1px;
    text-decoration:none;
    color:#364c63;
    background-color:#e3e6e8;
    }
```

### Describe the :active pseudo-class

What will your main navigation links look like when your reader clicks on them? Mine will primarily remain the same as the `:hover` state; only the background color will change:

```
#section_links_list a:active{
    padding-top:3px;
    padding-right:1px;
    padding-bottom:3px;
    padding-left:1px;
    text-decoration:none;
    color:#364c63;
    background-color:#c2ced6;
    }
```

### Describe the :visited pseudo-class

What will your main navigation links look like after your reader has visited them? Mine will primarily remain the same as the links; only the color will change:

```
#section_links_list a:visited{
    padding-top:3px;
    padding-right:1px;
    padding-bottom:3px;
    padding-left:1px;
    text-decoration:none;
    color:#737f8c;
    }
```

Again, you are adding the syntax in the order in which a reader will interact with the links you design for them. *This is not the correct order for the syntax to work.* Add the `a:visited` *before* the `:hover` and `:active` syntax (LoVe HAte).

**Create and Describe a "You Are Here" Class**

The section links now look the way you want them to... but "Butter Crust" doesn't because it's not a link. What do you want the "you are here" item to look like?

I want mine to have a white background, with a dotted border on the top and bottom, referencing the "you are here" in the main navigation links.

Create and define a class in CSS for the line item

My class looks like this:

```
li.youarehere_section{
    padding-top:5px;
    padding-bottom:5px;
    padding-left:1px;
    border-top:1px dotted #a3b2c2;
    border-bottom:1px dotted #a3b2c2;
    }
```

Add the class in the HTML

Add the class directly into your `li` tag, as shown:

```
<ul id="section_links_list">
    <li class="youarehere_section">
        Butter Crust</li>
    <li><a href="fpo_crumb.html">Crumb
        Crusts</a></li>
    <li><a href="fpo_lard.html">Lard
        and Suet</a></li>
    <li><a href="fpo_savory.html">
        Savory Dough</a></li>
    <li><a href="fpo_shortbread.html">
        Shortbread Crust</a><li>
    <li><a href="fpo_sweet.html">Sweet
        Dough</a></li>
    <li><a href="fpo_wheat.html">Whole
        Wheat</a></li>
</ul>
```

**View your web page**

Save your HTML document, and refresh your browser. The section links are done. You have unvisited links, visited links, a hover state, and a "you are here" item (Figure 13.13).

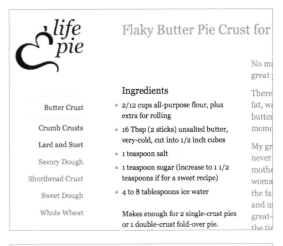

FIGURE 13.13 The section links are done. *Top:* What my links, visited links, and the "you are here" item look like. *Bottom:* My hover state adds a light blue-gray background.

## Adding the Link Syntax: Ads

The third kind of text link on the page is in the ads. If you'd like to get more practice working with links, I recommend defining your ad links. There are a couple of new things to learn.

### Designate pseudo-classes using a div ID

Use the same process you just used for the main navigation and the section links. One thing you'll find different is that the ad links are not in a list. So how will you designate the pseudo-classes for ad links only? Use a div ID.

Put the name of the ad container in front of the pseudo-classes. This tells the browser to use the pseudo-classes described only for links in that div. All other links will use different pseudo-classes.

For example, the pseudo-classes for the links in my PBS ad would be:

```
#advertisement_pbs_container a:link{}
#advertisement_pbs_container
   a:visited{}
#advertisement_pbs_container a:hover{}
#advertisement_pbs_container
   a:active{}
```

Depending on how you designed your page, each ad may need different pseudo-classes. Make as many as you need.

### Link to an external site

The ads link to hypothetical external sites. While there is not an actual *Life & Pie* show on PBS, you can still link your ad to the PBS homepage.

When linking to an external site, use the entire URL including the protocol (for example, `http://`) in your HTML syntax. The code for my link would look like this:

```
<div id="advertisement_pbs_container">
   <h4>Life &amp; Pie is on PBS!</h4>
   <p><a href="http://pbs.org">Check
      your local station.</a></p>
   </div>
```

When you are finished describing the links, you are ready to expand your design to the remaining pages in this site. You'll do that in the next chapter.

---

### Recommended Resources

For this lesson, I recommend the following on-line resources:

- To download the new pages for this lesson, visit `www.wiley.com/go/typographicwebdesign`

- To see examples of this lesson, visit `typographicwebdesign.com`

- To learn more methods for designing links with lists, I recommend Listamatic at `css.maxdesign.com.au/listamatic/`

- To learn more about pseudo-class selectors, including more about `:focus`, go to `css-tricks.com/5762-pseudo-class-selectors/`

- To pick colors for your link states, I recommend the Hues Hub at `www.december.com/html/spec/colorhues.html`

---

## Moving Forward

This chapter introduced you to designing navigation systems that communicate. Links should remain readable, and long lists of links should be chunked. The four states (link, visited, hover, active) help readers see what is clickable, as well as where they've been. The chapter also introduced you to setting the four states using pseudo-class selectors in the CSS.

In the next chapter, you will learn about applying systems across multiple web pages in a site.

# CHAPTER 14

# Applying Systems across Pages

A web page is part of a greater entity. As web typographers, we don't just design elements to create a whole page; we design a set of pages to create a whole site. Thus, we need to establish systems of voice, grid, and navigation to use across multiple pages. These systems are "rules" for combining elements to form a complex whole, so even if pages differ in the *kind* or *amount* of content, the pages still feel like part of the whole site.

## Five Reasons to Apply Systems

Designers and typographers don't just apply systems because we like them. Systems make designing—and interacting with—web sites an easier, more pleasurable experience. The following sections present five reasons why you should apply systems.

### Systems Are Easier on Your Readers
Applying systems across pages creates similarity. As readers move through a site, they learn to recognize the different voices (I am a narrative; I am a list of ingredients; I am a set of instructions;

I am a caption; I am a link to another page). They also learn where to find content on the page.

If you don't apply a consistent system, readers will have to work harder to find what they are looking for (Figure 14.1).

### You've Already Done the Hard Work. Why Start Over?
You have created chunking and hierarchy to help your readers scan the content. You have established voices so readers can identify the different elements on the page. Font, font size, line height, and div width have been set to promote reading. Headlines, text, navigation, and images have been arranged to create rhythm and tension, while not diverting readers from their quest. Why start over?

### Diverse Pages Still Feel Like Parts of a Whole
Websites can contain a variety of information. Some pages may contain primarily text, while others contain primarily images, tables, or a combination of the three. Consistency of voice, grid, and navigation helps readers recognize that diverse content is still part of a single site (Figure 14.2).

FIGURE 14.1 These two pages are part of the same site, but don't look like it. If the visual systems change throughout the site, readers have to work harder to find and identify information.

FIGURE 14.2 Systems help readers recognize that diverse content is still part of a single site (ThomasLadd.com). *Top:* An image-based page. *Bottom:* A text-based page from the same site.

## Multiple People Can Work on the Site and Retain Consistency

Websites are rarely designed, built, and maintained by a single person over a long period of time. Systems allow for various people (junior designers, contractors, clients) to expand a site or modify content while retaining consistency.

## Data-Driven Sites Create Pages on the Fly

Luckily, HTML and CSS are perfect for creating and applying systems. Using a single CSS file automatically creates a system. Using multiple CSS files based on a system creates a system with appropriate variations. Content pulled into pages from a database will follow the system you've established (Figure 14.3).

FIGURE 14.3 The pages for HistoricType.com are dynamically created. Content is stored in a MYSQL database. *Top:* An image-based page. *Bottom:* A text-based page. Images, text, and search functions were carefully considered when creating this tight system.

## Plan for Diverse Pages from the Start

The recipe lesson purposely does not contain radically diverse pages; I wanted you to focus on specific tasks. But even working with relatively similar pages, you'll find a system works better when you consider more than one page from the start. Subtle differences (length of heading, amount of text) should influence your system as you build it.

In the future, start every project by looking across the breadth of the site. Are some pages text heavy? Are others image heavy, or do they contain tabular material? Do any pages combine the three? Even if pages are similar, what are their differences?

In the future, perform the steps you did in Lessons 11 and 12 for a variety of pages simultaneously. With some negotiation, you can create a system of voice, grid, and navigation that works across the pages. Do you need to create a system of variations? If so, how many do you need? Balance variation and consistency—honor content while creating pages that feel like parts of a whole.

## Allow for Flexibility

Not all content is the same. If an element doesn't work in a carefully constructed system, create a variation. In fact, careful variations can add value to a website by helping a reader recognize when they've entered a different section of the site (Figure 14.4), or drawing attention to an important page.

**FIGURE 14.4** Careful variations add to the readers' experience. Here, a shift in color tells readers they've entered a different section of the site. *Top:* This section has more links, and needs an extra level of navigation under the main navigation across the top. *Bottom:* This section is simpler—there is no reason to use the extra level of navigation. Don't force a system that isn't necessary.

Again, balance variation with consistency—don't make your readers work harder to find what they are looking for. Above all, systems should help, not hinder.

---

### Web Pages Are Parts of a Greater Whole

To summarize, systems are most helpful when:

- Voices and placement are consistent. If you change things around, readers will have to work harder to find and understand content.

- Diverse pages are considered from the start. You can create systems that work for a variety of content.

- Variation is used (when necessary) to honor content and help the reader. Systems should help, not hinder.

---

# Lesson 14: A Recipe, Part 4

You've already designed and built a page for a crust recipe. Now it's time to expand outward—to redefine the whole. No longer confined to a single web page, you must consider a group of pages, and strive to balance consistency with flexibility. By the end of this lesson, you'll have applied systems of voice, grid, and navigation across multiple pages (Figure 14.5).

This lesson helps you achieve the following objectives:

1  Practice building multiple pages in HTML and CSS.

2  Practice negotiating content and systems. Do any pages require a variation? Would subtle variations benefit the readers' experience?

3  Pay attention to the details.

4  Promise yourself that from now on, you'll always consider more than one page when designing a site.

5  Link new pages to each other, so the pages form a web.

Even if you are already HTML/CSS savvy, follow the walk-through provided. I show you what a typographer looks for in the process.

FIGURE 14.5 By the end of this lesson, you'll have applied systems of voice, grid, and navigation across multiple pages, as in this example of the Apple Pie recipe by Chris Nelson.

## Overview of the Lesson

Make your three new HTML pages by flowing in new content. Analyze how the systems you've developed work across all four pages.

Does your design hold up across multiple pages? Would slight changes to your systems benefit the pages? Do you need to create a variant system for any of the pages? If so, can you add the variant as a class within the existing CSS?

Make changes as needed.

If the system you've carefully created for the Flaky Butter Crust recipe doesn't work as well across the other pages, don't despair. This is an important lesson to learn—a lesson that is hard to learn unless you *experience* it. Always consider multiple pages when designing a website!

## Apply the CSS to Multiple Pages

In this lesson, you'll modify the recipe from the last lesson, so make a copy of the last lesson's folder and name the new folder *14_recipe*. Keep it in the *web_typography* folder.

Rename the CSS file *recipe_systems.css*. Link it to the *index.html* file by going into the HTML file and changing the syntax in the head element to the following:

```
<link href="recipe_systems.css"
   rel="stylesheet" type="text/css" />
```

Change the title as shown:

```
<title>Lesson 14: Recipe
   (Apply System)</title>
```

### Download the text and images for the new pages

Access the text and image files for this lesson from the book's companion website at www.wiley. com/go/typographicwebdesign. Once you have downloaded them, put them in a new folder called *resources* in your *14_recipe* folder.

### Create a New Web Page

There are many ways to create web pages. Because you are creating a system (and not producing dynamic pages), you'll make the new web pages for this lesson by repeatedly saving the existing page with a new name each time.

### Create apple.html

Open *index.html*, and save it as *apple.html*. The prompt will ask if you want to replace the existing *apple.html*. Click yes. The existing file is the FPO (for placement only) page you used in the last lesson.

### Flow in the content

Open *14_apple_pie_recipe.doc*. Find the title of the recipe. Copy and paste it into the *apple.html* file, replacing the title of the crust recipe. Do the same with the narrative, ingredients, directions, and caption—taking care to paste content between the appropriate HTML tags.

For example, the HTML syntax for my title recipe went from this:

```
<div id="recipe_title_container">
   <h1>Flaky Butter Pie Crust for
   Sweet or Savory Pies</h1>
</div>
```

to this:

```
<div id="recipe_title_container">
   <h1>Apple Pie</h1>
</div>
```

**View your web page often as you paste in new content**

Save your HTML document and view it in your browser. At some point, something might go wrong. If you check the web page often, it will be easier to fix mistakes.

### Identify and Fix Problems

When you are done placing the Apple Pie recipe content into the system, you'll probably see things that don't work the way you want them to. Your design is different from mine, so I can't tell you exactly what problems you'll see and how to fix them, but I can show you some of the problems I needed to fix. This will help you see the process—it will give you tips on how to approach modifying your system as needed.

First, write down the problems you see. Then, fix them one at a time. Tackling problems one by one will make the task manageable. Most changes can be done directly in the HTML (change a word, add a tag, create a link). But some fixes require CSS changes.

**View your web page often**

Save your HTML document and view it in your browser every time you fix a problem. Sometimes fixing one problem creates another—as you'll see in the following sections from the problems I fixed in my design. If you view your web page often, it will be easier to immediately catch and fix new problems.

### How I Fixed the Problems in My System

As recommended earlier, I started by noting what needed to change, and tackled the changes one by one. I started from the top of the page, and worked my way down, viewing the page in my browser at every step.

**I moved short recipe titles over**

The title *Apple Pie* is too short to work in my system. Colorwise, it feels like it should belong with the memory text, but the placement suggests it belongs with the ingredients list. To fix this, I created an h1 with a custom class to make short recipe titles line up with the memory text (Figure 14.6).

The CSS looks like this:

```
h1.short{
    padding-left:330px;
    }
```

The HTML looks like this:

```
<div id="recipe_title_container">
    <h1 class="short">Apple Pie</h1>
</div>
```

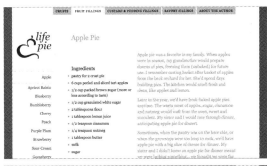

**FIGURE 14.6** *Top:* In my design, short recipe names floated over the ingredients. *Bottom:* I moved short recipe names over to line up with the memory text, using an h1 with a class.

**I updated the picture and then fixed the gap on the right**

The page had the wrong picture in it. I fixed this by moving *14_applepie.jpg* into the *images* folder and changing the HTML as follows:

```
<img src="images/14_applepie.jpg">
```

But the apple pie picture is narrower than the butter crust picture. It created an odd gap between the image and the directions (Figure 14.7). To fix this, I created a class to float the image right and added a bit of space beneath it (floating the image right makes the top padding on the caption stop working in some browsers). Here is the CSS:

```
.short_picture{
    float:right;
    padding-bottom:10px;
    }
```

The HTML looks like this:

```
<img src="images/14_applepie.jpg"
    class="short_picture">
```

**I chunked the caption into two paragraphs and then fixed the paragraph spacing**

The caption for the apple pie picture was too long to live in only one paragraph; I split it into two paragraphs. When I did this, the caption had huge paragraph spacing because the p.caption class inherited the bottom margin used for the p element (Figure 14.8). To fix this, I specified a smaller bottom margin on the p.caption class, like this:

```
.caption{
    padding-left:75px;
```

```
    padding-top:10px;
    margin-bottom:0px;
    font-style:italic;
    color:#B29E4D;
    }
```

**I made the heading language and chunking consistent**

When I flowed in the text, I realized the instructions use different language for the headings. The butter crust recipe uses the term *Directions*, while the apple pie recipe uses the term *Preparation*. I recommend keeping the term consistent, and fixed this by changing the heading language. All of my pages will use the term *Directions*. (In the real world, check with your client or editor regarding word choice.)

The instructions in the apple pie recipe also lack chunking. I created subheadings to break down the process for readers. (Again, always check with your client or editor.)

**I added space below my h3**

When I added subheadings to the apple pie directions, the space between the subheadings and the text below them felt too tight. The spacing felt fine in the butter crust recipe because each subhead was followed by a note about time—making the subheads feel more spacious.

I ended up adding 3 pixels of bottom padding on the h3 element. The space improved the apple pie recipe and did not negatively impact the butter crust recipe.

the recipe as
varieties.

## Directions

**PREPARE THE**
Prepare the Fla
instructed. Put
(with the remai

**PREPARE THE**
In a large bowl
ground cinnam
at room temper
saucepan, lettin
Add 2 tablespo
to a low boil. B
syrupy and ligh

**BUILD THE PI**
Preheat the ove
to a large bowl
flour). Pour the
the apples and

*Macerating the apples in sugar and spices for a few hours removes their water before baking. This results in a firmer, fuller pie.*

*The juices are boiled down and poured back into the pie before baking, so we won't lose a bit of flavor.*

the recipe as
varieties.

## Directions

**PREPARE THE**
Prepare the Fla
instructed. Put
(with the remai

**PREPARE THE**
In a large bowl
ground cinnam
at room temper
saucepan, lettin
Add 2 tablespo
to a low boil. B
syrupy and ligh

**BUILD THE PI**
Preheat the ove
to a large bowl
flour). Pour the
the apples and

*Macerating the apples in sugar and spices for a few hours removes their water before baking. This results in a firmer, fuller pie.*

*The juices are boiled down and poured back into the pie before baking, so we won't lose a bit of flavor.*

**FIGURE 14.7** *Top:* The narrower apple pie picture created a gap of space on the right. *Bottom:* I created a class to float the image right. This restored the strong vertical line created by a consistent gutter, which improves visual tension.

the recipe as needed t
varieties.

## Directions

**PREPARE THE CRUST**
Prepare the Flaky Butter
instructed. Put the prepa
(with the remaining ball

**PREPARE THE APPLES**
In a large bowl combine
ground cinnamon, nutme
at room temperature for
saucepan, letting the app
Add 2 tablespoons of uns
to a low boil. Boil over m
syrupy and lightly caram

**BUILD THE PIE**
Preheat the oven to 425°
large bowl and mix them
Pour the reduced syrup o

*Macerating the apples in sugar and spices for a few hours removes their water before baking. This results in a firmer, fuller pie.*

*The juices are boiled down and poured back into the pie before baking, so we won't lose a bit of flavor.*

the recipe as needed t
varieties.

## Directions

**PREPARE THE CRUST**
Prepare the Flaky Butter
instructed. Put the prepa
(with the remaining ball

**PREPARE THE APPLES**
In a large bowl combine
ground cinnamon, nutme
at room temperature for
saucepan, letting the app
Add 2 tablespoons of uns
to a low boil. Boil over m
syrupy and lightly caram

**BUILD THE PIE**
Preheat the oven to 425°
large bowl and mix them
Pour the reduced syrup o

*Macerating the apples in sugar and spices for a few hours removes their water before baking. This results in a firmer, fuller pie.*

*The juices are boiled down and poured back into the pie before baking, so we won't lose a bit of flavor.*

**FIGURE 14.8** *Top:* A caption with two paragraphs has too much paragraph spacing. *Bottom:* Clearing out the bottom margin inherited from the p element fixes the problem.

**I updated the section links, and then fixed the two-line links**

The page had the wrong links in it; it still showed the section links for crusts. I fixed this by putting the correct links in the `section_links_list`. But one of the links for the Fruit Fillings section is a Sour-Cream Gooseberry pie. The name of the pie is so long it breaks into two lines. The links are spaced vertically using `line-height:32px`, so the two-line link felt like two separate links!

At first, I fixed this by creating a class for the two-line links. The class has a tighter line height, but a little top and bottom padding keep the entire link properly spaced in the list (Figure 14.9).

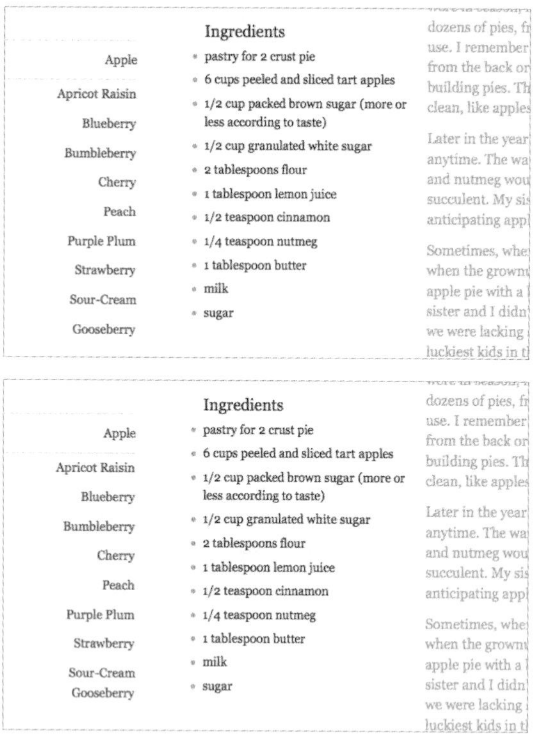

FIGURE 14.9 *Top:* A two-line link (Sour-Cream Gooseberry) looks like two separate links. *Bottom:* Tightening the line height helps the two-line link look like a single link.

The CSS clearly specifies the ID and element (`li`):

```
#section_links_list li.double-line{
    line-height:16px;
    padding-top:6px;
    padding-bottom:6px;
    }
```

Here's the HTML:

```
<li class="double-line">
<a href="fpo.html">Sour-Cream
    Gooseberry</a>
</li>
```

**I realized one of my systems needed to change**

If I need to fix two-line links with a class, the system may not be working as well as it could. Chances are there will be more two-line links to deal with, and I don't want to have to apply a class to each one, so I decided to fix the original vertical spacing system.

I removed the class, and changed the vertical spacing system for the `li` to accommodate the needs of the two-line links. The original `li` for the section links had a `line-height` of 32px:

```
#section_links_list li{
    list-style:none;
    color:#364C63;
    line-height:32px;
    }
```

I tightened the `line-height` so two-line links chunk properly. Top and bottom padding keep the open vertical spacing between all links in the list.

Here is the new CSS:

```
#section_links_list li{
    list-style:none;
    color:#364C63;
    line-height:16px;
    padding-top:8px;
    padding-bottom:8px;
    }
```

Links styled with the new system look just like the links in the original design, and the new system solves the vertical spacing problem. Now I don't have to apply a class to every two-line link.

### I updated the "you are here" list item

The page had the wrong list item specified as "you are here"—it still said I was in the Crust section. I made the Crust section an active link to the *index. html* page, removed the link syntax from the Fruit Fillings list item, and made Fruit Fillings the "you are here" list item.

### I made the section list "you are here" item stand out more

With the short recipe name moved over and placed above the memory text, I felt like the "you are here" item in the section list needed to stand out more. It was too subtle to help a reader see immediately what page in the section they're on. I fixed this by changing the color in the section_links_list li so it matches the color of the recipe name (Figure 14.10).

Here is the CSS code:

```
#section_links_list li{
    list-style:none;
    color:#bfa640;
    line-height:32px;
    }
```

**FIGURE 14.10** *Top:* The "you are here" item is the same color as the links. It's too subtle. *Bottom:* Making the "you are here" item the same color as the recipe name helps emphasize what page the reader is on.

**I made the footer information more separate from the text**

When I flowed in the apple pie directions, the space between the directions and the footer information below them felt too tight. The footer felt like an extension of the directions. I fixed this by adding space and a subtle rule line between the footer and the directions (Figure 14.11).

The CSS for the `p.footer` now looks like this:

```
p.footer{
    margin-top:75px;
    padding-top:3px;
    border-top:1px dotted #a3b2c2;
    }
```

**I created in-line links for the text**

When I flowed in the apple pie directions, I suddenly needed an in-line link at the start of the directions ("Prepare the Flaky Butter Pie Crust..."). When I added the link syntax to link the text back to the Flaky Butter Crust page, the link used default colors and an underline (Figure 14.12). Why? Because all of my link states are specific to lists and divs. I don't have any plain link states to use for regular links in the text.

To fix this, I created "plain" pseudo-class selectors for links in the CSS:

```
a:link{
    text-decoration:none;
    color:#364C63;
    }
```

```
a:visited{
    text-decoration:none;
    color:#737F8C;
    }
```

```
a:hover{
    text-decoration:none;
    color:#364C63;
    background:#E3E6E8;
    }
```

```
a:active{
    text-decoration:none;
    color:#364C63;
    background:#C2CED6;
    }
```

**BAKE**
Place pie on a baking sheet (to catch juices) on an oven rack set at the lowest level in the oven.

Bake for 30 minutes.

Cover the edges of the pie with aluminum foil to prevent over-browning, and return to oven.

Bake for an additional 15–25 minutes, or until the juices start to bubble up trough the slits and the apples feel tender, not mushy when tested with a fork.

Cool for 3–4 hours before cutting.

Stores at room temperature for 2 to 3 days.

Life and Pie J. Smith, © 2010    Web Design by Laura Franz

**BAKE**
Place pie on a baking sheet (to catch juices) on an oven rack set at the lowest level in the oven.

Bake for 30 minutes.

Cover the edges of the pie with aluminum foil to prevent over-browning, and return to oven.

Bake for an additional 15–25 minutes, or until the juices start to bubble up trough the slits and the apples feel tender, not mushy when tested with a fork.

Cool for 3–4 hours before cutting.

Stores at room temperature for 2 to 3 days.

Life and Pie J. Smith, © 2010    Web Design by Laura Franz

FIGURE 14.11 *Top:* The footer was too close to the directions, and looked like an extension of the directions. *Bottom:* Adding more space and a subtle rule above the footer fixed the problem.

## Directions

**PREPARE THE CRUST**
Prepare the Flaky Butter Pie Crust. Roll and line a pie dish as instructed. Put the prepared piecrust into the refrigerator (with the remaining ball of dough) to chill.

**PREPARE THE APPLES**
In a large bowl combine sliced apples, sugar, lemon juice, ground cinnamon, nutmeg, and salt. Let the apples macerate at room temperature for about two hours. Strain into a saucepan, letting the apples drain for about 15–30 minutes. Add 2 tablespoons of unsalted butter to the juices and bring to a low boil. Boil over medium height heat until the liquid is syrupy and lightly caramelized.

## Directions

**PREPARE THE CRUST**
Prepare the Flaky Butter Pie Crust. Roll and line a pie dish as instructed. Put the prepared piecrust into the refrigerator (with the remaining ball of dough) to chill.

**PREPARE THE APPLES**
In a large bowl combine sliced apples, sugar, lemon juice, ground cinnamon, nutmeg, and salt. Let the apples macerate at room temperature for about two hours. Strain into a saucepan, letting the apples drain for about 15–30 minutes. Add 2 tablespoons of unsalted butter to the juices and bring to a low boil. Boil over medium height heat until the liquid is syrupy and lightly caramelized.

**FIGURE 14.12** *Top:* An in-line link uses default colors and underline. *Bottom:* Creating "plain" pseudo-class selectors in the CSS fixed this problem.

### I fixed all punctuation as needed

As always, I made sure to use the proper syntax for curly quotes (`&ldquo;` and `&rdquo;`), apostrophes (`&rsquo;`), and em (`&mdash;`) and en (`&ndash;`) dashes. I also made sure to use the proper syntax for the degree symbol (`&deg;`). Again, a good resource for character entity codes is available at `digitalmediaminute.com/reference/entity/index.php`.

## Build the Rest of the Recipe Pages

Repeat the process to set the last two recipes: Chess Pie and Allie's Meat Pasty. As you apply the systems, be willing to make modifications or add new syntax. When you apply the systems to the savory recipe (Allie's Meat Pasty), for instance, you may need to create in-line links specifically for the memory text. I know I did.

### I needed to create in-line links for the memory text

When I flowed in the content for Allie's Meat Pasty, I turned "lard and suet" and "sweet dough" into links. The links used the "plain" link states I created for the Apple Pie recipe, and didn't look right. The links were too small and dark in the memory text. I fixed this by making another group of pseudo-class selectors—this time associating the link states with the `p.memory` class (Figure 14.13).

The new link states look like this in the CSS:

```
p.memory a:link{
    text-decoration:none;
    font-size:16px;
    color:#8F99A3;
    }

p.memory a:visited{
    text-decoration:none;
    font-size:16px;
    color:#737F8C;
    }

p.memory a:hover{
    text-decoration:none;
    font-size:16px;
    color:#364C63;
    background:#E3E6E8;
    }
```

```
p.memory a:active{
    text-decoration:none;
    font-size:16px;
    color:#364C63;
    background:#C2CED6;
    }
```

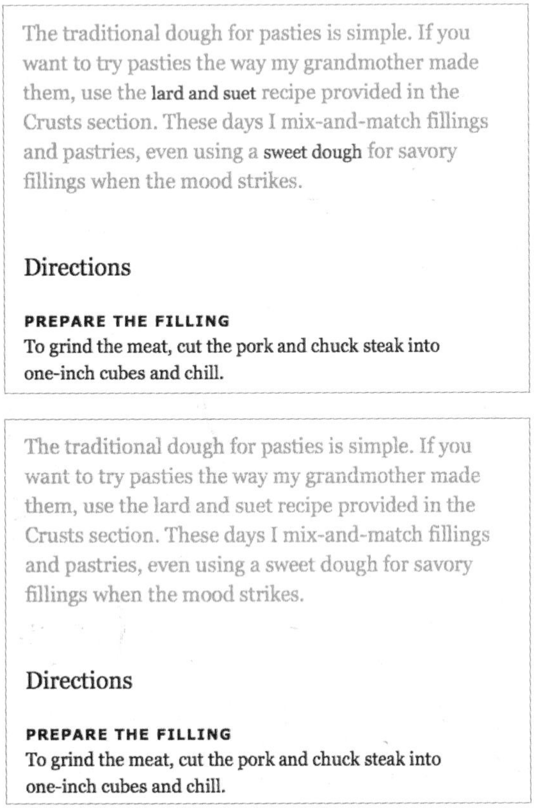

The traditional dough for pasties is simple. If you want to try pasties the way my grandmother made them, use the **lard and suet** recipe provided in the Crusts section. These days I mix-and-match fillings and pastries, even using a **sweet dough** for savory fillings when the mood strikes.

### Directions

**PREPARE THE FILLING**
To grind the meat, cut the pork and chuck steak into one-inch cubes and chill.

The traditional dough for pasties is simple. If you want to try pasties the way my grandmother made them, use the lard and suet recipe provided in the Crusts section. These days I mix-and-match fillings and pastries, even using a sweet dough for savory fillings when the mood strikes.

### Directions

**PREPARE THE FILLING**
To grind the meat, cut the pork and chuck steak into one-inch cubes and chill.

**FIGURE 14.13** *Top:* An in-line link uses the "plain" pseudo-class selectors, and the text is too small and dark for the memory text. *Bottom:* Creating another set of pseudo-class selectors to be used with the p.memory class fixed this problem.

When you are done building all of the recipe pages, it is time to move on to the next chapter.

### Recommended Resources

For this lesson, I recommend the following on-line resources:

- To download the text and images for this lesson, go to `www.wiley.com/go/typographic webdesign`

- To see examples of this lesson, go to `typographicwebdesign.com`

## Moving Forward

This chapter introduced you to applying systems of voice, grid, and navigation across multiple pages in a website. The chapter also introduced you to creating flexible solutions for a system as needed. Classes truly are important tools for web typographers!

In the next chapter, you will learn about options for choosing and incorporating new fonts into your website.

# Interlude: Building a Font Library

*Selecting type with wit and wisdom requires knowledge of how and why letterforms evolved.*

ELLEN LUPTON, THINKING WITH TYPE (2004)

# CHAPTER 15

# Building a Font Library

A good web typographer can create countless lovely, readable web pages armed with nothing but Verdana and Georgia. But having a variety of web fonts to work with opens up a world of possibilities: New forms and subtle layers of meaning influence how readers experience the text. Thus, you need to carefully build a "library" of fonts: a list of quality fonts you can count on when setting typographic web pages. It helps to know three things when building a font library: classification (based on the history of type), how to identify a good font, and how to access good fonts.

## Classification

Typographers classify fonts—grouping them together based on form. It's like classifying cars: hatchback, sedan, wagon, SUV—classification allows us to create general mental models and helps us talk about fonts. Classification helps us picture what a font might look like—even if we've never seen it. It also helps us choose fonts appropriate for the medium (screen) and content.

Many classification systems have been developed over the years. One such system is the Vox-ATypI

system (`en.wikipedia.org/wiki/VOX-ATypI_classification`), which makes it possible to classify typefaces into 11 general groups. Robert Bringhurst, author of *The Elements of Typographic Style*, developed a 13-class system aligned with shifts in Western Art history starting with the early Renaissance.

While complex classification systems are great for the true typophile, and allow type designers to discuss subtle differences in serifs, terminals, and stroke weight, they aren't easy to use. They require expert knowledge of type history, form, and letter-making techniques. For a basic overview of the both the history of type and general shifts in *letterforms* (the forms of the letters), I recommend a simpler classification system: the five families of type.

## Five Families of Type

The Five Families of Type consists of five general categories: Old Style, Transitional, Modern, Slab Serif, and Sans Serif (Figures 15.1 to 15.3). Usually we add a sixth category when discussing fonts: Display Faces, meant for headlines only (never for text).

# read read

FIGURE 15.1 *Left:* Andron, an Old Style web font. *Right:* Georgia, a Transitional web-safe font. Both are set at 72px.

# read read

FIGURE 15.2 *Left:* Serif 72 Beta, a web font with Modern elements. *Right:* Museo Slab, a Slab Serif web font. Both are set at 72px.

# read read

FIGURE 15.3 *Left:* PT Sans, a humanist Sans Serif font. *Right:* Museo Sans, a geometric Sans Serif font. Sans Serif fonts can vary greatly. Both are set at 72px.

The Five Families of Type is a good system to start with for classifying fonts. It does not require an expansive knowledge of type history or the eye to differentiate between a dozen (or more) "classes" of fonts. In addition, the terms are commonly used by other typographers (even if they prefer a different classification system, they'll know these terms, too).

But there are two problems with this classification system. First, it is too general. For example, Sans Serif typefaces can vary greatly from each other. The term *Sans Serif* does not help us "picture" a font.

Second, it is based on fonts (typefaces) developed for print. Good web fonts tend to have a different internal structure than typefaces developed for print. Designers who work in both web and print mediums will have to develop different mental models for each term.

## Expanding the Five Families Classification System

Because the Five Families of Type classification system is too general, we can use adjectives to help typographers better visualize fonts. Two adjectives I'll use in this chapter are *humanist* and *geometric*.

More detailed classification systems use the term *humanist* for the earliest roman fonts (Figure 15.4). Humanist/Venetian fonts are older than Old Style fonts. Humanist is also used with Sans Serif fonts to describe letters that reference the human hand.

# read read

FIGURE 15.4 *Left:* Calluna has some humanist elements, such as the rising crossbar on the *e* and the pen-formed terminal on the *a*. Calluna, by Jos Buivenga, is a web font and holds up well on the screen. *Right:* Centaur, a humanist-inspired font for print. Both are set at 72px.

## Old Style

Old Style fonts feel more traditional or "old." They are based on forms created by writing letters with pen and ink, but are not calligraphic or script fonts. Adobe Garamond (print) and Andron (print and web) are examples of Old Style fonts (Figure 15.5).

# read read

FIGURE 15.5 *Left:* Andron, an Old Style web font by Andreas Stötzner. Unfortunately, it lacks legibility at small text sizes on the web, due to its small x-height and small closed counters in the *a* and *e*. *Right:* Adobe Garamond, a digital version of an Old Style font (originally attributed to Claude Garamond) for print. Both are set at 72px.

Old Style fonts have pen-formed terminals (Figure 15.6), wedge-shaped serifs (also called "adnate" serifs) that flow into the stems of the letters (Figure 15.7), and less contrast between thick and thin strokes (Figure 15.8). They also have a diagonal stress (Figure 15.9). The "stress" is the imaginary line drawn between the thinnest parts of the bowl. All of these structural elements mimic letters formed by pen and ink.

FIGURE 15.6 *Left:* Andron. Old Style fonts mimic pen-formed letters. They have pen-formed terminals and a smaller x-height. *Right:* Compare to Georgia, a Transitional font. Both are set at 90px.

FIGURE 15.7 *Left:* Andron. Old Style fonts have adnate serifs—they flow into the stem. Head serifs are wedge-shaped. Foot serifs have curved bottoms. *Right:* Compare to Georgia, a Transitional font. Both are set at 90px.

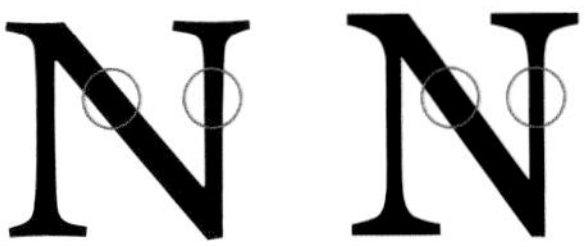

FIGURE 15.8 *Left:* Andron. Old Style fonts have less contrast between the thick and thin strokes in letters. *Right:* Compare to Georgia, a Transitional font. Both are set at 90px.

FIGURE 15.9 *Left:* Andron. Old Style fonts have a slanted stress (the invisible line between the thinnest parts of the bowl). *Right:* Compare to Georgia, a Transitional font. Both are set at 90px.

Old Style fonts designed for print have smaller x-heights and small closed counters on the lower-case *a* and *e*. Good web fonts deviate from this structure in order to retain legibility.

Old Style fonts can be used for text or headlines, and give a traditional or "old" feeling to the text, partially because they are reminiscent of the mid-fifteenth to mid-eighteenth centuries. They need to be set larger because of their small x-height.

Beware fonts that have overly emphasized pen-formed terminals and serifs—they can draw attention to themselves and undermine the flow of words.

**Transitional**

Transitional fonts feel traditional, but are "crisper" than Old Style fonts. More concerned with ideal letters than pen-formed letters, Transitional fonts have teardrop-shaped terminals (Figure 15.10, left), more contrast between thick and thin strokes (Figure 15.11, left), and generally horizontal serifs that flow into the stems of the letters (Figure 15.12, left). Stress tends to be more vertical, and changes as needed throughout the font (Figure 15.13, left).

fa fa fa

FIGURE 15.10 *Left:* Georgia. Transitional fonts have teardrop-shaped terminals. *Middle:* Although Serif 72 Beta still has teardrop-shaped terminals, they are crisper, which makes the font feel Modern onscreen. *Right:* Bodoni BE. Modern fonts have ball-shaped terminals. All are set at 90px.

N N N

FIGURE 15.11 *Left:* Georgia. Transitional fonts have contrast between thick and thin strokes. *Middle:* Serif 72 Beta's high contrast between thick and thin strokes makes the font feel Modern on the screen. *Right:* Bodoni BE. Modern fonts have extreme contrast between thick and thin strokes. All are set at 90px.

dn dn dn

FIGURE 15.12 *Left:* Georgia. Transitional fonts have crisp adnate (flowing into the stem) serifs. *Middle:* Although Serif 72 Beta's serifs aren't Modern, the thin foot serifs make the font feel Modern onscreen. *Right:* Bodoni BE. Modern fonts have very fine serifs that meet the stem at a right angle. All are set at 90px.

oe oe oe

FIGURE 15.13 *Left:* Georgia. Transitional fonts have a slight, nonuniform stress. *Middle:* Serif 72 Beta. Serif 72 clearly has a Transitional stress. *Right:* Bodoni BE. Modern fonts have a vertical stress. All are set at 90px.

Transitional fonts were originally designed in the mid-eighteenth century with control (of form, of the printing process) in mind. A well-known Transitional font for print is Baskerville (Figure 15.14, right), designed by John Baskerville, who dedicated most of his career to controlling the printing process. He created new techniques for making and drying paper and ink. His contemporaries accused him of trying to blind his readers with his higher-contrast typefaces.

A well-known Transitional web font is Georgia (Figure 15.14, left). Transitional web fonts continue to have teardrop-shaped terminals and crisp, adnate serifs, but lose the delicate beauty associated with Transitional print fonts.

read read

FIGURE 15.14 *Left:* Georgia, a Transitional web-safe font designed by Matthew Carter. Designed for the screen, it has more substantial strokes, larger closed counterforms in the *a* and *e*, a larger x-height, and more defined terminals than you'd usually see in a traditional Transitional font. *Right:* A contemporary version of Baskerville (Monotype), a Transitional font originally designed for print by John Baskerville. Both are set at 72px.

Transitional fonts can be used for text or headlines, and give a traditional feeling to the text without feeling quite so "old."

**Modern/Didone**

Modern fonts feel very crisp and elegant. They are based on drawn letterforms with extreme contrast of thicks and thins (Figure 15.11, right), ball-shaped terminals (Figure 15.10, right), and thin, delicate serifs that create a crisp corner with the stem (Figure 15.12, right). They also have a vertical stress (Figure 15.13, right).

Modern fonts are not contemporary; they were modern in the late eighteenth century. Continued advancements in printing technology and paper allowed for such crisp, elegant letterforms to be printed cleanly. This classification is sometimes called *Didone* after the first Modern font. Another well-known Modern font for print is Bodoni (Figure 15.15, right). Serif 72 Beta is a web font with both Transitional and Modern characteristics (Figure 15.15, left). It's gorgeous at large sizes, but difficult to read as text.

# read read

FIGURE 15.15 *Left:* Serif 72 Beta, a web font with both Transitional and Modern characteristics designed by Christian Robertson (Betatype). *Right:* A contemporary version of Bodoni (BE), a Modern font originally designed for print by Giambattista Bodoni. Both are set at 72px.

Modern fonts should never be used for text, as their thin strokes get lost on the screen. They are great for headlines, and add elegance to a typographic layout.

## Slab Serif

Slab Serif fonts were originally designed to say, "Look at me!" Characterized by uniform strokes (Figure 15.16) and heavy serifs equal to the strokes (Figure 15.17), Slab Serif fonts came of age during the Industrial Revolution in the early nineteenth century.

Changes in printing and paper-making technology allowed for increased (quick, inexpensive) advertising. Fonts shifted use from subtle text in books to loud words on broadsides (posters).

Traditionally, Slab Serif serifs are *unbracketed*—they are not adnate. They do not flow into the stem

(Figure 15.17). Slab Serifs are the same thickness as the other horizontal strokes in letters, and can be blunt and square or rounded (Figure 15.18).

As with every class in this system, there are a variety of Slab Serif fonts. Some contemporary Slab Serif fonts (Figures 15.16 to 15.20) have contrast between thick and thin strokes. Serifs end up thinner than traditional Slab Serif serifs. Geometric Slab Serif fonts have a mathematical consistency to them. Museo Slab is a Slab Serif font with geometric characteristics, while DejaVu Serif is not geometric (Figure 15.21). Both are available for font-linking.

Traditional Slab Serifs should be used with care in text. Thick strokes and serifs can result in smaller counterforms, and reduced space hinders legibility. Look for a Slab Serif with open counterforms, a generous amount of space between letters, and more delicate strokes, like Museo Slab and DejaVu Serif.

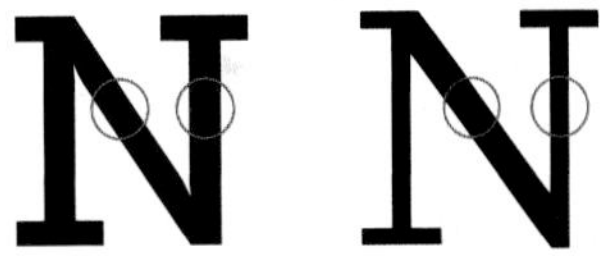

FIGURE 15.16 *Left:* Museo Slab. Traditionally monoline, Slab Serif fonts do not have an appreciable contrast between thick and thin strokes. *Right:* DejaVu Serif is a contemporary Slab Serif font. Both are set at 90px.

# dn dn

FIGURE 15.17 *Left:* Museo Slab. Slab Serif serifs are unbracketed, or not adnate; they meet the stem at a right angle. Serifs are the same weight as the other horizontal strokes in the letters. *Right:* DejaVu Serif. Both are set at 90px.

FIGURE 15.18 *Left:* A contemporary version of Rockwell, from the Monotype library. Serifs are square. *Right:* A contemporary version of Courier, originally designed by Howard "Bud" Kettler for IBM. Serifs are rounded. Both are set at 66px.

FIGURE 15.19 *Left:* Museo Slab. Slab Serif fonts were originally monoline. Strokes ended abruptly and did not create a terminal shape. *Right:* DejaVu Serif is a contemporary Slab Serif font. Both are set at 90px.

FIGURE 15.20 *Left:* Museo Slab. Traditionally monoline, Slab Serif fonts do not have a stress; bowls are usually circular. *Right:* DejaVu Serif is a contemporary Slab Serif font. Both are set at 90px.

FIGURE 15.21 *Left:* Museo Slab is a Slab Serif font by Jos Buivenga. Designed for print, it has consistent strokes, round bowls, and a mathematical consistency to the letters. Due to open counterforms and generous letterspacing, the font remains legible on screen. *Right:* DejaVu Serif is a Slab Serif font with a narrower bowl, chiseled terminals, and contrast between thick and thin strokes. Both are available for font-linking. Both are set at 66px.

## Sans Serif

Sans Serif fonts (Figures 15.22 through 15.28) feel more contemporary than serif fonts, even though

sans serif letters have been around since the Fifth century BCE.

Characterized by uniform strokes (Figure 15.22) and no serifs (Figure 15.23), Sans Serif fonts are often associated with the twentieth century because they gained popularity after World War I. Helvetica (Figure 15.26, right) is probably the most well-known Sans Serif. Arial (Figure 15.26, left) was one of the original Sans Serif fonts created for (as opposed to designed for) the screen.

Like every class in the system, there are a variety of Sans Serif fonts. Sans Serif fonts can be used for either text or headlines.

**Geometric Sans Serif** fonts have a mathematical consistency to them; their bowls tend to be perfect circles. Museo (available for font-linking) and Futura (print) are geometric Sans Serif fonts (Figure 15.27).

**Humanist Sans Serif** fonts reference the human hand. Gill Sans (print) and Verdana (web) are humanist Sans Serif fonts (Figure 15.28). With modulating strokes, they feel less mechanical than other Sans Serif fonts.

FIGURE 15.22 *Left:* PT Sans. Sans Serif fonts do not have an appreciable contrast between thick and thin strokes. *Right:* Museo Sans. Both are set at 90px.

FIGURE 15.23 *Left:* PT Sans. Sans Serif fonts do not have serifs. *Right:* Museo Sans. Both are set at 90px.

FIGURE 15.24 *Left:* PT Sans. Humanist Sans Serif fonts tend to have a modulated stroke; terminals do not have an extra shape. *Right:* Museo Sans, a geometric Sans Serif, has more monoline strokes. Both are set at 90px.

oe oe

FIGURE 15.25 *Left:* PT Sans. Sans Serif fonts do not usually have a true stress because strokes are usually monoline. *Right:* Museo Sans. Both are set at 90px.

read read

FIGURE 15.26 *Left:* Arial. Created but not designed for the screen by Monotype, Arial lacks generosity of x-height, counterforms, and letterspacing, all of which promote legibility onscreen. *Right:* A contemporary version of Helvetica, designed by Max Miedinger, a Sans Serif font design for print. Both are Neo-Grotesque Sans Serif (also called Anonymous Sans Serif due to their plain appearance). Both are set at 72px.

read read

FIGURE 15.27 *Left:* Museo Sans, designed by Jos Buivenga, has a "double-decker" *a*. *Right:* A contemporary version of Futura, designed by Paul Renner for print. Most geometric Sans Serif fonts have a "single-decker" *a* (the *a* is a circle with a line on one side), making them feel even more geometric. Both are set at 72px.

read read

FIGURE 15.28 *Left:* Verdana, designed by Matthew Carter, is a humanist Sans Serif font designed for the web. Referencing the hand, humanist Sans Serif fonts usually have modulated strokes, narrower bowls, and open apertures. *Right:* A contemporary version of Gill Sans designed by Eric Gill for print. Both are set at 72px.

## Display Fonts

Display fonts are used for large type (headings, pull quotes) only. They are not appropriate for text. Classification of display fonts is less consistent than text fonts. They are often grouped according to a single characteristic—distressed/grunge, retro, script, art deco, and so on. But display fonts are so varied, they are difficult to describe using a single term. For instance, some of my favorite display fonts are Selfish (a distressed, elegant script), BlackJack (a script with some lovely thicks and thins), and EastMarket (a retro font with soft corners, substantial thick strokes, and a funky lowercase *s*).

## Identifying Good Web Fonts

A good web font makes no excuses. It never says, "If only you could see me in print." For example, an exquisitely designed font with extremely thin strokes and delicate serifs might be beautiful printed on high quality paper, but if strokes and serifs get lost on the screen, it's not a good web font. Always evaluate web fonts based on how they perform onscreen, not in print.

### Good Text Fonts for the Web

What qualities should you look for when choosing text fonts for the web? A good web text font usually has a generous x-height, open counterforms, and a generous aperture (Figure 15.29). It has generous (but not too generous) letterspacing (Figure 15.30).

It does not have thin strokes or delicate serifs, which can get lost on the screen (Figure 15.31). Nor does it have strident serifs or terminals (which draw attention to themselves and undermine the flow of words).

| A good web font has a generous x-height and open counterforms. | A good web font has a generous x-height and open counterforms. |
| --- | --- |

FIGURE 15.29 *Left:* Calluna is more legible because it has a generous x-height and open apertures (though the font is not as smooth on Windows). *Right:* Andron is less legible at text sizes due to a smaller x-height and smaller closed counterforms in the *a* and *e*.

| A good web font has generous (but not too generous) letterspacing. | A good web font has generous (but not too generous) letterspacing. |
| --- | --- |

FIGURE 15.30 *Left:* PT Sans has generous letterspacing, which helps with readability onscreen. *Right:* Droid Sans's letterspacing is a little too loose, and undermines readability.

| A good web font does not have delicate strokes or serifs. | A good web font does not have delicate strokes or serifs. |
| --- | --- |

FIGURE 15.31 *Left:* DejaVu Serif has a contrast between thick and thin lines, but remains legible onscreen at text sizes. *Right:* Serif 72 Beta's thin strokes and serifs are too delicate. The font is hard to read at text sizes onscreen.

A great web text font has all of the characteristics already mentioned, plus multiple styles (roman, italic, bold) to meet your needs (even a simple bibliography needs a good italic). A great web text font works well as text but also looks great big (for headings).

Some delightful and well-designed web fonts available for font-linking don't have multiple styles. You can use size, case, and color to meet your needs. But a *great* web text font has the styles and weights you need.

**Good Display Fonts for the Web**

A good display font has consistent letterspacing (Figure 15.32). Script fonts especially need excellent *kerning* (spacing between pairs of letters); otherwise, letters will overlap or have big gaps between them (Figures 15.33 and 15.34). If you want a script that connects, connections should be as clean as possible.

FIGURE 15.32 Demand consistent and healthy kerning. *Left:* A script font with inconsistent spacing. *Right:* A Sans Serif font with little spacing.

FIGURE 15.33 Avoid using a script font with bumpy connections. *Left:* BlackJack's connections are well integrated into the font. *Right:* This font's connections are not very good, making the stroke of the script look odd in places.

*display font*

*display font*

FIGURE 15.34 Do you want a script with connections? *Top:* Lobster doesn't connect every letter, but the breaks are integrated into the design. *Bottom:* This font looks broken. The forms of the letters make us expect them to connect, and they don't. It's disconcerting.

A display font should look good at the size you need it, have all the characters you need, and maintain legibility (Figure 15.35). It should be well proportioned. In Figure 15.36, Calluna is well proportioned. All the parts of the letters work together in harmony; no element demands our attention. In Figure 15.37, Museo 700's letters complement each other. The curves feel like they belong to the same pattern, or group of curves; the black and white shapes in the letters are balanced.

Finally, a display font should work with the word or words you need to set (Figure 15.38). Some display fonts look great until you use them with your text—and realize one or more letters don't work with the overall design of your page.

use Use

FIGURE 15.35 Do details hold up at the intended size? Even with good, fun fonts, if you use them too small, you'll lose the details that make them unique. *Left:* GrutchShaded. *Right:* Astonished.

use use

FIGURE 15.36 Choose a well-proportioned font. *Left:* Calluna is well proportioned. *Right:* This font is not well proportioned. The thick angled serifs on the *u* demand more attention than they should. The crossbar on the *e* feels too thin compared to the bowl of the letter.

use use

FIGURE 15.37 Choose a well-designed font. *Left:* Museo 700 is a well-designed font. *Right:* This font is not well designed. The serifs are overpowering, the white space in the *u* is awkward, and the white spaces in the *s* are way too small. The top and bottom of the *e* look like they belong to two different letters!

use Use

FIGURE 15.38 Choose a font that looks right with your word or words. Even beautiful, well-designed fonts you love can have a letter that feels odd in the context of your page design. *Left:* EastMarket. I love this font, but the *s* is not appropriate for every design. *Right:* HamburgerHeaven is another favorite, but the *e* is unique, and is not right for every design.

## Building Your Font Library

A good typographer can work with the same font over and over, making it sing every time. Building a font library is not about collecting fonts just to have them (although we all do it). It's a matter of introducing a font to your palette because you're working with content that needs it.

Build your library slowly and surely. Work extensively with each font until you know it intimately. To start, choose a couple of serif fonts and a couple of sans serif fonts. Figure out everything you can do with them. This will help you identify what you need in a new font.

Look at what others are doing. Find people who strive for quality typography and learn from them (Figure 15.39). It's okay to disagree with or modify what others do as well. Test your own ideas.

FIGURE 15.39 Tim Brown shares a couple of his favorite font pairings on NiceWebType.com. Learn from people who strive for quality typography. And test your own ideas, too.

When expanding your library, look for what you're missing that your content needs. Be willing to pay for a font. You'll have more options and get better quality—more styles and weights, better spacing, and fonts that work both large and small.

## Free or Open-License Fonts

Using free or openly licensed fonts is a great place to start your library (Figure 15.40)—especially if you are a student, or just starting to look for web fonts to use. There are a handful of free fonts (Museo, PT Sans, Droid Serif are three that come to mind) that you can use to set beautiful pages of web typography for many years.

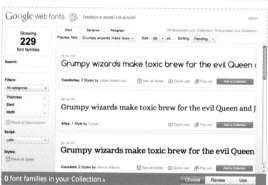

FIGURE 15.40 I love free web fonts. FontSquirrel.com and google.com/webfonts are great places to start when learning web typography—especially if you are a student. But if you want a better variety of well-designed font families (complete with a variety of weights and styles), you need to be willing to pay.

But unfortunately, most free fonts are not great text fonts. They lack legibility and beauty. I keep a resource (`www.goodwebfonts.com`) of lively, subtle, perfectly legible fonts for the web. After months of searching and testing, my grad student and I only found ten free web fonts we'd recommend using for text. And unfortunately, even those ten don't all look great in Windows.

With a handful (or two) of good free web fonts, your choices are still limited. Many free fonts only include roman (and if you are lucky, italic and bold). If you want to use the whole font family—if you want light and heavy weights—you usually need to pay for it.

Plan to expand your font library beyond what you can use for free. Luckily, between Verdana, Georgia, and a handful of quality free fonts, you can take your time figuring out what you need.

## Purchasing Web Licenses

A few foundries (fontspring.com, typotheque.com, fontshop.com) sell web licensing for fonts (Figure 15.41). As a consumer, you can purchase a print license, a web license, or a combined license.

*Upon purchase, you own a license to use the font.* There is no yearly fee. Purchasing a web license expands your library legally, honestly, and with professionally designed font families. When you purchase a web font, you install the font on your own server and use the `@font-face` syntax to use the fonts on your web pages.

Many of these fonts were originally designed for print, so consider them carefully before purchasing a license. Also be aware that, while many licenses include unlimited website use and unlimited page views, this is not true for all licenses. Double-check the number of permitted websites and page views before purchase.

**FIGURE 15.41** Fontspring is one of the few web foundries that sell web licensing for fonts. When you buy a web license, you own the right to use the font, with no yearly fees, and you can use the @font-face declaration. Always look to see if there is a restriction on page views or domains when purchasing a web license.

## Buyer Beware

Beware of popular fonts designed for print that are licensed for the web. They may not hold up onscreen.

Don't buy a font unless you know it will work the way you need it to. If you've tested fonts with a resource like fontsquirrel.com or google.com/webfonts, you've probably experienced a common problem: thinking a font looked great until you used it with your text. If possible, test new fonts at text size, not display size, before purchase.

Does the foundry provide a list of websites using the font (Figure 15.42)? If not, can you find any on your own? Does the foundry provide examples of the font in use—in HTML, not pretty illustrations of the font at display sizes?

Finally, shop around. There are various ways to build your font library. Use the method that works best for you.

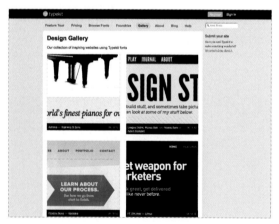

FIGURE 15.42 Good foundries and subscription-based services provide a gallery of websites using their fonts. Look for a gallery like Typekit's (typekit.com), where you can visit the actual sites and see fonts in use (a gallery of just images is not as helpful).

## Subscription-Based Services

Subscription-based services keep the fonts on their servers. Designers use a bit of code in their HTML to access the fonts. The fonts are more secure, so type designers are more comfortable allowing fonts to be used for font-linking (Figure 15.43).

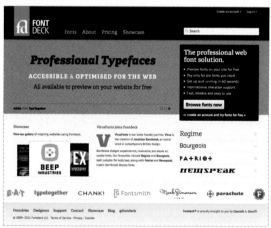

FIGURE 15.43 Subscription-based services keep the fonts on their servers and charge a yearly fee. *Top:* Typekit offers packages that include a large variety of fonts. *Bottom:* Fontdeck also provides access to a large variety of fonts, but only charges for the fonts you use.

**Typekit** (`typekit.com`) offers a variety of reasonable packages. A portfolio package, allowing you to use an unlimited number of its fonts on an unlimited number of websites (not just your own, but your clients' sites, too) is $49.99 per year. Some of the fonts offered are also available as free fonts, but you'll get more with a subscription (more styles and weights—and less syntax to manage). Its text font offering has improved substantially over the past year. Paying for a yearly package is great for building a foundation of web fonts, which you can supplement as needed with web licenses you purchase or subscribe to elsewhere.

**Fontdeck** (`fontdeck.com`) offers a variety of high-quality fonts at reasonable subscription rates. You pay only for the fonts you use, and you pay per website, per year. Be aware, you'll need to subscribe to each style in a font you want to use. One great thing about Fontdeck is that it allows you to test-drive all of its fonts for free.

When choosing a subscription-based service, examine the following characteristics:

- Ease of use (Can you get the fonts working, on your own, immediately?)

- Quality of fonts provided (Don't be swayed by the number of fonts they offer—how many will you actually use? How many are print fonts that don't hold up well on screen?)

- Cost (Access to better fonts with more styles is worth more money, but read the fine print—know how many websites, page views, and styles you get for the price.)

## Building a Font Library

To summarize, when building a font library for the web, remember that:

- Typographers classify fonts—grouping them together based on form.

- Having a classification system helps you picture what a font looks like based on its classification: Old Style, Transitional, Modern, Slab Serif, and Sans Serif.

- A good text font usually has a generous x-height, open counterforms, a generous aperture, and generous spacing between letters.

- A good text font usually does not have thin strokes or delicate serifs, strident serifs, or terminals.

- You can build your library slowly, over time. Get to know the fonts you have. Choose new fonts based on what the content needs that your current fonts can't provide.

- Most free fonts are not appropriate for text. Those that are often have limited styles. So be willing to pay for fonts.

# Lesson 15: Critically Analyze Fonts

You've already designed and built the start of a website. You've applied systems of voice, grid, and navigation across multiple pages. By the end of this lesson, you'll have analyzed web fonts, chosen one to use for the text in your recipes, and replaced the web-safe font you've been using thus far (Figure 15.44).

This lesson helps you achieve the following objectives:

1   Practice looking critically at fonts, considering their history/feeling, legibility/readability, and capability to do the job at hand.

2   Practice testing multiple fonts. Don't settle for the first one you think might work. It often won't.

3   Practice choosing two fonts to work together.

4   Practice making subtle changes to your design (size, line height, color) to accommodate the new font(s).

5   Practice building font stacks.

6   Become familiar with font resources beyond fontsquirrel.com. I particularly recommend checking out google.com/webfonts (a free web font service), typekit.com (a reasonable, easy-to-use web-font subscription service) and goodwebfonts.com (a list of hand-picked fonts for use with web text).

7   Practice trying to find the font you need. You'll identify what kind of font to purchase when building your library.

**INGREDIENTS**

- 2/12 cups all-purpose flour, plus extra for rolling
- 16 Tbsp (2 sticks) unsalted butter, very-cold, cut into 1/2 inch cubes
- 1 teaspoon salt
- 1 teaspoon sugar (increase to 1 1/2 teaspoons if for a sweet recipe)
- 4 to 8 tablespoons ice water

**INGREDIENTS**

- 2/12 cups all-purpose flour, plus extra for rolling
- 16 Tbsp (2 sticks) unsalted butter, very-cold, cut into 1/2 inch cubes
- 1 teaspoon salt
- 1 teaspoon sugar (increase to 1 1/2 teaspoons if for a sweet recipe)
- 4 to 8 tablespoons ice water

FIGURE 15.44 By the end of this lesson, you'll have replaced your web-safe text font with a web font, like this example by Chris Nelson. *Top:* Crimson, a free web font with lining figures. When Chris developed this web page, Crimson bold was not available for the heading. *Bottom:* Georgia, his original web-safe font with Old Style figures.

Even if you are already HTML/CSS savvy, follow the walk-through provided. I show you what a typographer looks for in the process.

**Overview of the Lesson**

In this lesson, you'll visit three sites that provide access to web fonts. You'll test the fonts they have available, and choose fonts to incorporate into your recipes.

**Go to fontsquirrel.com, google.com/webfonts, or typekit.com**

Look for (text) fonts that match the feeling of your site—"classic, quality, but with warmth" or "fresh, local, simple, delicious, sustaining." Use the expanded Five Families of Type from this chapter to help you choose fonts.

**Test the fonts**

Test-drive the fonts first to narrow down your selection. Then use `@font-face` or syntax provided by the subscription service to use the selected font(s) throughout your site.

**Implement the best font, build a font stack, make subtle changes**

You will probably need to change size and line height in the CSS to make the new font work. You designed your pages around a different font, and even if the new one is similar to the original, no two fonts are the same. If your new font has a larger or smaller x-height, or a narrower or wider bowl, you'll need to make slight adjustments.

In the future, you should always pick your font early in the design process. I purposely waited until late in the project to choose a web font for the text for two reasons. First, it's allowed you to focus on other issues such as grid and navigation (which are more exciting than type history for most people). Second, you'll get the opportunity to see how much your design and text shift when you change the font.

**What to Look for in the New Font**

There are a lot of web fonts out there! You can narrow down your search by looking for quality fonts. Always look for a font that

- **Is legible and readable.** To ensure legibility, look for the following: a generous x-height, open counterforms, a generous aperture; an even, generous (but not too generous) spacing between letters; substantial strokes and serifs (so they don't get lost on the screen); and serifs and terminals that don't scream out, "Look at me!" Check out goodwebfonts.com, a resource for lively, subtle, and perfectly legible fonts on the web.

- **Can do the job at hand.** Do you need an italic or bold? Does the font family have these? Do you need to use the font small and large? What do the numbers look like? Does the font hold up in the color palette you are using? Does it have all the characters you need? Be willing to negotiate your design as needed. In the future, you'll pick your font much earlier in the design process.

- **Works with the other fonts in your design.** If you want to use a display font for headlines or other text, or weave a second text font into the design, now is the time to try it. Review Chapter 4 to help you choose a second font.

## Using a Web Font from Font Squirrel

I show you how to use web fonts from three different sources in this lesson. The first source is `www.fontsquirrel.com`. For this example, you'll modify the recipe from the last lesson, so make a copy of the last lesson's folder and name the new folder *15_recipe_fontsquirrel*. Keep it in the *web_typography* folder.

Create a new folder called *fonts*. You'll put your web font files in this folder. Keep the *fonts* folder in the *15_recipe_fontsquirrel* folder.

Rename the CSS file *recipe_newfonts_fontsquirrel.css*. Link it to the *index.html* file by going into the HTML file and changing the syntax in the `head` element to the following:

```
<link
   href="recipe_newfonts_fontsquirrel
   .css" rel="stylesheet"
   type="text/css" />
```

Change the title as shown:

```
<title>Lesson 15: Recipe (New Fonts
   FontSquirrel)</title>
```

**Link the new CSS file to all the HTML files**
Link the new CSS file to *apple.html*, *chess.html*, and *pasties.html* by going into the HTML files and changing the syntax in the `head` element.

**Test and choose one or more fonts to incorporate**
At `fontsquirrel.com`, test and choose one or more fonts to incorporate into your design. If a font doesn't look right to you (or doesn't have all the styles you need), don't settle. Keep looking.

**Download the @font-face kit**
The directions on the site are self-explanatory. If you need additional instructions, review the "Download the @font-face kit" section in Chapter 4.

**View the demo.html file in your browser**
The demo file is helpful. It lets you see that everything downloaded properly before you start using the syntax and the web font files.

**Put a copy of the EOT, TTF, SVG, WOFF, and license files in your fonts folder**
Put a copy of the font files in the *fonts* folder you just created in *15_recipe_fontsquirrel*. Put the

license file in the folder as well. It's good to keep the license agreement with the fonts. (Read it, too!) Leave the other files; you don't need them in the *fonts* folder. The *stylesheet.css* file is a valuable reference file, however, and you'll use it in the next step.

**Describe @font-face in your CSS document**
Find the *stylesheet.css* file provided by Font Squirrel in the `@font-face` kit. Open the file in your text editor. Find and copy the syntax for the styles you need to use in your web page. I'm using *Crimson Roman* and *Crimson Italic*. Use your own font information wherever I used Crimson-specific information.

Open your CSS for this lesson (*recipe_newfonts_fontsquirrel.css*), and paste the syntax at the top of the file. Do not copy and paste the syntax for any styles you won't use in the site, as it will slow down the site. Only copy and paste the syntax for the styles you are actually using, like this:

```
@font-face{
    font-family:'CrimsonRoman';
    src:url('Crimson-Roman-webfont
        .eot');
    src:url('Crimson-Roman-webfont
        .eot?#iefix')
        format('embedded-opentype'),
      url('Crimson-Roman-webfont
        .woff') format('woff'),
      url('Crimson-Roman-webfont.ttf')
        format('truetype'),
      url('Crimson-Roman-webfont
        .svg#CrimsonRoman')
        format('svg');
    font-weight:normal;
    font-style:normal;
    }
```

```
@font-face{
    font-family:'CrimsonItalic';
    src:url('Crimson-Italic-webfont
        .eot');
    src:url('Crimson-Italic-webfont
        .eot?#iefix')
        format('embedded-opentype'),
      url('Crimson-Italic-webfont
        .woff') format('woff'),
      url('Crimson-Italic-webfont
        .ttf') format('truetype'),
      url('Crimson-Italic-webfont
        .svg#CrimsonItalic')
        format('svg');
    font-weight:normal;
    font-style:italic;
    }
```

This syntax is not going to work . . . yet. You need to tell the various browsers to find the files they need in the *fonts* folder. Thus you need to add fonts/ to all of the URLs, like so:

```
@font-face{
    font-family:'CrimsonRoman';
    src:url('fonts
        /Crimson-Roman-webfont.eot');
    src:url('fonts
        /Crimson-Roman-webfont.eot
        ?#iefix')
        format('embedded-opentype'),
      url('fonts/Crimson-Roman-webfont
        .woff') format('woff'),
      url('fonts/Crimson-Roman-webfont
        .ttf') format('truetype'),
      url('fonts/Crimson-Roman-webfont
        .svg#CrimsonRoman')
        format('svg');
    font-weight:normal;
    font-style:normal;
    }
```

```
@font-face{
    font-family:'CrimsonItalic';
    src:url('fonts
        /Crimson-Italic-webfont.eot');
    src:url('fonts
        /Crimson-Italic-webfont.eot
        ?#iefix')
        format('embedded-opentype'),
      url('fonts/Crimson-Italic-webfont
        .woff') format('woff'),
      url('fonts/Crimson-Italic-webfont
        .ttf') format('truetype'),
      url('fonts/Crimson-Italic-webfont
        .svg#CrimsonItalic')
        format('svg');
    font-weight: normal;
    font-style: normal;
    }
```

**Use the font-family name in your selectors**

You've named the font-family and told browsers where to find the font. Now you're ready to use it.

Change the font-family in any selectors (*, h1, h2, h3, p, and so on) in which you'll use the new font. For example, my universal selector (*) font-family has been Georgia up to now. I need to change it to Crimson Roman:

```
*{
    font-family:'CrimsonRoman';
    }
```

**Build a font stack**

Choose a web-safe font and a generic font name that best match your chosen web font. My font stack for Crimson Roman looks like this:

```
font-family:'CrimsonRoman', Georgia,
    serif;
```

257

Once you've built your font stack, carefully scroll down your CSS file. Find all the places you need to change the `font-family`, and do so—replacing the old font with the new font stack. To avoid errors, it's best to use the "find and replace" function if your text editor provides one.

### Provide copyright information

Use a comment to identify any fonts linked in your file. Most licenses require that you provide the copyright information. Providing copyright information also helps web typographers identify and find good fonts! You'll appreciate it when others do it in their CSS.

Crimson doesn't request any specific notice, and there is not a designer listed, so I'll just add the information about their license above the `@font-face` declaration:

```
/* This Font Software is licensed
   under the SIL Open Font License,
   Version 1.1. This license is
   available with a FAQ at
   http://scripts.sil.org/OFL */
```

### Identify What Needs to Change

You designed your pages around a different font, and even if the new one is similar to the original, no two fonts are the same. Your design is different from mine, so I can't tell you exactly what problems you'll see and how to fix them, but I can show you some of the problems I needed to fix. This will help you see the process—it will also give you tips on how to approach fixing your text as needed.

### How I Fixed the Problems in My System

When I changed my font from Georgia to Crimson Regular, I immediately noticed a change in the size of my text. Upon closer inspection, I also found a problem with the italic text in my caption.

### I made all of the text bigger

Crimson Regular looks much smaller than Georgia, even at the same size. I increased the font size and line height on every element that uses Crimson Regular: the universal selector (`*`), `h1`, `h2`, `h4`, the `p.memory` class, the main navigation links, and the `p.memory` links.

I did not have to increase the size of my section links or caption because those are controlled by the universal selector. I did not have to increase the size on my `h3` because my `h3` uses Verdana, bold, caps as a contrast to the serif font.

My original text size was 14/20px (Georgia). I ended up using 16/21px (Crimson). I prefer Crimson at 17/22px due to the small closed counterforms in the lowercase *a* and *e*. But the div widths in my layout made the line length too short. If I were to use Crimson again from the start of a project, I would set it at 17/22px and make the divs wider.

### I made the bullets in the ingredients list smaller

Crimson's bullets are too big (Figure 15.45). To fix this, I added a line to the `ingredients_list li` to make the font size smaller, and then added a line in the `.list_text` class to bump the text back up to the correct size. I already had these styles in my CSS. I used them to make the bullets a different color from the text in the list. The CSS looks like this:

```
#ingredient_list li{
    font-size:13px;
    list-style: round;
    margin-bottom:6px;
    color:#B29E4D;
    }

.list_text{
    font-size:16px;
    color:#423624;
    }
```

## Ingredients

- 2/12 cups all-purpose flour, plus extra for rolling
- 16 Tbsp (2 sticks) unsalted butter, very-cold, cut into 1/2 inch cubes
- 1 teaspoon salt
- 1 teaspoon sugar (increase to 1 1/2 teaspoons if for a sweet recipe)
- 4 to 8 tablespoons ice water

Makes enough for 2 single-crust pies or 1 double-crust fold-over pie.

## Ingredients

- 2/12 cups all-purpose flour, plus extra for rolling
- 16 Tbsp (2 sticks) unsalted butter, very-cold, cut into 1/2 inch cubes
- 1 teaspoon salt
- 1 teaspoon sugar (increase to 1 1/2 teaspoons if for a sweet recipe)
- 4 to 8 tablespoons ice water

Makes enough for 2 single-crust pies or 1 double-crust fold-over pie.

FIGURE 15.45 *Top:* Crimson's bullets are too big. They jump out from the list. *Bottom:* I fixed the bullets by making the list items (li) smaller. I used a class to make the list item text the correct (bigger) size. I already had the li ID and the class in my CSS. I created them earlier when I changed the color of the bullets.

### I made the italics work!

When I scrolled down the page, I realized my italics weren't working. Why? The browser was trying to italicize Crimson Roman. But Crimson Roman doesn't have an italic version, so the browser was "faking" the italic (Figures 15.46 and 15.47).

*Roll out the dough with a rolling pin on a lightly floured surface. Move quickly and do not over-handle. The separate little bits of butter are the secret to a flaky crust.*

*Roll out the dough with a rolling pin on a lightly floured surface. Move quickly and do not over-handle. The separate little bits of butter are the secret to a flaky crust.*

FIGURE 15.46 *Top:* The caption with Crimson Roman and fake italics. *Bottom:* The caption with Crimson Italic. I fixed this by using the 'CrimsonItalic' font family and removing the font-style:italic syntax.

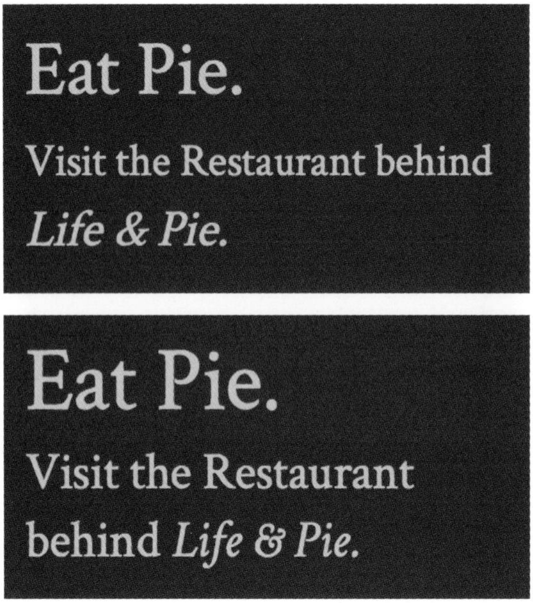

# Eat Pie.
## Visit the Restaurant behind
## *Life & Pie.*

# Eat Pie.
## Visit the Restaurant
## behind *Life & Pie.*

FIGURE 15.47 *Top:* An ad when I first added Crimson Roman. *Bottom:* The same ad after I increased the font sizes and fixed the italic. Note the ampersand.

## Using a Web Font from Google Web Fonts

Now you'll use web fonts from `www.google.com/webfonts`. Google Web Fonts is a hosting provider of freely licensed fonts. Google Web Fonts acts much like a subscription provider: It keeps the fonts on its server and provides you with a bit of syntax to make the fonts work in your site.

Once again, you'll modify the recipe from the last lesson. *Do not try and modify the pages you just made* with the Font Squirrel web fonts. You've made too many changes to the files. Instead, make a copy of the folder *14_recipe* and name the new folder *15_recipe_googlefonts*. Keep it in the *web_typography* folder.

Rename the CSS file *recipe_newfonts_googlefonts. css.* Link it to the *index.html* file by going into the HTML file and changing the syntax in the `head` element as follows:

```
<link
   href="recipe_newfonts_googlefonts
   .css" rel="stylesheet"
   type="text/css" />
```

Change the title as shown:

```
<title>Lesson 15: Recipe (New Fonts
   GoogleFonts)</title>
```

**Link the new CSS file to all the HTML files**
Link the new CSS file to *apple.html, chess.html*, and *pasties.html* by going into the HTML files and changing the syntax in the `head` element.

**Test and choose one or more fonts to incorporate**
Go to `www.google.com/webfonts` and look at some of the fonts it has available (Figure 15.48, top). On the day I took this screenshot, there were 229 font families to choose from. (A *font family* is a family of styles and weights available for a specific font.)

Narrow down the number of font families by choosing a filter. Figure 15.48, bottom, shows the fonts filtered by the keyword "Serif." The fonts are also sorted by "Number of styles," which makes it easier to find fonts that have a bold or italic style.

When you see a font that might work, click on the "See all styles" button (Figure 15.48, bottom). All styles available for that font pop up, allowing you to evaluate the weights and styles you need (Figure 15.49, top). Notice that many of the fonts on Google Web Fonts don't offer italics or bold.

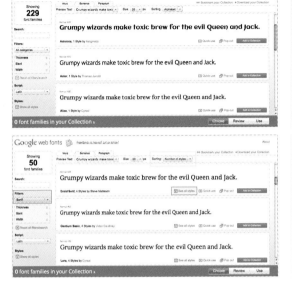

**FIGURE 15.48** *Top:* Google Web Fonts has a wide variety of free web fonts to choose from. *Bottom:* Use Filters (highlighted in red) to narrow down your search. Sort the fonts (highlighted in yellow) and use the "See all styles" button (highlighted in green) to help find a font that's right for your project.

Preview a paragraph of text to see if the font works for text (Figure 15.49, bottom). If a font doesn't look right to you (or doesn't have all the styles you need), don't settle. Keep looking.

If a font looks like it might work for you, you can add it to your collection and continue searching for other options. If you've found the right font and are done with your search, click on the Quick Use link, which is the small right-arrow in the box (Figure 15.49, bottom).

**FIGURE 15.49** *Top:* Evaluate all weights and styles of any font under consideration. *Bottom:* View a paragraph of the font to make sure it works well for text. If it does, add it to your collection or click the Quick Use button (highlighted in red).

## Use one of the web fonts

On the Quick Use page (or, if you've built a collection, after clicking the Use button for a font), pick the styles you want to work with. Only choose the styles you actually need—for example, I'm only using normal and italic (Figure 15.50). The more fonts and styles you link to, the slower your page will load.

Once you've chosen the styles you want to work with, Google Web Fonts provides you with the syntax to make the font work on your site. Follow these instructions to add the syntax to your code files:

1 Triple-click on the syntax (Figure 15.50) to select all of it.

2 Copy the syntax.

261

3   Open your HTML document.

4   Paste the syntax as the first element in the `<head>` of the document. If your Google Web Fonts don't work in a browser, confirm that you have the syntax as the first element.

5   Copy the font-family name from the page shown in Figure 15.50, and paste it in your CSS wherever you want to use the font in your website. I don't always agree with Google's font stacks, so I specify my own.

For example, in my site, I'll be using the font stack `'Droid Serif', Georgia, serif` in the universal selector. I don't need to use it anywhere else.

FIGURE 15.50 When you're ready to use a font, choose the styles you want to work with (highlighted in red). Copy and paste the syntax (highlighted in yellow) into your HTML document. Copy the font-family name (highlighted in green) for use in your CSS.

## Identify What Needs to Change

When you changed your font, the overall feeling of your text changed. And because no two fonts are exactly alike, the new font probably caused some problems in your design. Your design is different from mine, so I can't tell you exactly what problems you'll see and how to fix them, but I can show you some of the problems I needed to fix.

## How I Fixed the Problems in My System

When I changed my font from Georgia to Droid Serif, I immediately noticed my text looked too big, and the lines of text looked too close together. Upon closer inspection, I also found a problem with my "Ingredients" headline.

### I made the text smaller, but increased the line height

Droid Serif looks much bigger than Georgia, even at the same size; Droid Serif's x-height is very generous, and the bowls are squarer and take up more room. I decreased the font size and increased the line height on the universal selector (`*`), the `p.memory` class, and the `p.memory` links.

I enjoyed the larger-looking font in the main navigation links, the `h1` and `h4`, and even increased the size on the `h2`. Droid Serif is enjoyable at slightly larger sizes.

My original text size was 14/20px (Georgia). I ended up using 13/21px (Droid Serif). I prefer Crimson at 14/22px due to the slightly lighter strokes. But the div widths in my layout made the line length too short. If I were to use Droid Serif again from the start of a project, I would set it at 14/22px and make the divs wider.

**I pushed my ingredients headline down, so the list aligned with the links**

When the page was set with Georgia, the top section link aligned with the top item in the list of ingredients. Using Droid Serif, the list of ingredients moved up slightly. I added 2px to the top padding on the `h2.ingredients` to move the ingredients list back into place (Figure 15.51).

**FIGURE 15.51** *Top:* Droid Serif made the ingredients list shift up slightly. The first ingredient was no longer aligned with the first section link. *Bottom:* I fixed this by adding 2px of top padding to my h2.ingredients class.

## Using Web Fonts from Typekit

Now you'll use web fonts from `http://typekit.com`. Typekit is a subscription provider; it keeps the fonts on its server and provide you with a bit of syntax to make the fonts work in your site. It does this for a yearly fee. If you do not have a Typekit subscription, you can still do this part of the lesson. It offers a 30-day free plan, with access to a limited font library.

Before we begin: *In order for Typekit fonts to work, you need to have your pages on a web server.* If you can't put your web pages on a server, you won't be able to do this part of the lesson. But you can still follow along, or you are welcome to move on to the next chapter.

Once again, you'll modify the recipe from the last lesson. *Do not try to modify the pages you just made with Google Web Fonts.* You've made changes to the files. Instead, make a copy of the folder *14_recipe* and name the new folder *15_recipe_typekit*. Keep it in the *web_typography* folder.

Rename the CSS file *recipe_newfonts_typekit.css*. Link it to the *index.html* file by going into the HTML file and changing the syntax in the `head` element as follows:

```
<link href="recipe_newfonts_typekit
    .css" rel="stylesheet"
    type="text/css" />
```

Change the title as indicated:

```
<title>Lesson 15: Recipe (New Fonts
    Typekit)</title>
```

**Link the new CSS file to all the HTML files**

Link the new CSS file to *apple.html*, *chess.html*, and *pasties.html* by going into the HTML files and changing the syntax in the `head` element.

263

## Test and choose one or more fonts to incorporate

Go to Typekit.com and look at some of the fonts it has available. You can browse the Trial Library, the Personal Library, or the Full Library. When you see a font that might work, click on it to see a page showing the font styles. From here, you can go to the *Specimens* page to see the font at various sizes (there's a drop-down menu to change the style). You can also go to *Browser Samples* to see screenshots of how the font looks on various operating systems and in various browsers. Nice!

## Create a fontkit

Instead of creating a *fonts* folder on your desktop, create a kit at typekit.com (you must register and log in if you haven't done so already).

If this is your first time using Typekit, it prompts you to create a new kit, to name the kit (name it something meaningful, such as *15_recipes_typekit*), and to tell Typekit what URL the kit will be used on. You do not have to tell the exact URL of the page, just the general URL of the site (for example, *mywebsite.com*). Choose whether or not to include a Typekit badge on your site; if you are using the free plan, then you must include the badge.

## Add Typekit code to the recipe pages

Typekit automatically provides you with unique JavaScript to embed in the `<head></head>` section of all the HTML files that will use the kit (Figure 15.52). The JavaScript tells browsers to access the unique kit you have created. To embed the code, copy it from the Typekit page, open your HTML files, and paste the code in the head section of each page. If you ever need to get the code again, simply click on the *Embed Code* link in the top-right corner of the Kit Editor (Figure 15.53).

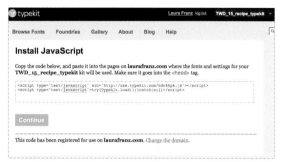

FIGURE 15.52 Typekit automatically provides you with unique JavaScript to embed in the head section of all the HTML files that will use the kit.

## Add fonts to the kit

Now that the HTML files are ready to tell the browsers to use the type kit you have created, you need to add some fonts to the type kit. If this is your first time using Typekit, it should prompt you to add fonts. If you miss the prompt for any reason, then to add a font, go to the page of the font you want to use, and click the green Add to Kit button in the top-right corner. Deselect any of the styles you don't intend to use; this will help the system run faster (Figure 15.53).

FIGURE 15.53 In the Kit Editor, you can choose exactly the styles you want to use (highlighted in red), identify what selectors should use the font (highlighted in blue), and go to the page where the unique JavaScript code is provided (highlighted in yellow).

**Tell the kit where to use the fonts in your design via selectors**

You've chosen your fonts; they are in the kit. But how does the browser know where to use the fonts in your design? You need to apply the fonts to the `font-family` for the correct selectors.

For example, in my design, I only need to apply the font I've chosen (Calluna) to the universal selector. So all I have to do is type the asterisk (`*`)—the symbol for universal selector—into the form where Typekit requests the selectors, and click the Add button (Figure 15.53).

Then, in the CSS, I go in and delete the `font-family` information from that selector because the `font-family` is now provided by Typekit for that selector.

Thus, my CSS does not include the `font-family`, and looks like this:

```
*{
    margin:0px;
    padding:0px;
    font-size:14px;
    line-height:20px;
    font-weight:normal;
    font-style:normal;
}
```

**Or use the advanced method**

If for any reason you'd rather add the `font-family` in your CSS yourself (we web designers and typographers do tend to like to control things), you can.

Typekit provides you with the `font-family` names to copy and paste into your CSS (much like you did with Google Web Fonts). Follow the "Advanced…" link near the selector box, and you are taken to a page that provides you with the `font-family` names (Figure 15.54). Copy and

paste both `font-family` names into the selectors in your CSS.

FIGURE 15.54 If you prefer to add the font-family directly in your CSS, click the Advanced link instead of adding a selector in the type kit. A page pops up with the font-family names. Copy and paste both font-family names into the selectors in your CSS.

For example, if I had accessed the Calluna font using this method, the CSS would look like this:

```
*{
    margin:0px;
    padding:0px;
    font-family:"calluna-1",
        "calluna-2", Georgia, serif;
    font-size:14px;
    line-height:20px;
    font-weight:normal;
    font-style:normal;
}
```

**Publish the kit**

When you're finished building the kit, and telling the browsers where to use the fonts on your pages, click Publish. This finalizes the kit and it's ready to work. Every time you make changes to a kit (add or delete fonts, add or delete selectors), you need to click Publish again to tell Typekit to make the changes.

It can take a couple of minutes for the published kit (new or changes) to go live, so don't panic if it seems like it isn't working. But usually it won't take that long.

**Put the pages on your web server**
Your pages can't "get" the fonts from Typekit if the pages are on your hard drive. In order to see the fonts you've chosen, put the pages on your web server.

**View your pages**
Go to your URL to see what the pages look like with your new font.

**Identify What Needs to Change**
Once again, your new font has probably created a few problems in your design. I can't tell you exactly what problems you'll see and how to fix them, but I can show you some of the problems I needed to fix.

**How I Fixed the Problems in My System**
When I changed my font from Georgia to Calluna, I immediately noticed my text looked too small. Upon closer inspection, I also realized the italic caption was a bit hard to read.

**I made the text bigger**
Calluna looks a little smaller than Georgia, even at the same size; Calluna's x-height is smaller. I increased the font size (but not the line height) on the universal selector (which increased the font size on the text, caption, ingredients list, and section links). I also increased the font size on the h1, h2, p.memory text, p.memory links, and the main navigation links. In the ads, I needed to increase the h4, but reduce the size of the text. The newly increased font size was too big (Figure 15.55).

FIGURE 15.55 *Top:* After I increased the font size on the universal selector, I realized the font size was too big for the ads. The h4, however, was too small. *Bottom:* The same ad after I fixed the font sizes.

My original text size was 14/20px (Georgia). I ended up using 15/20px (Calluna).

**I made the caption even bigger**
I looked for my font styles, and found the Calluna Italic worked just fine. But it's narrower and a little harder to read than Georgia Italic, so I increased the .caption font size by another 1 pixel (Figure 15.56).

**I made the recipe title lighter**
The recipe title was too small in Calluna, so I increased its size. But then it looked a little too clunky. Calluna is a slightly heavier font than Georgia. Calluna Regular is available as a free font, but by linking to Calluna through Typekit, my

subscription gives me access to a variety of weights and styles. For a more delicate, elegant look, I used Calluna Light in my h1 (Figure 15.57). My syntax looks like this:

```
h1{
    font-size:30px;
    line-height:24px;
    padding-left:75px;
    color:#BFA640;
    font-weight:lighter;
}
```

*Roll out the dough with a rolling pin on a lightly floured surface. Move quickly and do not over-handle. The separate little bits of butter are the secret to a flaky crust.*

Pinch some
ready, if not
time, pulsing
together. Co
dough it hol

**DIVIDE IN**
(65 minutes

Remove dou
surface. Divi
each into a l

*Roll out the dough with a rolling pin on a lightly floured surface. Move quickly and do not over-handle. The separate little bits of butter are the secret to a flaky crust.*

Pinch some
ready, if not
time, pulsing
together. Co
dough it hol

**DIVIDE IN**
(65 minutes

Remove dou
surface. Divi
each into a l

FIGURE 15.56 *Top:* Calluna Italic is narrower than Georgia Italic, so it's a little harder to read. *Bottom:* I fixed this by making my .caption class 1 pixel bigger.

# Chess Pie

Long associated with the Sou
every Christmas when I was a
where my great grandmother
was delicious.

# Chess Pie

Long associated with the Sou
every Christmas when I was a
where my great grandmother
was delicious.

FIGURE 15.57 *Top:* The larger Calluna heading looked too heavy. *Bottom:* I fixed this by using Calluna Light, a weight available at Typekit, but not available in the free web-font version of Calluna.

## View changes in your browser

Every time you make changes, reupload your CSS file to the server. Then refresh your page so you can see the changes in your browser. It takes a little extra work this way, having to constantly reupload a file, but the slight changes to the typography are worth it.

---

**Recommended Resources**

For this lesson, I recommend the following online resources:

- To download free fonts, visit `fontsquirrel.com`
- To link to free fonts, visit `google.com/webfonts`
- To link to commercial fonts, visit `typekit.com` or `fontdeck.com`
- To purchase web font licenses, visit `fontspring.com`

---

# Moving Forward

This chapter introduced you to the history of type design and choosing a web font for text. It also introduced you to three methods for incorporating web fonts into your recipe project: linking to a web font using `@font-face`, linking to a font at `google.com/webfonts`, and creating and using a type kit at `www.typekit.com`.

In the next lesson, you'll continue learning about the history of typography.

# Designing with Type: Historical Styles

*Bad design history says, here, this is nice, use it. . . .*

*Good design history says, this is how designers thought about their work then, and this is how that work fits into the culture. Now, what can **you** do?*

TIBOR KALMAN, J. ABBOTT MILLER, AND KARRIE JACOBS, "GOOD HISTORY / BAD HISTORY," PRINT MAGAZINE (1991)

# CHAPTER 16

# The Traditional Page

There are three general approaches to the typographic page: Traditional (classic), Modernist, and Post-Modernist. The typographic page changed as the content, audience, role of the designer, and available technology changed.

The Traditional typographic page developed from the old methods of book-making: first in scriptoriums, written by hand, and later with the advent of the printing press. The Modernist page grew out of a fascination with industrialization and a desire for order after years of living through the chaos of World War I. The Post-Modernist page was influenced by both the Deconstructionist movement and the advent of the personal computer. Suddenly, designers could take apart and rebuild texts in the comfort of their own studios (see Figure 16.1).

Traditional, Modernist, and Post-Modernist typographers had different ideas about how people read. This chapter briefly describes the Traditional page: the roles of the author, the designer, and the printed artifact. It also describes the formal characteristics of Traditional typography. The next two chapters describe the Modernist and Post-Modernist typographic page.

Beyond the bounds of these three historical styles is contemporary practice. Contemporary typographers combine formal and theoretical elements from Traditional, Modernist, and Post-Modernist typography. It is neither necessary nor practical to completely separate the three approaches.

## Characteristics of Traditional Pages

Traditional pages reflect some common characteristics.

**Traditional Pages Use a Text Frame**

In a Traditional page, text lives in a block, framed by generous margins (Figure 16.2). Deviations on this form include using two columns of text within the frame, filling the margins with blocks of text, filling the margins with a detailed border, and interlocking blocks of text in a complex system within the frame (Figure 16.3).

FIGURE 16.1 There are three general approaches to the typographic page. *Left:* A Traditional page by Rich Leonardo feels "old." *Middle:* A Modernist page by Chris Nelson is designed to guide the reader's eye from section to section. *Right:* A Post-Modernist page by Sarah Richards responds to the question "No one reads anymore?" by creating an unreadable visual texture.

Text frames came into use in the Middle Ages when the codex (manuscript book) replaced the scroll for written media. Scribes scored vertical and horizontal lines on the vellum pages, thus creating the first text frames.

### Traditional Pages Use Serif Fonts

Text frames continued to be used after the invention of moveable roman type and the printing press, but the typographic page was not stagnant.

The first printers' fonts mimicked manuscript text. Over time, fonts changed as printers' location, intent, and technology changed. Humanist, Old Style, Transitional, and Modern/Didot fonts were all used at various times and places to create Traditional page layouts (Figure 16.4).

FIGURE 16.2 The Society of Typographic Aficionados (SOTA) uses a classic text frame layout. Most websites don't use this structure—they use as much of the screen as possible. Contemporary typographers combine formal and theoretical elements from a variety of historical styles. Notice the use of a sans serif font and heavy, bold headlines. This is more typical of the Modernist typographic page, which you'll learn about in Chapter 17.

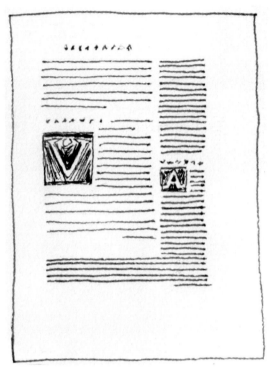

FIGURE 16.3 Thumbnail sketch by the author of a page created by Swiss printer, Johann Froben, in 1515. Commentary on the text is set in the right-hand column. Both the main text and the commentary fit within the text frame.

## Traditional Pages Strive for an Even Tone

Text on the Traditional typographic page is meant to be read in a relaxed, contemplative manner. Thus, there is an even tone on the page: Hierarchy is subtle, using changes in size, case, and style (italic) to create emphasis and to chunk text. Capital letters usually have letterspacing added to keep them feeling lighter on the page (Figure 16.5).

FIGURE 16.4 A detail from jontangerine.com. Jon Tan creates a Traditional typographic page complete with serif fonts; the use of size, italics, and small caps (but not bold) to create subtle emphasis; and (on lower-level pages) the use of justified text to create a traditional text frame. Contemporary typographers draw from a variety of historical theories about and approaches to typography. The playful application of his name in the upper-left corner is reminiscent of Post-Modernist typography, which you'll learn about in Chapter 18.

FIGURE 16.5 A detail from alistapart.com. A List Apart creates a Traditional feeling to its text using a serif font for its headings, italics for subtle emphasis, and letter-spaced caps (the date, "ALA staff," the word "list" in its logo). Headings are centered, which is also traditional. The use of a sans serif font is a contemporary addition to the Traditional page.

## Traditional Pages Convey an Elegant Feeling

In order to emphasize the frame, text is fully justified and other small amounts of text are often centered. Carefully spaced capital, serif letters feel both formal and delicate. Ornaments are used to add emphasis or help chunk text (Figure 16.6). The aspiration to keep an even tone on the page leads to seemingly simple and obviously elegant solutions.

FIGURE 16.6 A detail from ilovetypography.com. Some of the pages designed by John Boardley are very Traditional. He uses two ornaments on this page: the fleuron in the main heading and the initial cap to start the article. Letterspaced capital letters (the date, the subheading, the main navigation) feel more formal and delicate.

## The Role of the Typographer

Throughout the centuries, the Traditional page was seen as an agent to diffuse thought. Unlike posters, broadsides, and bills, books were meant to be contemplated. Books were created to share religious texts, classic literary texts, and scholarly works.

The earliest Traditional "typographer"—the scribe working in a scriptorium—was considered to be an agent of the divine. The artist-as-creator did not emerge until the Renaissance.

Later Traditional typographers—printers—reveled in their control of the page. In 1501 Aldus Manutius developed economic "little books of handy size" to share Greco-Latin literature with a larger audience. In the 1750s, John Baskerville developed new inks, paper, and drying techniques to achieve lighter, crisper letterforms.

Regardless of their ability to control the page, Traditional typographers believed books served the greater good and a common purpose. They believed careful use of type and space helped readers contemplate and comprehend the text.

### The Traditional Page Was Designed for Contemplation

To summarize, the Traditional page:

- Tends to use a text frame and serif fonts, keep an even tone to the page, and convey an elegant feeling.

- Has elegance, subtle contrasts, and an overall lightness to the page.

- May have ornaments, borders, and Old-Style numerals.

- Was designed by Traditional typographers who believed books served the greater good and a common purpose. These typographers carefully used type and space to help readers contemplate and comprehend the text.

# Lesson 16: Design and Produce a Website from a Traditional Approach

You designed and built the start of a working website in Chapters 11 through 15. Now it's time to expand your typographic toolbox. By the end of this lesson, you'll use all the skills previously learned to design and build a Traditional typographic web page. You'll also build a small website, linking the Traditional page to all of the previous lessons (Figure 16.7).

This lesson helps you achieve the following objectives:

1   Practice creating a website, complete with working links.

2   Practice using the design process provided in this book in a more fluid, simultaneous manner.

3   Practice using elements of the Traditional page when designing a website.

4   Practice walking the line between inspiration and duplication. Do not merely copy what was done before. Your medium, content, and audience are different from those of the classic typographers. What elements are appropriate to your design? What can be set aside or modified?

Even if you are already HTML/CSS savvy, follow the lesson. I provide an outline for the design process and point out where to find more information in the previous chapters.

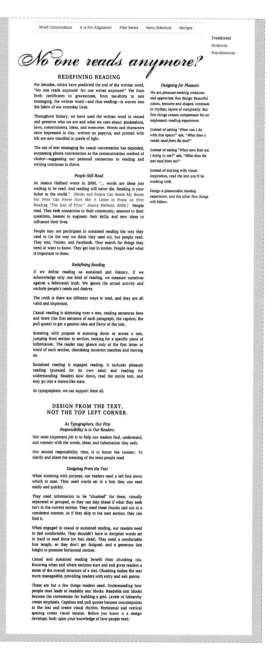

FIGURE 16.7 By the end of this lesson, you'll build a Traditional typographic web page. You'll link the page to two future typographic pages (Modernist and Post-Modernist) as well as to the pages built for previous lessons (*Word Connotations, Bibliography, A is for Alignment, Film Series, Ferry Schedule, Recipes*).

## Overview of the Lesson

In this lesson, you will design and build a Traditional typographic web page that links to all of the previous lessons.

1 Download the text file `redefining_reading.doc` from the book's website at www. wiley.com/go/typographicwebdesign.

2 Read the text.

3 Use the design process that you learned from the previous chapters (and outlined in the following section) to lay out elements.

## The Design Process

Remember, most of this happens simultaneously!

- Choose your font(s) based on legibility, aesthetics/emotion, and styles available (you'll need an italic).

- Set font size, line length (div width), line height, and alignment to promote readability and create a Traditional page.

- Create voices with style, size, case, letter-spacing, and color. Consider your text, headings, and links.

- Use systems of space and similarity to create hierarchy.

- Print out and re-arrange text blocks (divs) to find the appropriate grid for the text in a Traditional page.

- Build your site.

## Elements of the Traditional Page

While creating your design, keep in mind the characteristics of a Traditional page:

- Text frame
- Serif fonts
- Size, case, and italics used for emphasis
- An even tone
- An elegant feeling
- Careful use of type and space to help readers contemplate and comprehend the text

## Background Images Revisited

You used a background image in Chapter 5 to place the A in *A is for Alignment*. For your Traditional page, you may want to use an image to create a background pattern. First you need to get your page started.

In the *web_typography* folder, create a folder for the lesson. Call it *16_traditional_page*.

Create two new folders in the *16_traditional_page* folder. Call one of the folders *fonts*. The font files (should you choose to use a font you need to use the `@font-face` declaration for) will go here. Call the other folder *images*. Any images you use will go here.

**Start the HTML File**

In your text editor, create a new document and save it as *index.html* in your *16_traditional_page* folder.

Copy and paste in the basic HTML syntax, add the title, and link to the CSS file:

```
<!DOCTYPE html PUBLIC "-//W3C//
    DTD XHTML 1.0 Strict//EN"
    "http://www.w3.org/TR/xhtml1/DTD/
    xhtml1-strict.dtd">
<html xmlns="http://www.w3.org/1999/
    xhtml">
<head>
<title>Lesson 16: Traditional
    Page</title>
<meta http-equiv="content-type"
    content="text
    /html;charset=utf-8" />
<link href="traditional_page.css"
    rel="stylesheet" type="text/css" />
</head>
<body>
</body>
</html>
```

Add your `main_container` div between the `<body></body>` tags:

```
<div id="main_container"></div>
```

## Start the CSS file

In your text editor, create a new document and save it as *traditional_page.css* in your *16_traditional_page* folder.

### Describe the div ID for main_container

The `main_container` div is a white rectangle (990 pixels wide, auto height for now—you can change this later) centered in the browser. It has some space above and below it. It has an auto height, and will have divs floated inside. To force the div open, you need to include an

`overflow:hidden;` property. Write the syntax like this:

```
#main_container{
    width:990px;
    height:auto;
    margin-top:20px;
    margin-right:auto;
    margin-bottom:40px;
    margin-left:auto;
    background-color:#ffffff;
    overflow:hidden;
    }
```

### Clear margins and paddings with the universal selector

Because this is a Traditional page layout, I also recommend setting the `font-weight:normal;` (you can use size and style to create contrast):

```
*{
    margin:0px;
    padding:0px;
    font-weight:normal;
    }
```

## Add a Background Image

If you want to create an ornamental border for your text frame, you can use a repeating background image to make a pattern.

When choosing or creating an image to use for the background, ask yourself: What kind of image will help communicate a Traditional feeling? An image with organic shapes? One with geometric shapes? An image with bright colors? One with subtle colors? Pay attention to the size of the image. How much of the image will show around the border of the `main_container`?

278

## Make and place the image

In the photo-editing software of your choice (I use Adobe Photoshop), create an image. A small ornament can be repeated to make a pattern; a single large image can be placed behind the entire page.

For example, in Photoshop, I made an ornament using Bodoni Ornaments ITC. I saved it as *background.jpg* in the *images* folder. I brought it into the web page background by adding a line of syntax in the CSS for the body:

```
body{
    background-image: url(images
    /background.jpg);
    }
```

The preceding syntax tells the browser, "Put a background image in the body of my web page. Use *background.jpg* found in the *images* folder for this lesson." By default, the image will repeat across and down your browser.

## View your web page

Save your HTML document and open it in your browser. You should see a background filled with a repeating pattern. The `main_container` isn't filling the browser window because there's nothing in it to hold it open. You need to add some content (Figure 16.8).

## Insert and Prepare the Text

Read *redefining_reading.doc* to get a sense of the text. In the HTML file, flow the text from *redefining_reading.doc* into the `main_container`.

Mark the main headings with `<h1></h1>` tags, the secondary headings with `<h2></h2>` tags, and the paragraphs with `<p></p>` tags.

## View your web page

Save your HTML document and view it in your browser window. You should see a white rectangle filled with text on a patterned background. Now you need to design your typographic page (Figure 16.9), keeping in mind the elements that reflect the Traditional approach.

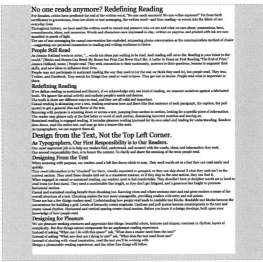

FIGURE 16.9 The background pattern surrounds a `main_container` holding the text for the lesson. Use the skills covered previously in this book to design and build your typographic page.

FIGURE 16.8 The background image is in place, repeating to create a pattern. The main_container doesn't have any content in it yet.

279

## Designing the Typographic Page

To design your page, use all the skills learned and practiced in previous chapters, keeping the Traditional approach in mind:

• Choose a font for legibility as well as a Traditional feeling (see Chapters 1 and 2 for a review).

• Determine the appropriate size, line height, alignment, and line length (div width) for text (see Chapter 6 for a review).

• Use case, style, and color to create multiple voices (text, links, pull quotes if you create them) on the page (see Chapter 11 for a review).

• Chunk information using systems of space and hierarchy (see Chapters 7 and 8 for a review).

• Develop a Traditional grid (text frame) that still creates rhythm and tension on the page (see Chapters 5 and 12 for a review).

• Build the grid with multiple divs as needed (see Chapter 12 for a review).

• Attend to typographic details (numbers and acronyms, rule lines, and punctuation). (See Chapter 9 for a review.)

• Link to finished previous pages (see Chapter 13 for a review).

• View your page in the browser often to check your progress.

## Linking to Files in Other Lesson Folders

At some point, you'll be ready to make your links work, and some of the links are different in this project. You need to tell browsers to *leave the folder your current page is in* and go into a *different folder* to retrieve files.

To link to pages in other folders, include this syntax:

```
../
```

This tells the browser, "Go up a level out of the folder the current page is in." Thus, to link to the finished *A is for Alignment* file, type the following:

```
<a href="../5_alignment_counterpoints
    /index.html">A is for Alignment</a>
```

This tells the browser, "Go out of the current folder, find the *5_alignment_counterpoints* folder, go into that folder, and open the *index.html* page."

### Test your links

Save your HTML documents, and view them in your browser. Make sure all links work as expected. When you link to previous lessons, those pages don't have links on them. Just use your back button to return to your Traditional page. This is not spectacular web design practice, but serves the purpose for this exercise.

---

**Recommended Resources**

For this lesson, I recommend the following online resources:

- To download the text and image for this lesson, go to `www.wiley.com/go/typographicwebdesign`

- To see examples of this lesson, go to `typographicwebdesign.com`

- To learn more about creating a complex background pattern, go to `pshero.com/photoshop-tutorials/graphic-design/complex-repeating-patterns-part-i`

- To learn about how medieval books (the first Traditional pages) were made, go to `www.getty.edu/art/exhibitions/making/`

- To learn about the Gutenberg Bible (one of the first printed books, based on manuscripts), go to `en.wikipedia.org/wiki/Gutenberg_Bible`

---

## Moving Forward

This chapter introduced you to theories and themes of the Traditional typographic page. The chapter also introduced you to using a background image to create a pattern and linking to pages in other folders.

In the next chapter, you will learn about the theories and themes of the Modernist typographic page.

# CHAPTER 17

# The Modernist Page

The Modernist page was a product of World War I. German designers—having lived for years in a country at war—wanted to help create a better society. They did not want to look back, and condemned Traditionalists for doing so. Inspired by new technologies and the systematic approach to mass production, Modernist typographers believed in *clarity of form* as opposed to beauty.

German printer Jan Tschichold, believing in the tenets of Modernism, published *The New Typography* in 1928. The rise of Modernism in typography is attributed to his writings, which influenced decades of typographers. Later, Tschichold returned to working in a more Traditionalist manner.

The period after World War II saw the rise of the International Typographic Style, which influenced corporate design well into the 1960s. Although *formally* similar to Modernist typography, the International Typographic Style lacks the dogmatic search for clarity and truth.

Contemporary typographers move freely between the Traditional and Modernist styles. But in the early 1930s a heated debate waged over which was the "one true approach." Philip Meggs wrote in his introduction to *Texts on Type: Critical Writings on Typography*, "Artistic struggles are seldom limited to disagreements about what constitutes the noble virtues of beauty and truth... Underlying the conflict are concerns about economic survival: Who will get the work?"

## Characteristics of Modernist Pages

Modernist pages reflect some common characteristics.

### Modernist Pages Use Space in an Architectural Manner

The text frame of the Traditional approach is gone. Text blocks can live anywhere on the page and are spatially related to each other via the grid. White shapes (not just gutters and margins) are equally important architectural elements (Figure 17.1).

FIGURE 17.1 *Top:* Landor.com (Landor Associates) uses space in an architectural manner. The layout is asymmetrical; white shapes and blocks of text are equally important formal elements. Most websites don't use this structure—they use as much of the screen as possible. *Bottom:* The site uses a grid of vertical and horizontal alignments to place text and information. Notice the repetition of the strong horizontal line, created by images on the home page and a main headline on the contact page.

## Modernist Pages Use Sans Serif Fonts

Sans serif fonts were used sparingly before they found favor on the Modernist page (Figure 17.2). Jan Tschichold wrote in *The New Typography*, "Our age is characterized by an all-out search for clarity and truth, for purity of appearance. So the problem of what typeface to use is necessarily different from what it was in previous times. We require from type plainness, clarity, the rejection of everything that is superfluous."

## Modernist Pages Use Contrast to Create Emphasis

Text on the Modernist typographic page is meant to be glanced at quickly, with readers deciding what to read of the text, if any. Thus, hierarchy is created via placement, size, and weight. Different levels of emphasis guide readers around the page (Figure 17.3).

## Modernist Pages Convey an Asymmetric, Lively Feeling

Text on the Modernist page is neither centered nor justified. Modernist typographers railed against symmetry as an aesthetic form determined by previous typographers. Asymmetry was considered more logical (chunking text for readers) and a better expression of modern life (Figures 17.1 and 17.2).

**FIGURE 17.2** The Ministry of Type uses Modernist typographic elements. The page is asymmetrical, the font is sans serif (Bliss Pro, a typeface designed by Jeremy Tankard), and color is used to guide the reader's eye down and across each entry.

**FIGURE 17.3** SixLog (designed by Studio van Son) *Top:* The page structure is less architectural, and the body font is serif. But the use of big red type to lead the reader's eye helps chunk the text and make it easier to skim. This is a Modernist typographic approach to hierarchy. *Bottom:* The contact page adheres to the grid system; the image is cropped into a square.

## The Role of the Typographer

A Traditionalist typographer would say, "Here is an important text; I've set it in a pleasing manner so the reader can enjoy and contemplate it." A Modernist typographer, on the other hand, would say, "People don't read in a leisurely manner anymore. This text might be important to readers, so I've used emphasis and space to help people skim it, and then read what is most important to them."

Modernist typographers interpreted texts, breaking them down and deciding what to emphasize— determining how to guide the reader's eye. Done in the name of clarity and truth, the movement also marks a shift in the typographer's relationship to the text: from scribe to editor.

### The Modernist Page Was Designed for Clarity

To summarize, the Modernist page:

- Tends to use a grid to create architectural space.
- Tends to use sans serif fonts, contrast to create emphasis, and asymmetry to guide a reader's eye.
- Has rhythm, clarity, and obvious contrasts.
- May have rule lines when necessary to communicate the text clearly.
- Was designed by Modernist typographers who believed careful use of type, space, and contrasts could help readers ascertain the content of a text at a glance. These typographers believed that by promoting clarity, truth, and purity of appearance, they could help move society forward.

# Lesson 17: Design and Produce a Website from a Modernist Approach

You designed and built a Traditional web page in the last chapter. Now it's time to further expand your typographic toolbox. By the end of this lesson, you'll use all the skills previously learned to design and build a Modernist typographic web page. You'll link the Modernist page to your Traditional page and to all of the previous lessons (see Figure 17.4).

This lesson helps you achieve the following objectives:

1   Practice creating a website, complete with working links.

2   Practice using the design process provided in this book in a more fluid, simultaneous manner.

3   Practice using elements of the Modernist page when designing a website.

4   Practice walking the line between inspiration and duplication. Do not merely copy what was done before. Your medium, content, and audience are different from those of the Modernist typographers. What elements are appropriate to your design? What can be set aside or modified?

Even if you are already HTML/CSS savvy, follow the lesson. I provide an outline for the design process and point out where to find more information in the previous chapters.

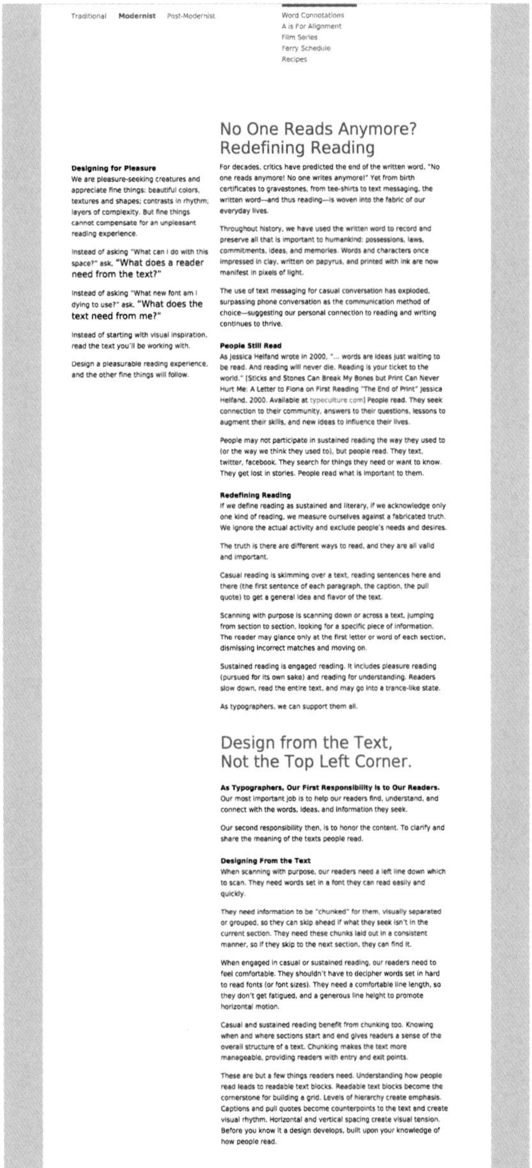

FIGURE 17.4 By the end of this lesson, you'll build a Modernist typographic web page. You'll also link this page to the page you built in the previous chapter.

## Overview of the Lesson

In this lesson, you will design and build a Modernist typographic web page that links to all of the previous lessons.

1  Use the design process provided in this book (and outlined below) to lay out elements.

2  Revise the CSS from the previous assignment or start from scratch.

## The Design Process

Remember, most of this happens simultaneously!

• Choose your font(s) based on legibility, aesthetics/emotion, and styles available (you'll need a bold).

• Set font size, line length (div width), line height, and alignment to promote readability and create a Modernist page.

• Create voices with style, size, case, letterspacing, and color. Consider your text, headings, and links.

• Use systems of space and similarity to create hierarchy.

• Print out and re-arrange text blocks (divs) to find the appropriate grid for the text in a Modernist page.

• Build your site.

## Elements of the Modernist Page

While creating your design, keep in mind the characteristics of a Modernist page:

• Architectural space and grid

• Sans serif fonts

• Obvious contrasts to create emphasis

• Asymmetry to guide a reader's eye

• Rhythm

• Clarity

## Create a New Design by Changing the CSS

While you could start this lesson from scratch, I recommend you modify the files from the last lesson.

Make a copy of the last lesson's folder and name the new folder *17_modern_page*. Keep it in the *web_typography* folder.

Rename the CSS file *modern_page.css*. Link it to the *index.html* file by going into the HTML file and changing the syntax in the head element to the following:

```
<link href="modern_page.css"
    rel="stylesheet" type="text/css" />
```

Change the title to:

```
<title>Lesson 17: The Modernist Page
    </title>
```

**Design the Typographic Page**

To design your page, use all the skills previously learned and practiced in previous chapters, keeping the Modernist approach in mind:

• Choose a font for legibility as well as a Modern feeling (see Chapters 1 and 2 for a review).

• Determine the appropriate size, line height, alignment, and line length (div width) for text (see Chapter 6 for a review).

• Use case, style, and color to create multiple voices (text, links, pull quotes if you create them) on the page (see Chapter 11 for a review).

- Chunk information using systems of space and hierarchy (see Chapters 7 and 8 for a review).

- Develop a Modernist grid (think architectural space) that creates rhythm and tension on the page (see Chapters 5 and 12 for a review).

- Build the grid by modifying divs as needed. In the CSS, change width, float, padding, margin, and so on. In the HTML, change the div order if needed (see Chapter 12 for a review).

- Attend to new details (numbers and acronyms, rule lines). Punctuation will probably remain the same (see Chapter 9 for a review).

- Links to finished previous pages are already done. You will probably have to modify your link lists and your link states. Don't forget to change the "you are here" list item (see Chapter 13 for a review).

- View your page in the browser often to check your progress.

### Changing the CSS Changes Everything

Thus far, you've built HTML and CSS documents side by side. Creating a new page layout—primarily by making changes to the CSS—requires a shift in thinking.

Here are some tips to make it easier:

- Sketch out your new Modernist page design in detail before changing the CSS. Don't just guess; have a plan!

- If you get lost or overwhelmed, sketch (or print out) the page as is, identify where the problems are, and tackle them one by one.

- Add a border or background color to your divs to help you see margin and padding (I need to do this at least once during every project). It's hard to visualize space while looking at syntax.

Once your Modernist page is done, it's time to move on to the Post-Modernist page in Chapter 18.

---

### Recommended Resources

For this lesson, I recommend the following on-line resources:

- To see examples of this lesson, go to typographicwebdesign.com

- To learn more about Modernism and typography, go to typophile.com/node/12610

- For inspiration, view posters and books using the Modern or International Style. You can find examples at www.aisleone.net/

---

## Moving Forward

This chapter introduced you to theories and themes of the Modernist typographic page. The chapter also introduced you to changing the design of a page by changing the CSS.

In the next and final chapter, you will learn about the theories and themes of the Post-Modernist typographic page.

# CHAPTER 18

# The Post-Modernist Page

The Post-Modernist page emerged in the 1980s. Influenced by the typographic experimentation of New Wave design in the 1970s, Post-Modern typography was made manifest with the invention of personal computers and page-layout software. Suddenly, Post-Modernist typographers could take apart (deconstruct) and rebuild texts (to create meaningful or aesthetic relationships) in the comfort of their own studios.

## Characteristics of Post-Modernist Pages

Post-Modernist pages reflect some common characteristics.

### Post-Modernist Pages Use Text Anywhere on the Page

The Post-Modernist page uses space in a hyper-architectural manner. Space becomes three- (and even four-) dimensional. Sometimes the z-axis is emphasized by layering text. Headings (or text) may be broken midword, leading readers to the next line. Sometimes text runs right off the page, perhaps to continue on the next page... or perhaps not.

In Figure 18.1, from Typophile.com, posts and new stories are set in a Modernist fashion, using a sans serif font, `weight:bold;` for emphasis, and a clear layout. The background contains text representing language and time. Recent posts layer one upon the other. Older posts are lighter, fading into the distance. Big, incomplete sentences are not meant to be readable. Instead, they represent the presence of multiple voices collaborating on Typophile. Subheadings in red boxes create emphasis and lead readers into the text.

### Post-Modernist Pages Use Any Font that Works

The Post-Modernist page may use serif or sans serif fonts, legible or illegible fonts. The purpose of the Post-Modernist page is to interpret the text and challenge the reader; the typographer uses whatever font she feels is most appropriate.

### Post-Modernist Pages Use Contrast to Create Emphasis

Contrasts of space, texture, shape, and size are all used to create emphasis. Emphasis is used on the Modernist page to chunk information or lead a reader through the text. On the Post-Modernist page, it is often used to provide an entry point into the landscape of text. Where might the reader start?

FIGURE 18.1 Typophile.com. *Top:* Text is layered. Posts are Modernist, while the background text is Post-Modernist and represents collaboration. *Bottom:* The Wiki section of the site. Using a serif font, large top and left margins, and italic for emphasis, the Wiki page is Traditional. Typophile shows how Traditional, Modernist, and Post-Modernist ideals can coexist.

## Post-Modernist Pages Use Form to Convey Meaning

The Post-Modernist page is not merely a formal exercise, devoid of meaning. Formal explorations are often a search for a way to physically (viscerally) represent the meaning of a text. In Figure 18.2, Post Typography uses a sea of words to communicate the diverse, vibrant work done in its studio. In Figure 18.3, Misprinted Type creates the opportunity for readers to explore and discover images of text.

## Post-Modernist Pages Convey a Textural Feeling

Text on the Post-Modernist page is neither centered nor justified. It is neither symmetrical nor asymmetrical. The relationship between text-and-text, text-and-space is explored, captured, and shared.

## The Role of the Typographer

A Post-Modernist typographer might say, "I have explored the text, taking it apart and putting it back together in a way that speaks to or entices the reader. If it catches a reader's eye, they will engage with it."

Some Post-Modernist typographers were inspired by the *Deconstructionist* movement. The typographers would interpret text, breaking it down in order to find contradictory meanings, and then piecing it back together in order to show the reader multiple interpretations.

Related to Deconstructionism is the potential for discourse between reader and text. Many Post-Modernist typographers (even those not familiar with Deconstructionism) wanted to offer readers the opportunity to create multiple meanings and personal interpretations of texts.

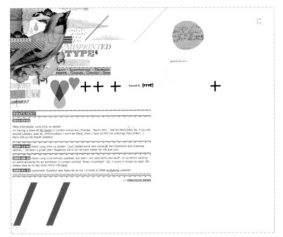

FIGURE **18.2** Post Typography (posttypography.com). *Top:* A sea of words covers the page, set for texture, not for legibility (too big, in all caps, with a tight line height). Color splits the text into manageable chunks, forming categories. On a:hover, links become bands of color, concealing the words. The color bands create emphasis, and lead readers into the text. *Bottom:* In the News section of the site, where text is meant to be read, the typography is clear and legible.

FIGURE **18.3** Misprinted Type (misprintedtype.com/v4). *Top:* Text is an extension of the image, while typographic characters are images unto themselves. Posts are set with texture in mind—the line height a little too tight, the line length a little too long. But the block of text mimics and balances the collage above it. Text is meant to be read, but comfort is sacrificed for form. Subheadings in red boxes create emphasis and lead readers into the text. *Bottom:* The same page scrolled down. Elements await discovery by the reader/explorer.

Some Post-Modernist typographers were simply heady with freedom. The personal computer afforded them the ability to do new things: easily create typefaces, layer text, and place text on curves with a mouse-click. Results of typographic exploration could be reviewed while in process. Typographers were artists and text their medium of choice. Experimentation was guided not by creating meaning, but by texture, shape, space, and intuition.

Whether inspired by Deconstructionism, discourse, or intuition/art, Post-Modernist typographers believed they could challenge and thus engage a generation of bored readers. If a reader was willing to stop and to ask, "What's this all about?" they'd be enticed to read further.

Post-Modernist typographers interpreted texts, breaking them down and recontextualizing them. Done in the name of Deconstructionism, discourse, or art, Post-Modernism marks a shift in the typographer's relationship to the text: from editor to "author."

### The Post-Modernist Page Was Designed to Challenge and Thus Engage Readers

To summarize, the Post-Modernist page:

- Tends to explore, capture, and share the text-text and text-space relationships.
- Has meaning as well as exploration.
- Was designed by Post-Modernist typographers who were inspired by Deconstructionism, discourse, and intuition/art. The typographers believed they could challenge and thus engage a generation of bored readers.

# Lesson 18: Design and Produce a Website from a Post-Modernist Approach

Thus far, you have designed and built a Traditional- and a Modernist-inspired page. Now it's time to expand your typographic toolbox. By the end of this lesson, you'll use all the skills previously learned to design and build a Post-Modernist typo-graphic web page. You'll link the Post-Modernist page to your Traditional and Modernist pages—and to all of the previous lessons (Figure 18.4).

This lesson helps you achieve the following objectives:

1   Practice creating a website, complete with working links.

2   Practice using the design process provided in this book in a more fluid, simultaneous manner.

3   Practice using elements of the Post-Modernist page when designing a website.

4   Practice walking the line between inspiration and duplication. Do not merely copy what was done before. Your medium, content, and audi-ence are different from those of the Post-Modernist typographers. What elements are appropriate to your design? What can be set aside or modified?

Even if you are already HTML/CSS savvy, follow the lesson. I provide an outline for the design process and point out where to find more information in the previous chapters.

FIGURE 18.4 By the end of this lesson, you'll build a Post-Modernist typographic web page. You'll link the page to your Traditional and Modernist pages, as well as all previous projects.

## Overview of the Lesson

In this lesson, you will design and build a Post-Modernist typographic web page that links to all of the previous lessons.

1   Use the design process provided in this book (and outlined below) to lay out elements.

2   Revise the CSS from the previous assignment or start from scratch.

## The Design Process

Remember, most of this happens simultaneously!

- Choose your font(s) based on aesthetics/emotion. For this lesson, do not worry about legibility.

- Set font size, line length (div width), line height, and alignment to explore texture, shapes, and meaning.

- Create voices with style, size, case, letter-spacing, and color. Consider your text, headings, and links.

- Use systems of space and similarity to create hierarchy.

- Print out and re-arrange text blocks (divs) to find the appropriate grid for the text in a Post-Modernist page.

- Build your site.

## Elements of the Post-Modernist Page

While creating your design, keep in mind the characteristics of a Post-Modernist page:

- The hyper-architectural grid includes the z-axis (depth).

- Emphasis creates an entry point for the reader.

- Text-text and text-space relationships create new relationships between elements, adding meaning to the text.

- Text is seen as texture, shape, and space.

## Exploring "Bad" Syntax

While you could start this lesson from scratch, I recommend you modify the files from the last lesson.

Make a copy of the last lesson's folder and name the new folder *18_postmodern_page*. Keep it in the *web_typography* folder.

Rename the CSS file *postmodern_page.css*. Link it to the *index.html* file by going into the HTML file and changing the syntax in the head element to the following:

```
<link href="postmodern_page.css"
    rel="stylesheet" type="text/css" />
```

Change the title to the following:

```
<title>Lesson 18: The Post-Modernist
    Page</title>
```

### Design the Typographic Page

To design your page, use all the skills learned and practiced in previous chapters, keeping the Post-Modernist approach in mind:

- Choose a font for legibility or beauty of form. You can choose emotional connotation over legibility in this lesson (see Chapters 1 and 2 for a review).

- Determine the appropriate size, line height, alignment, and line length... **Wait!** This is a Post-Modernist page!

- *Explore playing with the text.* Don't worry so much about legibility for this project. Make your type really big, really small, really tight, really loose. Let the ragged edge go crazy. Purposely set negative margins or remove floats on divs so blocks of text overlap each other. What happens if you use a negative line height or letter-spacing? *Now is the time to have fun, break the rules of good syntax, and see what you can do.*

- Use case, style, and color to create multiple voices (text, links, pull quotes if you create them) on the page (see Chapter 11 for a review).

- Chunk information using systems of space and hierarchy (see Chapters 7 and 8 for a review).

- Develop a Post-Modernist layout (think *hyper-architectural space*, think depth) that creates rhythm and tension on the page (see Chapters 5 and 12 for a review).

- Build the layout by modifying divs as needed. In the CSS, change width, float, padding, margin, and so on. In the HTML, change div order if needed (see Chapter 12 for a review).

- Attend to new details (numbers and acronyms, rule lines). Punctuation will probably remain the same (see Chapter 9 for a review).

- Links to finished previous lessons are already done. You will probably have to modify your link lists and your link states. Don't forget to change the "you are here" list item (see Chapter 13 for a review).

Here are some tips to make the design process easier:

- Sketch out your new Post-Modernist page design in detail *before* changing the CSS. *Don't just guess*!

- If you get lost or overwhelmed, sketch (or print out) the page as is, identify where the problems are, and tackle them one by one.

- Add a border or background color to your divs to help you see margin and padding (I need to do this at least once during every project). It's hard to visualize space while looking at syntax.

- Don't expect your design to work across multiple browsers. Some of your most satisfying explorations and results will use "bad" syntax (syntax that is not recommended and may not work across platforms or browsers). That's okay for now. The purpose of this lesson is to loosen up and experiment. Have fun.

Once your Post-Modernist page is done, you will have a portfolio of the work you've done for this book.

---

### Recommended Resources

For this lesson, I recommend the following online resources:

- To see examples of this lesson, go to typographicwebdesign.com

- To learn more about Post-Modernism, go to designhistory.org/Post_mod.html

---

## Moving Forward

This chapter introduced you to theories and themes of the Post-Modernist typographic page. The chapter also introduced you to exploring and having fun with "bad" syntax. There aren't any more chapters or lessons in this book, but you'll still move forward.

You have acquired a working knowledge of HTML, CSS, and typography. Take a moment to click through the portfolio you have created. Remember the struggles and successes you had with each project. Take a moment to write out or reflect on what you've learned throughout the course of the book, and what you still wish you knew more about.

If you love typography or web design—or both— you are living in an exciting time. Web typography is in its toddlerhood. You have the opportunity to build your skills and learn new techniques every day as your field continues to develop. Keep going—because good typography is always welcome.

# Moving Forward: Recommended Readings and Resources

## Choosing and Using Fonts

Bringhurst, Robert. *The Elements of Typographic Style*. Vancouver: Hartley and Marks, 1997.

Brown, Tim. "Fonts." *Nice Web Type,* `http://nicewebtype.com/fonts` (accessed June 20, 2011).

Franz, Laura. *Good Web Fonts: Lively, Subtle, Perfectly Legible Fonts for the Web,* `http://goodwebfonts.com` (accessed June 9, 2011).

## Working with Text on the Page

Bringhurst, Robert. *The Elements of Typographic Style*. Vancouver: Hartley and Marks, 1997.

Craig, James. *Designing with Type*. New York: Watson-Guptill, 2006.

Hochuli, Jost. *Detail in Typography*. London:Hyphen Press, 2008

Kane, John. *A Type Primer*. Upper Saddle River, New Jersey: Prentice Hall, 2003.

Lupton, Ellen. *Thinking with Type*. New York: Princeton Architectural Press, 2004.

## Developing a Grid

Brown, Tim. "More Meaningful Typography," *A List Apart Magazine*, 3 May 2011. `http://alistapart.com/articles/more-meaningful-typography/` (accessed June 28, 2011).

Kane, John. *A Type Primer*. Upper Saddle River, New Jersey: Prentice Hall, 2003.

Lupton, Ellen. *Thinking with Type*. New York: Princeton Architectural Press, 2004.

Marcotte, Ethan. "Fluid Grids," *A List Apart Magazine*, 3 March 2009. `http://www.alistapart.com/articles/fluidgrids/` (accessed June 28, 2011).

Vinh, Khoi. *Ordering Disorder: Grid Principles for Web Design*. Berkeley, California: New Riders Press, 2010.

## The History of Typography

Drucker, Johanna and Emily McVarish. *Graphic Design History: A Critical Guide.* Upper Saddle River, New Jersey: Prentice Hall, 2008.

Jubert, Roxanne, Serge Lemoine, and Ellen Lupton. *Typography and Graphic Design: From Antiquity to the Present.* Paris: Flammarion, 2006.

Kane, John. *A Type Primer.* Upper Saddle River, New Jersey: Prentice Hall, 2003.

## Critical Writings

Bierut, Michael, William Drenttel, Stephen Heller, and D.K. Holland, eds. *Looking Closer: Critical Writings on Graphic Design.* New York: Allworth Press, 1994.

Heller, Steven and Philip B. Meggs, eds. *Texts on Type: Critical Writings on Typography.* New York: Allworth Press, 1994.

## Keeping Current with Web Typography

*A List Apart Magazine,* 1998–2011. `http://alistapart.com` (accessed June 13, 2011).

Brown, Tim. *Nice Web Type,* 2002–2011. `http://nicewebtype.com` (accessed June 19, 2011).

## Syntax: CSS and Color

December, John. "The Hues Hub," *December Communications, Inc.* `www.december.com/html/spec/colorhues.html` (accessed June 13, 2011).

Griffiths, Patrick. *HTML Dog: The Best Practice Guide To XHTML and CSS,* 2003–2009. `http://htmldog.com/reference/cssproperties/` (accessed June 10, 2011).

## For the Love of Type

Boardley, John. *I Love Typography,* 2007–2011. `http://ilovetypography.com/` (accessed June 13, 2011).

Bringhurst, Robert. *The Elements of Typographic Style.* Vancouver: Hartley and Marks, 1997.

Shahn, Ben. *Love and Joy About Letters.* New York: Grossman Publishers, 1963.

# Bibliography

Bringhurst, Robert. *The Elements of Typographic Style*. Vancouver: Hartley and Marks, 1997.

Dair, Carl. *Design with Type*. Toronto: University of Toronto Press, 1967.

Haley, Allan. "It's About Legibility." *Fonts.com*. Monotype Imaging, www.fonts.com/ AboutFonts/Articles/Typography/ Legibility.htm (accessed June 18, 2011).

Helfand, Jessica. "Sticks and Stones Can Break My Bones but Print Can Never Hurt Me: A Letter to Fiona on First Reading 'The End of Print.'" *Screen: Essays on Graphic Design, New Media, and Visual Culture*. New York: Princeton Architectural Press, 2001.

Kalman, Tibor, J. Abbot Miller, and Karrie Jacobs. "Good History / Bad History." *Looking Closer: Critical Writings on Graphic Design*, ed. Michael Bierut et al. New York: Allworth Press, 1994.

Kane, John. *A Type Primer*. Upper Saddle River, New Jersey: Prentice Hall, 2003.

Lupton, Ellen. *Thinking with Type*. New York: Princeton Architectural Press, 2004.

Meggs, Philip. "Critical Writings on Typography." *Texts on Type: Critical Writings on Typography*, ed. Steven Heller and Philip B. Meggs. New York: Allworth Press, 2001, vii–xi.

Shahn, Ben. *Love and Joy About Letters*. New York: Grossman Publishers, 1963.

Tschichold, Jan. "The Principles of the New Typography." Trans. Rauri McLean. *Texts on Type: Critical Writings on Typography*, ed. Steven Heller and Philip B. Meggs. New York: Allworth Press, 2001, 115–128.

Will-Harris, Daniel. "Georgia & Verdana: Typefaces designed for the screen (finally)," *Typofile*, 2003. www.will-harris.com/ verdana-georgia.htm (accessed June 28, 2011).

# Index